PATHWAYS

*Be of the disciples of Aharon, loving peace and pursuing peace;
loving your fellowmen and bringing them near to the Torah.*
—Hillel in *Avos* 1:12

I dedicate this book to my parents,
Dr. Raymond and Gloria Greenberg,
who endowed me with the proper *middos*;
to my beloved wife, Kath,
whose questions started it all;
and to the community of Kemp Mill,
where we found the path.

Contents

Acknowledgments

I'd like to thank the following people and organizations who helped make this book possible by providing information and helping me find *ba'alei teshuvah* to interview: The American Jewish Committee, Rabbi Shimon Apisdorf, Janet Aviad, Rabbi Avrohom Braun, Rabbi Ephraim Buchwald, Rabbi Eli Gewirtz, Rabbi Menachem Goldberger, Sidney Goldstein, Rabbi Irving "Yitz" Greenberg, Samuel Heilman, William B. Helmreich, Rabbi Simon Jacobson, *The Jewish Observer*, Rabbi Shmuel Kaplan, Rabbi Kasriel Kastel, Barry A. Kosmin, Seymour P. Lachman, Rabbi Pesach Lerner, Rabbi Jack Luxemburg, Dr. Paul Marcus, Egon Mayer, Rabbi Daniel Mechanic, Rabbi Jacob Neusner, Rabbi Shlomo Porter, Dr. Bernard Reisman, Rabbi Yitschak Rudomin, Jeffrey Scheckner, Lawrence J. Schiffman, Rabbi Pinchas Stolper, Rabbi Chaim Veshnefsky, Chaim Waxman, Rabbi Moshe Weinberger, Jerry Weisberg, Rabbi Menachem Zupnik.

I'd also like to thank M. Herbert Danzger for his guidance and for his exhaustive research and insightful writing on the subject of *ba'alei teshuvah*. His book on the topic was an invaluable resource. Thanks also to Rabbi Leib Tropper of the Kol Yaakov Torah Center for his extra measure of support.

I'd like to express my gratitude to the *rabbeyim* in my community—particularly Rabbi Gedaliah Anemer and Rabbi Jack Bieler—for being role models and sources of inspiration and knowledge. The same goes for Ruthie Konick and Moishe Leiser, among others. To Esti Zemelman and Harriet Sheinson: Thanks for the keyboard work. To Jack Calman: Thanks for adding pictures to words.

To my beloved wife, Kath: Thanks for your patience and love, not to mention your computer acumen and editing skills. To Max and Jake: Thanks for putting up with *Abba* when his head was stuck in the computer. Finally, thanks to all the interviewees who participated in this book. Their stories should be an inspiration to us all.

I

Introduction

1
The Road
Less Traveled

In the place where *ba'alei teshuvah* stand, even the completely righteous
are not able to stand.

Talmud *Berachot* 34b

It's fitting that the idea for this book originated on *Shabbos*, a day of
spiritual transformation. The inspiration for it came not during *shul*, but
afterwards, during leisurely lunches with friends in the neighborhood.

It was at these get-togethers that I heard the stories of lives that were
transformed. The stories were told by people who had reconnected with
their religious roots by committing themselves to living as Torah-true
Jews. They are known as *ba'alei teshuvah* (literally, "those who return"),
and their stories put the hook in me.

First of all, they made for good listening, these spiritual travelogues
over *cholent*. The best of them had all the necessary literary elements—
conflict, struggle, interesting characters, and intriguing plots. And a
strong theme—redemption. There is something compelling about someone making a fundamental lifestyle change. When God and the possibility of miracles are added to the equation, it's even harder not to take
notice. I was also drawn to these stories because it was genuinely re-
freshing to hear Jews talk passionately about something other than real
estate or computers.

The fact that I'm a *BT* myself gave these tales added resonance. The
accounts I heard helped validate the decision my wife and I had made

several years ago to take that "road less traveled"—observant Judaism—through the often barren landscape of American Jewry.

The stories inspired us to stay on the path when it was tempting to stray, which at first was often. It was reassuring to hear that our family was not unique. Others had wrestled with the same doubts, made the same sacrifices, and committed the same blunders we had. But the payoff made it worthwhile. I learned that we'd all experienced the same deep-in-the-*kishkes* feeling of fulfillment that comes when any Jew rediscovers God and embraces Judaism in its most elemental form.

Some of the stories were dramatic. Others were quietly eloquent. All of them were uplifting, which meant they had little in common with most of the stories I had written over the past 17 years as a professional secular journalist. That was reason enough to try to get them into print.

I am an idealist by nature, but only a small fraction of my journalistic output could be called ennobling or otherwise beneficial to society. Most of the stories I wrote were either mundane, glib, or cynical. Some were hurtful. I routinely gossiped in print—which in Judaism is the sin of *loshen hara*—and regularly exploited the personal tragedies of others in the guise of "informing the public." It all came with the territory, but it's not something I'm proud of. Think of this book as a form of *teshuvah*, repentance, an attempt to put journalism to good use.

Ten years ago, I would have scoffed at the whole notion of *teshuvah*, had I known what it meant. Repentance? Torah? *Mitzvos*? *Shabbos*? I was vaguely aware of all that "religious stuff," but it was irrelevant to me. It all seemed either weird or fanatical, and above all, antiquated. It was not part of my life. Had I genuinely believed in God, I would have been embarrassed to admit it to most of the people I knew.

My Judaism was the lox-and-bagels variety that is practiced—if that's the right word—by most American Jews. That all changed, thank God, when circumstances put us in an Orthodox neighborhood in suburban Washington, D.C., where we learned how to live authentically Jewish lives from some wonderful role models.

But most American Jews never have that opportunity, and the result has been a pandemic of assimilation. In hopes of counteracting that grim trend, I decided to collect and disseminate these stories of spiritual awakening. If they inspire even one expatriate Jew to form a connection with traditional Judaism, it will have been worth the effort.

I also hope these stories touch observant Jews, whether *FFB*s or *BT*s, who may have become jaded and find that their spiritual batteries need a recharge.

The aim of this book is to show that no Jew is irretrievably lost—in theory, at least. Judging by the first-person narratives that have been gathered here, virtually anyone is capable of returning home spiritually, regardless of his religious origins or subsequent circumstances. Some of the people I interviewed have come a long, long way.

But the return trip can be disorienting, sometimes painful. Those who are making the transition are often plagued by doubt and other conflicts, internal and external. They may find it difficult to juggle the demands of *Yiddishkeit* and those of the secular realm they also inhabit. They may clash with family and friends and larger society as a whole. Their world can be a very confusing and turbulent place, and in the interests of full disclosure, I tried to illustrate that as well as the benefits of a religious life.

Returnees who participated in this book come from all walks of life and they live throughout the United States and beyond.

Most of them were raised in secular households that seem to typify assimilationist America—no Christmas tree in the living room, but no *siddur* either. And if there was a *siddur*, chances are it was permanently shelved after the final *bar* or *bas mitzvah* in the family. Despite a smattering of religious observance or occasional outbreaks of Zionistic zeal, the link these families had to Judaism was almost purely cultural and superficial, often gastronomic.

For example, Joan Bieler, a 43-year-old biologist, remembered being asked by a rabbi at a youth social club, "What about you makes you Jewish?" She was 12 at the time. Her answer: "On Saturday night we had bagels." That was it. Nothing more.

Some interviewees were raised in more observant homes than that—there was a semblence of *kashrus* or *Shabbos*, for example—but they strayed far from *Yiddishkeit* once they left the nest.

At another end of the spectrum was John Young, who was not merely assimilated; he was actually raised as a Gentile by a father who had repudiated Judaism and a Jewish mother who herself had been raised as a Christian. Young, 35, an economist, didn't know he was Jewish until he stumbled onto his grandfather's burial certificate at the age of 16.

A few interviewees said that during their formative years they were so embarrassed by their Jewishness that they hated that part of themselves. Being different from the other kids was too heavy a burden for them to bear. Most of the interviewees, however, simply found Judaism to be unimportant. It had no connection to what was happening around them in their everyday lives. They might have felt intensely Jewish, but they saw nothing linking that innate sense of distinctiveness to the practice of Judaism.

For these kids and young adults, this almost-lost generation, there was nothing in their environment to counterbalance the secularism that shaped their lives. They might have had a grandparent who was a connection to their heritage, but otherwise, Jewish role models were in short supply at home. Meaningful religious experiences were rarely found in the synagogue, a place where people showed off their wardrobes and engaged in organized mumbling three days a year. *Cheder* was a washout too.

Virtually all the interviewees who attended Hebrew school loathed the institution and saw it for what it really was—a glorified *bar mitzvah* factory. The right-of-passage "simchas" these plants produced ordinarily signaled the end of the youngster's Jewish involvement, such as it was, instead of celebrating entry into an adulthood devoted to the service of God.

Those youngsters who managed to soak up real Jewish knowledge were hard-pressed to put it to use through the performance of *mitzvos*. For the most part, the environment outside the Hebrew school or Sunday school classroom wouldn't permit it. The Torah said keep kosher, but *trayf* was the rule at home and throughout the neighborhood. The Torah said keep *Shabbos*, but everybody worked, shopped, or played ball on Saturday. And so on. It was an untenable situation, and the result was predictable.

"At about the age of 11 or 12, I just completely lost interest," said Arthur Sapper, 45, an attorney. "And the reason was, as I look back on it now, what psychologists call cognitive dissonance. That is, you learn one thing and see or practice another. And you have to reconcile the two in your mind. And when you're a child, it's very hard to do. Something has to go. And I was basically a victim of that, so Hebrew school went."

Sapper had his *bar mitzvah*, a perfunctory affair, but for nearly the next two decades, he said, "I was out of the synagogue and had almost no connection with Jewish religious life at all."

His story is not at all atypical.

For many interviewees, the drift away from Jewish tradition accelerated and took strange new twists once they left home for college and the world beyond. Many found sex, drugs, rock 'n' roll, or political activism. Some dabbled in Eastern religions as they searched for spiritual meaning in their lives.

Interreligious dating was the norm on campus, and still is. That's how Julius Ciss got involved in Christianity. While he was in art school in Canada in the mid-1970s, he became deeply ensnared in so-called "messianic Judaism" through a Gentile girlfriend. He was even baptized before he realized his mistake, quit the cult, and found his way back to genuine Judaism.

Miriam Adahan went out West in the 1960s and threw herself into the civil rights and anti-war movements. "I was a universalist," she said. "When they would ask for religion, I would put 'human.' I had no identity with any group of people."

Adahan, who now lives in Jerusalem with her family, is a deeply committed Jew whose *Yiddishkeit* infuses every aspect of her life, including her work as a psychologist. What accounts for her transformation?

There's a tradition that says each Jew has a *pintela Yid*, a spark of Jewishness that cannot be extinguished no matter how thoroughly assimilated the person has become. It's amazing how many ways God finds to fan that spark into a flame.

The catalyst may have been an event. Or a person. Or an outreach program. Or even a place, most likely Israel. Or a time, most likely *Shabbos*. Its appeal may have been emotional or intellectual or both. Whatever the impetus, it revealed a basic truth about any Jew—that he or she is linked to something bigger: A people, a land, a moral–ethical system, a historic continuum, a covenant with God.

But that was only the start. Typically, the return to observant Judaism is a lengthy and complex process—an evolution rather than a revolution—that includes periods of stagnation and backsliding and floundering as well as genuine growth.

Ideally, though, the growth never ends, making each *BT*—actually, any committed Jew—a work in progress. In that sense, it's somewhat misleading to think of a person as "having returned," since *Yiddishkeit* is not a destination, but a pathway. Rather, one is continually in the "process of returning."

(Nevertheless, there are certain criteria that do identify an individual as member of a religious—i.e., Orthodox—community, such as strict observance of *Shabbos* and *kashrus*. I've included in this book only the stories of Jews who currently identify themselves as Orthodox. For my rationale, see chapter 3, "What Exactly Is a *Ba'al Teshuvah*?")

The return to Torah may have been a response to existential angst, that yearning for something more profound than professional accomplishment, social success, or material achievement. Some took the religious route when secular philosophy failed to help explain the vicissitudes of life and the mysteries of the universe. Several said their embrace of Orthodoxy was, in effect, a "graduation" from less traditional forms of Judaism which they found to be insubstantial. Finally, some returnees said they weren't searching for anything at all. They didn't find *Yiddishkeit* so much as it found them—perhaps through the soul of a deceased relative or other departed Jew.

The catalyst that began the process of return may have had an immediate spiritual impact or it may have lingered in the person's subconscious and resurfaced years later. For some, the impetus took the form of a revelation that demonstrated the exquisite orderliness of the universe and therefore proved the existence of God.

Yaakov Ort had such a revelation. It came more than 25 years ago during a sun-washed morning in the Swiss Alps. "I remember sitting there," he said, "and it just occurred to me . . . it just absolutely penetrated me, that there had to be a God, that everything that I was seeing, the blueness of the sky and the beauty of the trees and just the gloriousness of the day . . . it struck me as being absolutely impossible that all of that could have been a random accident."

Although the experience was a continuing "source of comfort," said Ort, it didn't bear fruit for nearly two decades. In the meantime, he continued living a secular life and remained, as he put it, an "utterly selfish hedonist."

Jack Calman had a different sort of revelation, and the episode that spawned it had a distinctly Woody Allen-ish texture. During graduate school, Calman, whose Judaism had been little more than an ill-defined ethnic "feeling," accompanied his Gentile girlfriend to her parents' home for Sunday dinner. The main course? Roast pork.

"I'd had pork in Chinese restaurants," he said, "but I'd never had a blatant, 100 percent, full-strength, pink plateful of pork on Sunday night. I don't remember if they said grace or not, 'cause that's the only thing I remember from that night. I felt like I'd died. That made a big impression on me, 'cause I thought to myself, 'how am I ever going to be a family with these people?'"

For some interviewees, the initial turning point was a life cycle event, such as the birth of a child, which many people regard as a miracle. A birth is normally attended by religious ritual, a *bris* for example, and it tends to awaken feelings of generational linkage in the parents. It puts things into perspective.

A traumatic personal episode, such as a brush with death or the passing of a parent, can also have a clarifying effect. Additionally, in the case of a parent's death, the male mourner, who may have been a stranger to *shul*, is now called on to say *Kaddish* for 11 months. Some interviewees said this intensive exposure to Jewish ritual helped pave the way for their return.

The trip back is not always event-driven, however. For some interviewees, the portal of reentry was Jewish learning, usually in a *yeshiva*. They fell in love with the *mind* of Judaism, and the rest followed.

Many returnees were introduced to traditional Judaism through an encounter with another person, and it wasn't always a Jew. Several interviewees said Gentiles played a role in turning them on to *Yiddishkeit*. Ironically, a number of these cases were proselytizing attempts that boomeranged. For several others, it was a religious Jew, a friend or relative, who showed the way. One man followed the lead of his psychotherapist.

In many instances, of course, rabbis were indispensable in helping lost Jews blaze new trails. The case of Phillip Namanworth is an example. After a long and futile search for a spiritual connection—during which he practiced everything from Buddhism to Christianity to Taoism— Namanworth met a rabbi in Brooklyn who changed his life. The rabbi's name was Simon Jacobson.

"I'll never forget it," said Namanworth, 51, who works in the music industry. "He was talking [and] it blew my mind so much that I felt like the top of my head was going to fly off. I said, 'What is this?' He said, 'This is *Yiddishkeit*.' I said, 'I never heard this my whole life.' He said, 'That's the shame of it.'"

It's worth noting that Rabbi Jacobson is a member of the Lubavitch sect, which probably has helped more Jews reconnect with their heritage than any other organization. Several interviewees said their return to *Yiddishkeit* was largely the result of Lubavitch outreach efforts and teachings.

Finally, a number of returnees said their reawakening was triggered by a visit to Israel or by the lessons of the Holocaust. Miriam Garfinkle was profoundly affected by both when she participated in the "March of the Living," a program in which Jewish students visit the concentration camps and then immediately fly to Israel. At one of the camps she saw a film in which a Jew who was later killed by the Nazis pleaded with future generations of Jews to maintain their heritage. He said they had a responsibility.

"And if we didn't fulfill it, [the Holocaust victim said], it would be like walking on his grave. He would have died for nothing," Garfinkle, now 21, remembered. "I . . . realized that if every American Jew became like me, then five generations down the line Hitler would have won. We would have done it to ourselves."

She and her group then flew to Israel.

"It was like going from death to life," she said before her voice broke. "There was this unbelievable surge that you belong to the Jewish people and that this land is yours. . . . I gained my belief in *Hashem* in Israel. . . . Now, I made a definite decision that being Jewish wasn't a sideline issue, something to put at the bottom of your emotional resume. It had to take the foreground in my life."

Garfinkle, who went on to do outreach work in Israel, is working on a book that documents Jewish life in Judea, Samaria, and Gaza.

The road back, however, is not always smooth. Return can produce culture shock and conflict. Several interviewees found themselves alienated from friends or family members whose secular lifestyle and philosophy were now radically different from theirs. Intolerance—originating on either side of the religious divide—is a common problem and so are family spats. Yet most interviewees said they eventually reconciled with relatives, some of whom became more observant in the process.

In cases where spouses don't agree on key issues, such as the desired level of observance in the home, the return of one of them to traditional Judaism can threaten to destroy a marriage. "It's about as difficult an issue as one could possibly have," said Allan Leicht, a TV writer and producer, whose marriage tottered but ultimately survived with the help of some understanding friends and rabbis. "You have to have a very special kind of spouse in order to deal with the conflicts."

Even when *shalom bayis* prevails, returnees and their spouses find there are other personal and family-related issues to wrestle with. An example: Should one feel compelled to wear a *keepah* in the office as a public statement of religious commitment? Some do and some don't. Another example: *Frumkeit* and feminism—are they mutually exclusive? Not necessarily, according to the women I spoke with. However, most of them said they can understand why unobservant women might disagree, in part because the secular world has a different view of egalitarianism than does traditional Judaism. Still, some said they are occasionally bothered by the role Orthodoxy has carved out for them, if only because it is so different from what they were used to.

In addition, several interviewees of both sexes said they found it difficult to make the transition from embracing Judaism's spirituality to also performing its *mitzvos*—a journey from an ethereal, philosophic realm to the concrete precincts of daily observance, mandated deeds, some of which might seem odd, picayune, or overly burdensome.

Ultimately, though, everyone I talked with managed to bridge that gap once they learned that spirituality and actions can and should dovetail. These two elements do not inhabit separate and isolated spheres, but are part of a larger whole, an integrated system. When that system is working, spirituality gives the deeds meaning and the deeds reinforce spirituality.

But the struggle never ends—nor should it. It just takes place on successively higher levels. Such is the nature of *Yiddishkeit*. It may not be a panacea, but those who have embraced it say it has brought stability, depth, and a heightened sense of purpose to their lives—even if they can no longer eat lobster and enjoy some of the other trappings of the secular world. For some, the journey back to the Torah truly has been (apologies to The Grateful Dead) a long, strange trip. And they can't help looking back from time to time and smiling incredulously.

"[Sometimes] I really think that maybe I'm really whacked out and I've gone bonkers," said Esther Rochel Russell, an ex-"valley girl" from California who once barely knew who Moses was. She is now a deeply observant Jew with a young family. "I grew up for 30 years one way, with one perspective and one framework of education and thinking, and I miss going out and doing wild things with my friends. But then I think again, what am I really missing on an essential level? . . . I look around at the external world and see what is going on out there, and I say, you know what? Even if this is a . . . crock, this is 100 times better than anything else. And it really is. That I never doubt."

2

The *Ba'al Teshuvah* Movement: An Overview

Midway through the April 21, 1977, issue of *Rolling Stone* magazine is a full-page portrait of a bearded, mustachioed young man with sleepy eyes.

Nothing unusual about that. Over the years the *Stone* has featured countless depictions of hirsute young men, some of them sleepy-eyed. Some of them glassy-eyed. Many have been rockers or countercultyralists of one type or another.

This one was a member of a counterculture, but not the type normally associated with *Rolling Stone*. Instead of a guitar, he had a *sefer Torah* at his side. And a *yarmulka* on his head. And nestled just above his hairline was the black leather cube Jewish men have donned for centuries as part of the ritual regalia known as *tefillin*.

The young man in the picture, 26-year-old Michaèl Willis, was a newly observant Jew, a *ba'al teshuvah*. And the accompanying 20,000-word article was his sister Ellen's fervid account of her struggle to understand why her naturally skeptical and thoroughly acculturated sibling would suddenly veer off course and decide to live a Torah-true life.

"In my universe," she wrote, "intelligent, sensible people who had grown up in secular homes in the second half of the 20th century did not embrace biblical fundamentalism."[1]

---

1. Ellen Willis, "Next Year in Jerusalem," *Rolling Stone* (April 21, 1977): 65.

What is noteworthy is not only the fact that Michael Willis found *Yiddishkeit*, but the fact that the story of his return was given prominent play in a major national publication. People took notice. People who might not have known *Purim* from *Simchas Torah*.

"It was a real groundbreaker," said Rabbi Ephraim Z. Buchwald, director of the National Jewish Outreach Program.

Consider also the venue for the story. *Rolling Stone* isn't some starchy magazine-of-record. It is best known as a chronicle of life on the cutting edge, which is roughly where the *BT* movement found itself in 1977. The story of Michael Willis and his spiritual odyssey was a declaration that something new and different—and maybe even hip—had arrived on the American scene.

Actually, *Rolling Stone* was a little behind the curve on this one. By the time the story ran, the *BT* movement had been in existence about 10 years. That's eons for some trends, but only a millisecond on the 3,300-year Jewish timeline. Nevertheless, it represented a unique development not only in the annals of American Jewry, but perhaps in the entire history of the faith.

For the first time, observant Judaism became a matter of personal choice rather than family tradition for significant numbers of Jews.[2] (Exactly how many of them have taken this route is not clear.) The immediate backdrop for this turnabout was a seemingly inexorable decline in traditionalism that began more than 200 years ago and threatened to overwhelm halachic Judaism.

Over the centuries, of course, there have been celebrated examples of individual Jews who, against all odds, connected with the Torah. One of the most famous is the great sage and martyr Rabbi Akiva (50 C.E.–132 C.E.), a onetime illiterate shepherd who, with the encouragement of his wife, left home at the age of 40 and immersed himself in the study of Torah for more than a decade. He became one of the most revered teachers and leaders in Jewish history.

Rabbi Akiva and others like him have been the exception, however. There has been little fluctuation in levels of observance for much of Jewish history simply because Jews traditionally had lived in what Rabbi Irving "Yitz" Greenberg calls "hermetically sealed" environments—

---

2. M. Herbert Danzger, *Returning to Tradition: The Contemporary Revival of Orthodox Judaism* (New Haven: Yale University Press, 1989), 327.

sharply segregated societies where there was little inclination, or opportunity, to stray from the fold.

That began changing more than 200 years ago. Since then, the prevailing flow of Jewishness has been from more observance to less, from traditionalism to revisionism. The floodgates of assimilation opened when the Jews of Europe were emancipated from the ghetto in late 18th century and the *Haskalah*, or enlightenment, movement gained momentum.

Imbued with the newfound spirit of freedom, many Jews abandoned traditional Judaism. Some converted, intermarried, or simply faded into the dominant culture and ceased being active, identifiable Jews. Others were drawn to secular Zionism, Reform Judaism, socialism or Yiddishist organizations.[3] Whatever the attraction, they were leaving Orthodoxy in droves—first in Western Europe and finally in Eastern Europe, which had largely been insulated from the emancipation movement even into the 19th century.[4]

The social disruptions caused by World War I quickened the decline of Orthodoxy, which increasingly became associated with poverty, superstition, and ignorance, according to author M. Herbert Danzger.[5] The relative merits of Orthodoxy, however, soon became a moot issue when the Holocaust eliminated an entire civilization of Jews, both secular and religious.

America may have been a refuge for Jews, but it was largely a wasteland for *Yiddishkeit*. Reform and then Conservative were the dominant forms of Judaism in this country for most of its history.[6] By the time the post–World War II era arrived, Orthodoxy had become severely marginalized. "Toward the end of the 1950s," Danzger wrote, "scholars had largely written off Orthodox Judaism as an option for American Jews."[7]

What the scholars didn't see is this: Another piece of the foundation for a resurgence of traditional Judaism was being laid, and it would carry with it the seeds of the *teshuvah* movement. This segment of the infra-

---

3. *Ibid.*, 17.

4. *Encyclopaedia Judaica* (Jerusalem: Keter Publishing House, 1972), 7:1433–34.

5. Danzger, *Returning to Tradition*, 18.

6. Mendell Lewittes, *Jewish Law: An Introduction* (Northvale, NJ: Jason Aronson, 1994), 184.

7. Danzger, *Returning to Tradition*, 25.

structure was formed by hundreds of thousands of European Jews who came to this country as refugees between the late 1930s and the mid-1950s.[8]

They included some of the most prestigious names in Orthodox Judaism, such as Rabbi Joseph B. Soloveitchik, Rabbi Aharon Kotler, Rabbi Moshe Feinstein, and the late Lubavitch Rebbe Menachem Mendel Schneerson, to name a few.

The members of this group distinguished themselves as halachic authorities, spiritual exemplars, educators, and ardent anti-assimilationists. "They ultimately overcame the prevailing trend toward compromise with secular American values that [had] existed in the Orthodox camp," William B. Helmreich wrote in his book *The World of the Yeshiva*.[9]

By the late 1940s, the Lubavitchers, the first group to begin doing outreach work on a large scale, were recruiting Jewish public elementary school students. Within a few years, the effort had extended to secular college campuses and involved chasidic troubadour Shlomo Carlebach, who became a fixture, albeit a controversial one, in the outreach movement.[10]

Meanwhile, Yeshiva University was also establishing itself as a trailblazer in the field. In the mid-1950s it created a program specifically for its students with minimal Jewish backgrounds, as well a *Shabbos*-oriented initiative catering to assimilated teenagers and young adults. YU also helped establish scores of Orthodox *shuls* through which congregants were introduced to traditional Judaism. One of these institutions was Lincoln Square Synagogue in New York, which became one of the nation's leading *kiruv* outlets.[11]

The National Conference of Synagogue Youth, an outreach organization stressing strict adherence to *halachah*, was founded in 1959. Its target audience was teenagers and subteens, a population which had resisted earlier attempts to develop an Orthodox youth movement. Apparently, the times had changed. "In 1963 I was saying that it [the *teshuvah* movement] was happening, but my colleagues thought I was crazy," said Rabbi Pinchas Stolper of the Orthodox Union, the founder

---

8. William B. Helmreich, *The World of the Yeshiva* (New York: The Free Press, 1982), 32, 36, 45, 46.

9. *Ibid.*, 46.

10. Danzger, *Returning to Tradition*, 58–59.

11. *Ibid.*, 64–65.

of NCSY. "Nobody believed me." (Today, NCSY serves about 40,000 young people, according to Rabbi Stolper.)

The back-to-Jewishness movement finally coalesced in the 1960s and early 1970s, due to several factors, most notably Israel's victory in the Six-Day War in 1967. This inspired an outpouring of ethnic pride and engendered a sense of biblical connectedness throughout the Jewish world.

Meanwhile, the hippie movement, which attracted lots of Jews, was celebrating the glories of transcendence—not to mention hedonism. That environment created an entire subculture of young people who were seeking spiritual sustenance, among other things, and who had rejected materialism and conventional lifestyles. Many were attracted to cults and Eastern religions. Some, however, found their way to outreach-minded *yeshivot*.[12]

While some Jews were reaching out, others were turning inward, away from a larger culture that increasingly seemed unsympathetic or hostile to the plight of Jews, according to the *1995 American Jewish Year Book*.[13]

"The turn to survivalism [among Jews] was prompted as well by the growing realization that the American Jewish community itself was rapidly changing—and possibly eroding," Jack Wertheimer wrote in the *Year Book*.[14] Beginning in the early 1960s, studies revealed that the community was being weakened by rootlessness, declining fertility rates, higher divorce rates, and a startling rise in intermarriage.[15]

The intermarriage rate had risen from the single digits in the 1950s to 31 percent between the mid-1960s and 1970.[16] The current intermarriage figure—covering the period 1985 to 1990—is 52 percent, according to the 1990 National Jewish Population Survey.[17] What's more, the survey found that 72 percent of the children of mixed marriages have been raised as non-Jews.[18]

---

12. *Ibid.*, 65.

13. Jack Wertheimer, "Jewish Organizational Life in the United States Since 1945," in *American Jewish Year Book*, ed. David Singer (New York: The American Jewish Committee, 1995), 33.

14. *Ibid.*, 33.

15. *Ibid.*, 34.

16. *Ibid.*

17. Barry A. Kosmin, et al., *Highlights of the Council of Jewish Federations 1990 National Jewish Population Survey* (New York: Council of Jewish Federations, 1991), 14.

18. *Ibid.*, 16.

These and other alarming trends jolted the Jewish community into action. Various campaigns were launched to fight assimilation and otherwise maintain Jewish "continuity," a term which has become the buzzword of the 1990s.

Some of these programs appear to have had a positive impact, at least in the short-term.[19] Nevertheless, optimism is sometimes hard to come by in the Jewish community—if the *number* of observant Jews (primarily the Orthodox) is considered the chief criterion for determining the overall health of Judaism.

The fact is, Orthodox Jews are so rare in America that they are almost a demographic nonentity. They are a minority of a minority. Estimates of their number generally range from 450,000 to about 700,000, which is only 7.6 to 11.8 percent of the "core" American Jewish population of 5.9 million as broadly defined in the 1990 National Jewish Population Survey.[20]

It has been even more difficult to quantify the American *BT* movement, in part, because there is no universally accepted definition of what a *BT* is. One thing is clear, however. The movement, however it is defined, is a minority of a minority of a minority. The highest estimate of its size in America is roughly 150,000 to 175,000.

"We don't see any clear-cut evidence that this is a major movement," said Jeffrey Scheckner, a research consultant at the Council of Jewish Federations. "It appears to be more significant than it really is because people who are *ba'alei teshuvah* are more likely to make a statement about what they've done. People who leave [Judaism] fade into the woodwork."

He compared the situation among American Jews to afternoon rush hour in Manhattan. "There's a massive amount leaving and a trickle coming in," he said, referring to the 1990 National Jewish Population Survey, which indicates that only about 12 percent of Orthodox Jews are new to the denomination.[21]

Danzger maintains there are far more than that. (His definition of

---

19. A February 1995 survey of participants in Aish Hatorah's Discovery seminar, taken six months to one year after the program, showed a general upswing in observant behavior.

20. "Council of Jewish Federations 1990 National Jewish Population Survey" as updated in *American Jewish Year Book*, 1995, 181.

21. *Highlights of the CJF 1990 National Jewish Population Survey*, Table 24, 33.

Orthodoxy, however, is somewhat different than that of the NJPS, which relied only on the undocumented self-definition of respondents.) Danzger, who used religious practice as his sole criterion, has estimated that as many as one-quarter of current Orthodox Jews in America were not raised *frum*. That would put the number of newly Orthodox at between 112,500 and 175,000.[22] (Danzger based his national estimate on data from a 1981 survey of Jews in the New York area.)

Several other observers said 25 percent is too high for a national figure. However, those who concurred with Danzger contended that most conventional estimates of the *ba'alei teshuvah* population are probably low because many returnees do not pass through outreach organizations and other institutions where they are likely to be surveyed or tracked. Instead, they become observant in a more ad hoc manner, either through attendance at an Orthodox *shul* or by following the example of their day-school-educated children. These people do not show up on surveys.

"They've been so successful in blending into the general community," said Rabbi Stolper, "that we are almost unaware of their presence."

But do they stay with *Yiddishkeit* for the duration or do they bolt after dabbling for a while? (This is one of several questions concerning the movement that can be answered only anecdotally, since reliable data in this area is sparse.)

"My sociological horse sense would say they do stay," said Egon Mayer, director of the Center for Jewish Studies in New York. "Their decision to become more traditional is connected with their settling into a path in life that marks the start of adulthood."

Rabbi Irving "Yitz" Greenberg, the president of CLAL, the National Jewish Center for Learning and Leadership, isn't convinced. He said that interviews with outreach workers indicate that there is a high level of turnover among *ba'alei teshuvah*.

If *BT*s do tend to stay, as Mayer contends, that may be a reflection of the changing face of the *BT* movement itself. It is no longer the domain of restless world-wanderers, spiritual experimenters and hippies, or their 1990s counterparts. The movement has become more mainstream and stable and now includes many professionals and businesspeople—*frum* yuppies, or *fruppies*, as Rabbi Buchwald calls them. "They've found that

---

22. Danzger, *Returning to Tradition*, 193, 343.

you don't have to give up your Jewish identity and you can still be successful in this world," he said. "It's a whole new idea."

But how long does a *BT* remain a *BT*? At what point do they cease being newcomers and become generic Orthodox Jews who are accepted members of the observant community? Or do they remain a distinct subgroup? Is there a stigma attached to being a *BT*? To where do they gravitate in the Orthodox spectrum—the centrist community or somewhere further to the right? Finally, to what extent have they affected attitudes and practices in the Orthodox community and beyond? In short, what impact has the *ba'alei teshuvah* movement had on American Jewry?

No one knows how long it takes the average *BT*, if there is such an animal, to transform into a fully integrated Orthodox Jew. In order for it to happen, though, the newcomer must endure certain rites of passage, such as establishing that his or her level of *kashrus* is sufficient for neighbors to accept invitations for *Shabbos* lunch.

Some sources reported that *BT*s sometimes have trouble being fully accepted as members of more right-wing communities where they may be stigmatized by their secular backgrounds or family lineage. The problem is especially pronounced when the newcomer seeks a *shidduch* with an *FFB*. "The *FFB* single girl goes out with a *BT* guy," said one rabbi who specializes in outreach work, "but when it comes time to meet her parents, they get cold feet."

What also sets some *BT*s apart is a worldview that may never fully jibe with that of their born-*frum* neighbors. Try as they might—and some apparently are encouraged to do so—they never completely purge The Beatles or Saturday at the mall from their memory banks.

Those secular experiences remain a part of their makeup, even if they now wear a black hat and a *bekesha* and *daven* three times a day. This duality may trouble some of their neighbors, but it also broadens them as people—if they can handle the psychological strain of living in two vastly different worlds at once. Such grounding comes in handy for *BT*s when they go into outreach work, as many have done, or when they enter the rabbinate or the *chinuch* field. They are better able than others to relate to not-yet-observant Jews.

*BT*s can be found at all points on the Orthodox spectrum, but some observers feel they tend to move to the right if they have the option. In part, this may exemplify the general rightward shift in Orthodoxy that has taken place over the past several years. But it may also reflect an individual newcomer's insecurity with his or her level of *frumkeit*. Or it may simply be a logical extension of one's continuing spiritual journey in search of more "authentic" and less "diluted" forms of religion.

All told, the influence of the *BT* movement on American Jewry has been greater than its mere numbers would suggest. The arrival of these newcomers has had a revitalizing effect on many segments of the community, including the *FFB* branch. "It has forced them [*FFBs*] to confront a belief system they didn't think of as a belief system," author William Helmreich said in an interview.

Several observers credit *BT*s with having injected a note of passion and idealism into the sometimes stultified world of Orthodox Judaism. "They have pulled people out of their lethargy," said Rabbi Simon Jacobson, a chasidic educator in New York.

A man named Hillel Gross, who grew up Orthodox, summed up this feeling in a speech he made in February 1986 to a *ba'al teshuvah* group in New York. "By your enthusiasm, by your embrace of everything that's Jewish, you challenge us," he said. "By your insatiable thirst for knowledge, you provoke us. And by your open-hearted love affair with Judaism, you ultimately shame us."[23]

The influence of *BT*s has also been felt on the far side of the religious gulf, among Jews who ordinarily are isolated from traditional Judaism. "In a very subtle and mysterious way, this has raised some sort of consciousness," said Rabbi Moshe Weinberger, a writer, lecturer, and *rebbe* at Ezra Academy of Queens.

"At this point, almost every Conservative and Reform Jew in the United States already knows of a friend or a relative or someone whose child has become *frum*," explained Rabbi Menachem Zupnik of *Bais Torah U'tfilah* in Passaic, NJ. "They are cognizant of the fact that there is a *BT* movement out there, and it's had a major impact on them psychologically. Orthodox Judaism has become more real, more demystified. It becomes a choice people make. After a while, it becomes impossible to say that everyone who becomes a *ba'al teshuvah* is crazy."

Nevertheless, the *BT* movement, particularly its chasidic branch, has come in for criticism. Certain Jewish leaders have branded it a glorified

---

23. Lincoln Square Synagogue flier (New York: October 1987).

cult which breeds extremism, intolerance, and hero worship while driving a wedge between nonobservant parents and newly observant children.[24]

It's true that *frumkeit* can become a divisive issue in families, but normative Judaism does not encourage such discord. On the contrary. It forbids children from being disrespectful to their parents and encourages them to love and honor their parents and seek ways of peace and reconciliation.[25]

The charge of intolerance has been leveled by Jewish leaders who accuse Orthodoxy, particularly its right-wing sector, of denigrating less traditional forms of Judaism, and of spawning divisiveness in the Jewish community.

Aspects of the *BT* movement "smack of an all-or-nothing view of Jewish life," said Rabbi Jack Luxemburg, who heads a Reform synagogue in suburban Washington, DC.

Without alternative forms of Judaism, he added, American Jewish life would resemble that in Israel, where absolutism reigns and there is little middle ground between fully secular Jews and ultra-Orthodox *charedim*. "If you cut the rope to those who are not Orthodox," he said, "I believe you send a tragic message."

Finally, there are those, even within Orthodoxy, who are concerned that too many *BT*s seem overly preoccupied with the "externals" of observant Judaism, such as distinctive modes of dress and other local customs and stringencies that may or may not be halachically mandated. "One wonders to what extent there has been an inner transformation [among these people]," Rabbi Ralph Pelkowitz of New York wrote in 1980 in the journal of the Orthodox Union.[26]

Rabbi Irving "Yitz" Greenberg, an Orthodox Jew, has some of the same concerns. While he lauded the *ba'al teshuvah* movement for having provided an alternative to runaway assimilation, he said that same success has helped spawn a mood of "triumphalism" and "arrogance" in the Orthodox camp and has helped lead to its rightward shift. He also criticized those in the movement who routinely encourage returnees to "reject all of the secular world" and "turn their backs on their past."

---

24. Danzger, *Returning to Tradition*, 300.

25. Mordechai Becher and Moshe Newman, *After the Return* (Jerusalem: Feldheim, 1994), 34–35.

26. Ralph Pelkowitz, "The Teshuva Phenomenon: The Other Side of the Coin," *Jewish Life* 4:3, 16ff, as quoted in Danzger, *Returning to Tradition*, 271.

The overall impact of the movement? "It's not a bankruptcy," he said, "but it's not as great a profit margin as we might have thought."

The return to traditional Judaism is not a cure-all, cautioned Dr. Paul Marcus, a psychoanalyst and psychologist, who regards *frumkeit* as a lifestyle option that can have either a positive or negative influence on an individual, depending on many factors.

"Some [returnees] escape into an insular, rigid world at the expense of not facing up to the more complex conflicts and decisions in life," he said. "It can be an escapist or extreme way of dealing with inner conflict."

For others, however, the journey is a life-affirming flight from alienation, anomie, and self-absorption. "They now feel tied to a community and they do good deeds and they try to make the world a better place, and that's positive," said Marcus. "My basic sense is that most of the people I've seen have been pleased with the change. Their lives seem enhanced. They've gone from more distress to less. They have more of a sense of direction."

Unfortunately, that cannot be said for most American Jews. "We still have masses and masses of bored Jews and nobody is reaching them," said Lawrence J. Schiffman, professor of Hebrew and Judaic Studies at New York University.

Despite any inroads made by the *ba'al teshuvah* movement, this can't bode well for the future of American Jewry. Can it?

Rabbi Jacob Neusner is disturbed when any Jew fades into the woodwork of secular American culture. Yet he is unconcerned about the survival of Judaism. In part, that's because Jews have been through this sort of thing before, and because they have an extraordinarily powerful ally. In fact, the Jews have weathered so many crises and disproven so many doomsayers over the centuries, said Neusner, that one professor referred to them admiringly as "the ever-dying people."

"Judaism will sell itself," said Neusner, who is Distinguished Research Professor of Religious Studies at the University of South Florida. "If a product has held its market for 4,000 years, why panic? I'm not ready to panic. You never get panicky if you believe in God. God will provide."

3
What Exactly Is a *Ba'al Teshuvah?*

Deciding whose stories to include in this book wasn't as easy as I first thought, and that in itself was illuminating.

The decision-making process highlighted some tough issues Judaism now faces and it raised questions that were difficult to answer—difficult because they may be unanswerable by man.

Journalists don't usually think in terms of unanswerable questions. But religious Jews do. I'm both, and that complicated matters. I found myself constantly trying to reconcile the demands of spirituality and journalistic rationality, and as a result, my perspective kept shifting back and forth between the worlds of *ruchnius* and *gashmius*.

Gashmius is the realm of the physical, the objective, the quantifiable. It is where reporters feel comfortable. *Ruchnius* is the spiritual. It embraces the unfathomable, the undefinable, and the transcendent. It is alien territory for most working journalists.

During my work on this book, these two worlds were often in open conflict.

On a spiritual level, it seemed presumptuous to try to answer some of the most basic questions that were raised in my research. A prime example: What is a serious Jew?

Ultimately, only God can decide that. But on a *gashmius* level, a journalistic level, I was obligated to try to arrive at an answer. It's futile to write about Jews returning to their religious roots without attempting to gauge the seriousness of their commitment to Judaism—as subjective as that concept may be.

In today's polarized environment, there are sharply conflicting perspectives on what constitutes meaningful Jewish practice. Everything is politically loaded.

For that reason, the act of defining certain terms was problematic, most notably *ba'al teshuvah*. It is translated by some as "master of return" and by others simply as "one who returns." Let's focus on the latter term. What exactly do those words mean? From where did this person come? And to what precisely is he returning? In short, what is a *BT*?

First of all, what is *teshuvah*?

It is a fundamental Jewish concept, the idea of self-renewal. The classic commentators, including Rambam, define it in terms of repentance from sin (and subsequent avoidance of sin) for any Jew, observant or not. Contemporary Talmudist and author Adin Steinsaltz goes one step further. "Broadly defined, *teshuvah* is more than just repentance from sin," he writes. "It is a spiritual reawakening, a desire to strengthen the connection between oneself and the sacred."[1]

In its most common current usage, however, *ba'al teshuvah* is essentially a colloquialism that implies not only repentance, but also a marked change in lifestyle brought about by a philosophical transformation and additional religious practice.

How much practice? Must one reach a critical mass of *Yiddishkeit* to qualify as a *BT*? Does it matter where on the denominational spectrum one finds himself?

"It should . . . be questioned whether any definition of *teshuvah* requires complete Orthodox observance before one is considered a *ba'al teshuvah*," educator Arnold D. Samlan wrote in the journal *Sh'ma*. "Doesn't a person who chooses greater observance of *mitzvot* do *teshuvah*, even if done under Reform or Conservative auspices?"[2]

Yes. But that person wouldn't be included in this book. I've selected only those interviewees who now consider themselves Orthodox Jews.

I've followed the lead of author M. Herbert Danzger, who wrote in detail about the *ba'al teshuvah* movement in his book *Returning to Tradition: The Contemporary Revival of Orthodox Judaism*.

---

1. Adin Steinsaltz, *Teshuvah: A Guide for the Newly Observant* (Northvale: Jason Aronson, 1996), 3.

2. Arnold D. Samlan, "The Contemporary Jewish Lexicon," *Sh'ma: A Journal of Jewish Responsibility* 22/431 (April 3, 1992): 87.

Discussing the "new phenomenon" of Jews returning to the fold, he wrote, "most of these *ba'alei t'shuva* have returned not to Reform or Conservative Judaism, movements that have made a separate peace with the modern world, but to Orthodox Judaism, which seems intransigently resistent to the demands of modernity."[3]

Danzger added: "Those who become Orthodox . . . not only undertake a new way of life but also give up or at least subject to strain many of their most important ties to others who are not Orthodox. . . . In sociological terms, becoming Orthodox involves an implosion of social relations."[4]

In short, the experience of Orthodox Jews is fundamentally different than that of other Jews because Orthodoxy, even modern Orthodoxy, makes demands on its adherents that the other denominations do not.

In order to provide readers with meaningful insights into the *BT* phenomenon, to convey its essence, I felt it was important to focus on those Jews who have come the farthest, risked the most and arguably are now the most deeply involved with their faith—newly Orthodox Jews.

Implicit in the contemporary definition of *ba'al teshuvah* is the idea that "Judaism can never again be a mere hobby" for the returnee,[5] according to Steinsaltz, who speaks of a "new kind of *teshuvah*"[6] that rejects the pick-and-choose Judaism that is often sanctioned by non-Orthodox denominations. "To the *ba'al teshuvah*, undertaking only part of what Judaism demands," he writes, "seems like self-deception, a kind of trick played on the Creator of the universe and oneself."[7]

Obviously, there are non-Orthodox Jews who have made strides in their observance, and for that they should be commended. They have done *teshuvah*, but that alone does not make them *ba'alei teshuvah*. Not yet; not according to the current definition of the term, which admittedly, has been framed solely by Orthodox Jewry. Samlan is concerned that the use of this term, among others, has "created needless, artificial ways of separating Jew from Jew" and has engendered an "all-or-nothing" approach to Judaism.[8]

---

3. M. Herbert Danzger, *Returning to Tradition: The Contemporary Revival of Orthodox Judaism* (New Haven: Yale University Press, 1989), 2.

4. *Ibid.*, 27.

5. Steinsaltz, *Teshuvah*, 16.

6. *Ibid.*, 9.

7. *Ibid.*, 16–17.

8. Samlan, "The Contemporary Jewish Lexicon," *Sh'ma* (April 3, 1992): 87–88.

True, there are some who have fostered divisiveness through their use of the term. I've done it myself, and I know it's wrong. I think *frum* Jews, *BT*s or otherwise, have an obligation to try to reach out to non-*frum* Jews with kindness and understanding, regardless of philosophical differences.

Nevertheless, use of the term *ba'al teshuvah* clearly indicates that a distinction is being made. That distinction stems from the recognition of a simple reality: Practically speaking, there's a basic difference between lighting candles on Friday night for the first time and making a genuine commitment to live a Torah-true life, with all the restrictions and obligations that entails.

At least that's the *gashmius* answer. God may feel differently. In His eyes, for all we know, the Jew whose *yetzer hara* prevents him from doing anything more than lighting candles may be as righteous and as deserving of reward as his *shomer mitzvos* neighbor. If I wrongly overlooked that person, I apologize.

The journalist in me, the *frum* journalist, has concluded that *ba'al teshuvah*, in its current context, connotes the embrace of a religious ideal as well as a break with the past and the adoption of new culture. Those who embrace this ideal are committed to elevating their lives and bringing *kedusha* to the world through the strict observance of the letter and spirit of *halachah*, whether or not they are now able to perform all the requisite *mitzvos*. They strive to *someday* do it all. Only Orthodoxy meets those criteria. If that's "all-or-nothing" Judaism, so be it.

Those who would argue that my views are colored by the fact that I am Orthodox, and a *BT*, are correct. I am not a disinterested observer, although I hope a fair one. I believe that Orthodoxy is the most powerful form of Judaism because it touches virtually every aspect of human existence. For that reason, it is unique among the denominations in its ability to enrich lives. That's provided, of course, that its practitioners are kind, moral, ethical, and open-minded in addition to being scrupulous in their observance of formal *halachah*.

I mention this because there are, unfortunately, ostensibly halachic Jews who perform *mitzvos* by the carload but have inculcated none of the moral and ethical values of Judaism or of its spirituality. I would no sooner include them in this book than I would include Jews who believe that the consumption of noodle kugel is the pinnacle of *Yiddishkeit*. Or those who believe that certain *halachot* can be discarded on a whim.

So, one of the chief criteria for inclusion in this book is that the person be classified as an "Orthodox Jew."

What is an Orthodox Jew?

(A neighbor of mine shuns the use of the term "Orthodox" because, he says, it muddies the water. He feels Jews are either unobservant or observant, or they aspire to be observant. They need no other labels. That's an oversimplification of his position, but he has a point. As a result, whenever the shorthand term "Orthodox" appears in this book, feel free to mentally substitute such words as "Torah-true," "observant," or "traditional.")

For the record, the *Encyclopaedia Judaica* defines an Orthodox Jew as one who accepts "as divinely inspired the totality of the historical religion of the Jewish people as it is recorded in the Written and Oral Laws and codified in the *Shulchan Aruch* and its commentaries until recent times, and as it is observed in practice according to the teachings and unchanging principles of the *halachah.*"[9]

For the purposes of this book, I've defined Orthodoxy more in terms of observance than belief because deeds are the essentials of Judaism. In particular, the observance of *kashrus* and *Shabbos*—two of the more publicly visible *mitzvos*—are the criteria I've chosen to use here, and not without precedent. These two are key elements in any self-definition of Orthodoxy and are generally considered minimal grounds for acceptance in an observant community.

Thus, interviewees were considered for the project only if they claimed to be *shomer Shabbos* and *shomer kashrus.* That seemed to be sufficient evidence that I was dealing only with serious, committed Jews.

In truth, not every case I encountered was quite so clear-cut. A few of them tested this standard rather severely and made for some agonizing decision-making. Despite these possible exceptions, I feel that Orthodoxy, as commonly defined, is generally the best indicator of strength of commitment to Judaism, which is why I used it. It may not be a perfect standard, but it is the best gauge that was available. Again, that's the *gashmius* view.

In conclusion, for purpose of this project, *ba'alei teshuvah* are defined as Jews who are now Orthodox but weren't always. That's the short answer. In a broader sense, they are Jews whose lives have been changed in a fundamental way. They are Jews for whom the Torah was once a peripheral part their lives—if it was present at all—and for whom the Torah is now the core of their existence.

---

9. *Encyclopaedia Judaica* (Jerusalem: Keter Publishing House, 1972), 12:1485–86.

4
The Stories

The 31 individuals whose stories were selected for this book were contacted through Jewish outreach organizations, synagogues, and other communal sources, as well as by word of mouth.

Their stories were recorded during telephone and in-person interviews conducted between January and September of 1995. The transcripts of the interviews were then edited for impact, clarity, and length as well as to eliminate possible *loshen hara*. The edited narratives also include my questions as well as sections of paraphrased or explanatory material. These portions appear in italics, as do most non-English terms in the narratives, which are defined in the glossary. The male pronouns "he," "him," and "his" were used generically throughout the book to refer to individuals of either gender. This was done to avoid awkward sentence constructions. Both Ashkenazic and Sephardic spellings of Hebrew terms were used to accurately reflect the speaking style of each narrator. In some cases, both forms appear within the same narrative.

The most interesting and insightful narratives were chosen, and only those told by people now identifying themselves as Orthodox Jews. In a few cases, names and certain details of the stories were altered to protect the privacy of the interviewees.

The participants constituted a wide cross section of once-disaffected Jewry, chiefly American. Two of them, however, were born and raised in Russia and three in Canada.

They came from many walks of life, including medicine, science, law, art, finance, show business, education, psychology, and the media. Six are now rabbis and one is the wife of a rabbi.

They ranged in age from 20 to 65, but nearly half were in their 40s (at the time of their interviews). In most cases, other information about the interviewees, such as marital and employment status as well as domicile, is current as of the time of their interviews only. It may have changed since.

Twenty-five of the thirty-one participants were male. Slightly more than half of them began returning to *Yiddishkeit* when they were in their twenties, before their lives were settled.

Sixty percent of those who were ever married started becoming observant before they were married. Only nine began the process after they had children, but in most of those cases children played a direct or indirect role in their decision to become more religious.

Regardless of when the process started, most of the returnees said it took several years before they had inculcated the values of *Yiddishkeit* and incorporated its practices sufficiently to call themselves Orthodox Jews.

The returnees are geographically dispersed, although most of them now live in the northeast United States. Two reside in Canada and four in Israel.

And at the time of his interview, one lived where he stuck out like a sore thumb. Jamie Mausberg, an environmental engineer and sometime ski instructor, until recently was a resident of Salt Lake City, Utah, where he was one of only a handful of religious Jews. At last count, the entire state had only 3,500 Jews, representing 0.2 percent of the population.

"You learn to live with it," he said. "It's funny; I guess maybe it makes you stronger in your Judaism. There's been a lot of religious [Jewish] kids . . . who come up here and go skiing and we all taught skiing at the resorts. And you run into these people and they're just blown away by the fact that there's a *frum* kid living out here in the middle of the *midbar* and somehow getting on with life in a decent way. Some of them actually said that I had inspired them to go home and live a more observant Torah lifestyle."

II

The Narratives

5
The View
from the Top

I remember being on top of that mountain and looking down, literally and figuratively, and wondering what life was all about. I knew I was about to die.

By the time he was in college in the early 1970s, Brad Abramson had long since abandoned the pro forma Judaism of his youth and was deeply ensconced in the counterculture.

During Columbus Day vacation, he and some friends went hiking in the mountains in New Hampshire. What began as a carefree outing became a harrowing ordeal when Abramson and another hiker became separated from the rest of the group and got lost on the rugged slopes. With their food dwindling, the temperature dropping, and darkness closing in, Abramson slipped and fell into a hole beneath a boulder. The two explorers spent the next three days huddled in the hole, which provided virtually the only protection from the bitter cold and a blizzard.

Weak from exposure and lack of food and water, the hikers gave up hope—and so did the rescue parties that climbed the mountain in search of their frozen corpses. Miraculously, they stumbled on the lost hikers before it was too late. Abramson was frostbitten, dehydrated, and badly shaken from his closest-ever brush with death. It was a nightmarish episode. But it gave him time to think.

I had never associated Judaism with spirituality or religion. I only associated it with relatives and *bar mitzvahs* and things that didn't touch

ul to me. I remember in high school I used
on anything really me *yarmulka*. I thought it was the weirdest thing
to pick on a kid who
anybody could do. college I had turned to spiritual things and East-
By the time I w n, mysticism, etc. When somebody was trying to
ern religions, Hin at my school [a small college in Massachusetts],
start a Hillel cha ard, where you'd check off what religion you were,
they sent around er. I checked "other." I didn't want to identify.
Jewish or wha
In college I was involved in a [religious society] which teaches that
the Godhead has incarnated itself in different figures in different cul-
tres, that any se man could be an inspiration. I wanted to look at an
inspirational figure, so I had a big picture of Jesus on my wall at college.
While I was away from school [recovering after the mountaineering
misadventure], some other kids saw the picture of Jesus, so they figured it would be a nice thing to get me another one. They bought one—
a nice big one of him on the cross—and they hung it on the wall next to
the other one.

When my parents went back with me to school, the first thing they
saw was these pictures, and my mother almost fainted. I remember her
saying, "Maybe you might want to visit a synagogue."

I went to the Conservative *shul* my parents belonged to, and they'd
have guest speakers from time to time. They had this Lubavitch *chasid*
speaking, and I thought, here's an amazingly mystical guy. It really
knocked me out, the commitment to Torah and tradition. I was flabber-
gasted. This was something I could put my feet on and live with. Other
Eastern religions were interesting and tantalizing, but something in me
always knew these things weren't me. There were never ways to incorporate it into your lifestyle, to put holiness into your day-to-day existence, like how to bring up a family, things like that.

I later wrote to him [the *chasid*] and poured out my life story. I was
drawn to this guy because he was pulling no punches, there was no intel-
lectualization. He was speaking from the heart.

Then I went to a *pegisha* in Crown Heights [in Brooklyn], and it was
a total emotional experience. I felt like I was inside a Chaim Potok novel.
When I opened the door it was like I had discovered a different world.
I was gently pushed, almost carried along, to the front of the room and
then I was literally lifted up by a big chasidic guy. It was like I'd been
there before; it was something good and something right. On *motzei*

Shabbos they had a *farbrengen* and I remember dancing and dancing. I was being swept away, totally emotionally. All along, I'd been looking for meaning, and this was it.

I went home to my parents' house [in Cherry Hill, New Jersey], glassy-eyed with *tzitzis* on. It was like I'd been dropped out of space. My *Yiddishkeit* didn't last. I went back to college very confused about my lifestyle. I got more and more involved in drugs and stuff. I realized that I had to get out of there because I didn't want to destroy myself. I decided to go to a *yeshiva* in Crown Heights, and at the last minute, I stopped. I started crying. I was confused and embarrassed. It ended up that I didn't go.

All I knew was extremes. I only knew of *Chabad* or nothing, the world of black hat versus total secularism, one world to another. Around this time, I was set up for Pesach at the home of a *rav* in Springfield, Massachusetts, who had gone through Yeshiva University, and I remember asking about it [YU]. It seemed like a slower, more gradual alternative to me. I knew *Yiddishkeit* was right and knew in some form or other that I wanted it.

I transferred to YU, which is where I met my wife. It was a confusing place. I met people there who had very, very different philosophies than what I was used to. I knew nothing of learning or Gemara. I thought everything was singing. I didn't know exactly what I was getting myself into. But I had some motivated *rabbeyim* who helped me see the light. At one point, I remember, I made it clear that I felt that Jews were cheats and liars and prejudiced. Rabbi [Shlomo] Riskin sat me down in such an emotional and sincere way and said, "Shmuel, what's wrong? Can I help you?" He kept me from becoming a total deserter.

I graduated from YU [in 1977] modern and confused. I had no real firm goal and no practical way of implementing what I had learned. I enjoyed learning, but I'd slide back a little to my old ways, this time with a *yarmulka* on.

The turning point came after YU when we went to Israel. We were visiting the *Ohr Somayach* community, looking for a possible *yeshiva* for me. Rabbi [Nachman] Bulman was the most personable and encouraging for me. He asked us, "Why do you want to come to Israel?" We talked about the holiness and the *Kotel* and everything, and he looked at me and said, "Don't be such a baby. What are you going to do, float around in a cloud and travel with the angels?" What he meant was we to become grounded if we wanted to implement *Yiddishkeit* into a practical everyday lifestyle. We had to figure out how we wanted to live it.

We finally did. What did it for us was at *Ohr Somayach* when we saw young people living together and learning together and you could just feel the *Yiddishkeit*. It was very moving. Maybe it was my '60s idealism coming through. I'd always been looking for people of common interests coming together and sharing. This felt sort of like going back to nature. It wasn't like in America where there was so much fragmentation.

When we came back to *Ohr Somayach* in Yonkers [with plans to move back permanently to *Ohr Somayach* in Israel], we met Rabbi [Leib] Tropper, who was another strong influence on me. He was a totally unique guy. He was a wild kind of guy. At first I didn't know how to read him. He got totally involved with his learning. He would end a *Gemara shiur* by jumping up and down [laughs]; or he'd smack you on the back when you found an answer, and his glasses would go flying off [laughs]. He got me very much into learning. He made learning fun. From the [one-year] Yonkers experience, I wanted to dedicate my life to learning.

The final stint in Israel was at *Aish Hatorah* [where Abramson eventually received rabbinic ordination]. The *rosh yeshiva* was Noach Weinberg, one of the most charismatic people I've ever met. He was very, very idealistic, almost revolutionary in his idea of saving the Jewish world. I remember their battle cry: They were waging a war on assimilation, there was blood in the streets, get out the troops. I was totally swept away by the enthusiasm. He [Weinberg] was like the Abbie Hoffman of *Yiddishkeit*. I wanted to come back to America and save the world. The plan was to come back and start a Philadelphia branch of *Aish Hatorah*, but the finances didn't work out.

The situation was very depressing. Our first *Shabbos* experience in Philadelphia . . . well, let me put it like this. When we were in Israel, the sounds we'd hear on Friday night were the *yeshiva bochrim* singing *zemiros*. It was wonderful. When we came to Philadelphia, our neighbors provided their own brand of noise on Shabbos—the stereo booming. It felt like hell on earth.

At the suggestion of one of his teachers, Abramson came to Monsey, New York, where he taught and did administrative work at a yeshiva.

I finally felt grounded, but I had a family to support [three children by then], and it was tough. I remember I'd call up the bank on the day the *yeshiva* paid me to make sure there was enough money in my account. One time I called the bank and they actually laughed when I asked. It was always a struggle between doing what God wanted me to do and supporting my family. Sometimes I'd wonder, why isn't He providing? I wondered if I was reading the message wrong.

He wasn't. Abramson eventually landed a job as a rebbe *at a well-funded special education* yeshiva *in Teaneck, New Jersey, which is operated under modern Orthodox auspices. He teaches Judaics and secular subjects and does vocational training. He has been there for the past six years and finds the work highly rewarding.*

I remember being on top of that mountain and looking down, literally and figuratively, and wondering what life was all about. I knew I was about to die. I told myself that if I ever make it out of here, with whatever time I have left, I was going to find out what it's all about and go with it. Would I go in the direction of being 100 percent nihilist and hedonist? Or would I go in the opposite direction and find meaning and purpose for living? You can guess which direction I took. *Hashem* had been giving me the message all along, but maybe I didn't get it until he pushed me into that hole in the mountain.

Brad (Shmuel) Abramson, 41, and his wife have six children and they live in Monsey, New York.

6
Meaninglessness Meets Its Match

I was a universalist. When they would ask for "religion," I would put "human." I had no identity with any particular group of people.

Although she was born and bred in America, Miriam Adahan grew up tormented by visions of the Holocaust. The anguish took its toll. For nearly the first three decades of her life, she firmly believed that "the world was a meaningless place and that there is no God." Even so—or perhaps because of that—she was highly idealistic and fought injustice at every opportunity. And then something unexpected happened.

In the early 1970s, at a low point in her life, Adahan received a potent spiritual jolt in a garden in California. She still isn't sure what happened. But from then on, one thing was certain—she knew there was a God. Unfortunately, she had no idea how to connect with this force. It never occurred to her to go to a rabbi because she didn't think of rabbis as people who could understand her spiritual needs. So she spent the next several years pursuing other paths in a futile attempt to make sense of her experience. It wasn't until her father died in 1976 that she found what she was looking for.

I grew up in a typical midwestern 1950s environment. I was kind of an unusual child in that I was always looking for meaning and purpose in life when everybody else was not interested. I went very minimally to afternoon [Hebrew] school, knew nothing about Judaism except for the holidays. You know, you celebrate the holidays.

However, her father, an attorney, had been passionately involved in efforts to get the Jews out of Europe and later to rid Israel of Arab refugee camps. "He was a very mission-oriented person," said Adahan, who along with the rest of the family, pitched in, and helped with his secular pro-Jewish causes.

And then I went to Berkeley in the '60s and I was part of the antiwar and civil rights movement. I was still looking for a mission and a purpose. I went to law school for a while. I went to medical school for a while and none of that worked out. And then I found my love, which was psychology, and I went for that. I still wasn't happy. I taught high school in the '60s in the Detroit ghetto, from the age of 21 to 25.

At this point, was there any Yiddishkeit *in your life?*

Nothing. It was totally meaningless to me. I was a universalist. When they would ask for "religion," I would put "human" [laughs]. I had no identity with any particular group of people. I opposed cruelty and oppression anywhere and everywhere, whether it was in the school system or in the world. That's what I wanted to do, to help people, to be of service to humanity. That was my goal. I loved teaching; that's where I really found myself.

When I was 14, I had one inspiring teacher called Avraham Karbal. I went to an afternoon Jewish school and learned *Pirkei Avos* there. And that was my one link to Judaism. When I worked in black schools, I remembered *Pirkei Avos* and I loved them. I even taught them to the kids.

Adahan was married in 1969 at the age of 27 to a secular Israeli. A year or two later, after she'd had her first child, she had what she called "a very illuminating experience."

I had never believed in God because of the Holocaust. I had a very mystical experience one day sitting in Berkeley. I was sitting in a garden and I had, like, a direct experience that there's a God in the universe [laughs]. It was very strange; I won't even go into it.

Can you tell me a little about it?

I was sitting in a garden and looking at some flowers and I'd really been looking for answers in life because there'd been a lot of disappointments in my life. And I was sort of at loose ends where to go with my life, and I had this direct experience that there is somebody running the show. That moment changed my life and it was totally unexpected.

From looking at a flower? From its structure or beauty or what?

I have no idea. I had never believed in God. I was the kind of kid, when I was 11, I was walking around with books on existentialism.

Camus and Sartre. I was a confirmed nihilist. I read Nietzsche. This was my way of thinking the world was a meaningless place and that there is no God.

At the time of this revelation, what exactly was troubling you?

It's better not to say. I just didn't want my daughter to go through the same sense of aloneness and anguish and feeling of absurdity that I had gone through. I didn't know what to turn to. What was it about the flower? All of a sudden the world took on . . . there was a golden glow. It was like I saw beyond the *gashmius* world. There was another dimension that was very apparent to me in that moment that had totally penetrated and was part of the physical world, but was beyond it. I had never known there was another dimension. I had lived my life in a very physical dimension.

All of a sudden I became very aware that there was a spiritual dimension, that there was a fifth dimension to this world. It became very real, obvious, not intellectual at all. Every place I looked was permeated with this golden glow and it was obvious that that glow was spiritual. It was like being graced with an apprehension of something, like a gift. Let's say you were blind and then you could see and you didn't know before what you were missing. So I understood what I had been missing.

This just came out of nowhere?

Nowhere. I knew that this world was basically spiritual and not basically physical and that the physical was just temporary. All of a sudden I got all this awareness, and I walked around like this for three days.

Your husband must have thought you were totally meshuggah.

I didn't tell him about it, for that reason [laughs]. He's a very down-to-earth Israeli. What happened was, the glow began to fade and I wanted it back. Then I understood why I couldn't live in the physical world. I wanted to be part of that spiritual reality.

So I went around trying to ask various teachers—religious teachers, spiritual teachers in Berkeley. It was a time of a lot of gurus. I never thought to go to a Jewish teacher, because rabbis to me were these very serious, dour people who would tell you about pots and pans and *kashrus* and it didn't seem very spiritual. Spiritual to me had to do with getting that experience back. So I started guru-hopping, and nobody could understand what happened. Nobody validated what had gone on.

I felt very alone now in this new spiritual world. So I started trying various forms of meditation and different groups, and that was unsatisfying because it was a lot of ego. You know, everybody was trying to outdo everybody else with the visions they had.

And then in 1976 my father died. And my older sister, who had since married that man [Avraham Karbal] who taught me when I was 14—I introduced them—we sat *shiva* at their home.

As it turns out, her sister was becoming observant; her husband had been raised in an Orthodox home. They had decided to send their children to the closest parochial school, which happened to be a yeshiva, rather than have them bused to inner city Detroit.

So by the time I got there when my father died, it was just before Pesach, I see this incredible . . . remember I had been studying other religions for the previous four years and had been very disappointed in everything.

Pesach comes, and three things impressed me [at her sister's home]. One, the idea of religion that's in this world, because every other religion says that if you want to be religious you have to go away from the world; you have to go onto a mountaintop, into an ashram, a convent, something else, and meditate, and you're not part of the world.

So here they are, taping the lights and switching the dishes and putting foil on the counters—it's so "in this world," but making this world spiritual, which I loved the idea of. I was there involved in all these frantic Pesach preparations and it was instant love. And I said, "Get me a rabbi."

It was like two, three days after my father died; I said I want to know more about this religion. So I devoured everything I could find. It was interesting; on my father's deathbed, I came to him not knowing anything about Judaism. He had come from an Orthodox home, but had gone away from it. And he knew that I was involved in all kinds of whatever. On his deathbed, about an hour before he died, I held his hand and I said, "Don't worry, I'm going to become an Orthodox Jew." I don't know where these words came from. I didn't know what Orthodoxy was; I didn't know what it meant. But I said that to him.

I knew he was worried about me, for reasons I can't go into. I had a number of serious illnesses and he was worried about me. I was not well at the time, and I told him, "I'm gonna be okay, I'm going to become Orthodox." Three days later, I am fully committed.

Usually, it takes people a lot longer than that.

Well, it took me a long time to get rid of my *goyisha* values. I knew that this was pure truth. I was fascinated with a religion that allows one to be in the world and yet separate from it. [Her sister] was very non-coercive and very loving.

He died on a Sunday night, and Wednesday night was the first *seder*. And I remember sitting down with three generations of people all dressed modestly, all singing the same songs, saying the same *brachas*, doing the same thing. I felt linked to generations of Jews. I felt linked to history. I felt linked to something very meaningful, whereas my life in Berkeley for seven years was such a transient life and [there was] no stability and no sense of family or history. It was just whatever new fad was coming up next.

I just started learning everything I could. I learned *Chabad Chasidus* and my rabbi was Rabbi Silberberg, in Bloomfield Hills [Michigan] with *Chabad*. I need the *Chasidus* because I love the inner, inner, inner meanings and the love and the joy. But there are also things in the *misnagdisha* world that I'm equally attracted to, and I like that grounding.

Was the transition to frumkeit *easy for you?*

I felt that Orthodoxy was perfect, but I saw a lot of things I didn't like in the practice. I had a lot of arguments, over whether Jews are better or they have a special soul or they have a special link, this and that, this was my big struggle.

What was your position on those issues?

At the beginning, I just felt that anybody with a loving heart has a special *neshama* [Jew or not]. That's how I divided the world, those with hearts and those without.

Did you evolve into a different position?

I think that people who keep *mitzvot* have a very special relationship with God. Now that I see there's a special, tremendous *koach* that keeping all the *mitzvot*, and not just seven, will give a human being, I'm very impressed. But also there's a lot of disappointment in how it's done.

Meaning?

Not everybody has a good heart [laughs]. I met very special people when I was first *frum*. And it was only later that I heard about all the disagreements and the arguments and the power struggles. Thank God I didn't see this or hear about it at the beginning. And that saddened me, that there's all this politics and this one hates that one. But I see that people are people, and depending on the personality type and their level of spiritual evolution, people are very different.

You already believed in God; how did you incorporate that into your emerging new lifestyle?

That I had to really work on. I believed that there was a God. That's *emunah*. But *bitachon*—belief that God cared about me personally and had a special relationship with me and that I could have a personal, direct relationship with God—that took a long time coming because I had not had particularly close relationships with anybody growing up. So my sense of alienation and aloneness was very strong, and that transferred itself over into my relationship with God.

It was a constant process, and also dealing with the Holocaust. I came into this lifetime with Holocaust memories, however you want to translate that. As a three-, four-, five-year-old, when I would go to sleep, I would always hear people screaming, crammed into a tight space. And if I would see stripes or hear German, I would go nuts. And then it was only later on that I realized these were Holocaust memories that were either in my cells, because I was born in 1942, or from a previous incarnation. I had a tremendous amount of fear and anxiety about being in the world.

As a child did you try to hide your Jewishness?

I went to a school that was 98 percent Jewish, and completely assimilated. What I had to hide was [the fact that] I learned that nobody was really interested in hearing about and trying to understand what we were here for. What is our existence all about? That was my obsession.

I was a very deeply feeling child and there was nobody to talk to, literally. Not one human being that could understand the depths of the emotional anguish I was feeling or explain to me why I would have these incredibly real nightmares in which I was being chased. There were certain sights I would see that would just paralyze me.

How does Yiddishkeit *help you deal with these images?*

I now know that there's an ultimate purpose, that we're going toward a specific goal, that there's meaning, even though the world looks completely meaningless and absurd and tragic and incomprehensible and unjust. That's the way it looks. And unless you have a connection to that other dimension, that's the way it's going to remain looking, and that's how it will seem.

Once you have the connection, how does it look to you?

I have those two sets of eyes, my *gashmius* eyes and my *ruchnius* eyes. And if I look with my *ruchnius* eyes, there is a higher meaning to it all.

And what is that meaning?

That we're here to love.

Which you initially believed.

Right. We're here to love God despite whatever happens to us. I've been though a lot of very, very difficult physical and emotional situations that have tested me to the limits of what a human being's faith can be tested to. The people I work with in Israel are also in that same situation of being tested to limits. I work with battered women. I work with abused children. I work mostly with young women with cancer, with little children.

Has your husband been on the same page as you, in terms of Yiddishkeit?

When I became observant, we were separated at that time. And I said, look, my condition of getting back together was that he also become observant, which he did. I can just say we're on very different paths, although we're both observant. If he had been listening to sports on *Shabbos*, it couldn't have worked.

There are those who feel Orthodoxy denigrates women. How do you deal with women's issues?

Orthodoxy is the most incredibly feminist philosophy around. I have never seen strength in women like I've seen strength in women with large families who are managing these kids. I see female strength and I see women who are not hooked into getting their sense of value from their men, which is what the secular world does—getting your strength from being beautiful and having a man love you or value you [for that]. I see women getting a sense of value from their relationship to *Hashem* which is where it should come from.

Does it bother you that woman have no leadership roles in an Orthodox shul?

Traditionally and psychologically, men need to fraternize and they need to be around other men and they need to have their exclusive group where women are not involved. And that's what Orthodoxy recognizes, a truth. It's not this obsession the secular world has with the mating game. In the secular world, regularly, men in their forties leave their wives for younger models.

Women don't need to go to *shul*; they don't have to be there. Men need that; they need to get away from women at times and not have the conquest and the sexual issues on their mind. The Buddhists do this and nobody complains at all; nobody says one word.

In sum, what impact has Yiddishkeit *had on your life?*

I always believed in being a loving human being, but I think I didn't know what that meant—truly to love.

What does that mean?

To love unconditionally, to love life. I think what *frumkeit* taught me was a love of life that is unconditional. I loved life if it would give me certain things. It was a conditional love of life. Okay, if I get this and this and this, then I'll like you, God. I was bargaining.

Now, I can treasure every moment, even the painful moments and see it as part of this journey, and [I] treasure people as they are, treasure myself, value myself, value life and find joy in life as it is, not as I wanted it to be. I'm not angry at how life is anymore. I'm upset about the injustice on a *gashmius* level. I have on the steering wheel of my car a little card that says, "I make God's will my will" [laughs]. And it's in my purse. It's my spiritual credit card, right next to my Visa.

How old are your kids?

13, 15, 17 and 25.

How are they with frumkeit*?*

Pretty good. I mean they're not like me. They're not these airy-fairy spiritual types. They're much more down to earth [laughs]. But boy am I happy to be bringing them up with these values, because I look in a newspaper here in America and I see the widespread drug use among young people. I'd be terrified if I was a parent without *Yiddishkeit*. What are parents doing? What are they giving their kids?

FINDING THE MIRACLES WITHIN

Miriam Adahan is a practitioner of Torah-oriented psychotherapy, which means she functions as "sort of a spiritual midwife. I don't do anything fancy. I'm there to guide people and help them think more clearly and not be bitter or angry about the cards they were dealt this lifetime."

I have an organization [headquartered in Jerusalem] called EMETT, which stands for Emotional Maturity Established Through Torah, and it provides guidelines for thinking in spiritual terms. The basis for all of Torah is love. Love God, love people, honor yourself, honor people, honor life. And it's the hardest thing to do.

The therapy that I do is having people contact that part of themselves which is love, which is the essence of the human being, and use that part to heal themselves.

How does that differ from more conventional types of therapy?

What I do as quickly as possible is have a person begin communicating with his or her own *neshama*. Like if a person is sad, have him draw a picture of himself sad and draw a picture of the part of themselves that is pure joy, and have them dialogue back and forth to make a connection with the loving life force with them.

The idea of communicating with your own *neshama* is very, very important. And that's really what heals people, when people can get in touch with that part of themselves. When a person has contact with that *neshama*, they have an ongoing source of connectedness, so they're not worried so much about being hurt. They're not worried so much about the pain of life. Life is painful, and most people don't know how do deal with pain except to get depressed and enraged and to look outside themselves for cures.

I tell people to use everyday events as opportunities to respond in what might be an unnatural manner, in a loving way. People think, "Yeah I'm a good person—unless I'm tired, bored, hungry, irritated, or provoked; and then I turn into a monster." What we do is look for those times when we're tired, hungry, bored, irritated, or provoked and act according to the Torah and celebrate those moments.

Adahan urges her clients to make entries in what she calls a "faith-building" notebook.

One side [is for listing] acts of self-discipline for people to get in touch with own inner godliness, because the ability to restrain a negative impulse comes from our godly soul. The other side is to write down little miracles that happen each day. Like a car narrowly missing you. Or getting an appointment with a doctor like, *boruch Hashem*, there just happened to be a cancellation or you would have had to wait three months; that kind of thing. So you write down the little miracles. It could be a smile or a good word or anything. You practice being grateful on a daily basis for little things. And on a very small level you begin to build a sense that God is with you and there are miracles in your life no matter how bad things might be going; that there are blessings and you focus on the blessings.

What kind of reaction do you get from clients when you start talking about Torah this and Torah that?

I work mainly with observant people, so there's no problem with people understanding that they do have a godly part that that they can tap into. We talk constantly about this *neshama*, this godly part of ourselves, but we don't take it seriously as a source of wisdom.

One might expect that people living in a frum *community are generally better adjusted and have less pain, etc.*

They have different pain. There's a pain that comes from living in too permissive a society and too liberal a society and there's a pain that comes from living in perhaps a society that can at times seem overly strict. To be *frum* is to be in the Olympics. There you are, you've got your mountain-climbing equipment, at least, and you've got a direction to go in. That's what *frumkeit* gives you. But the mountain climbing is your task. Are you gonna be a loving human being? What's going on in your heart? The climb is yours and yours alone.

I deal with people with problems with living, which everybody has. EMETT skills are basic skills for how to get along in the world and not lose your dignity—how can you maintain your dignity and live in a world which is so irritating and often so tragic.

That's the challenge. It's the same challenge if you're religious or if you're not religious. If you're religious, at least you know that there's a God there and that you have a godly soul that at least you can connect to. My job is to give the techniques which enable the person to connect to their godly soul.

The *Chazon Ish* said there's only one goal in life and that's *lahit aloht*, which means to go up, to refine yourself. So whether you're in a traffic jam or dealing with a kid that's having a tantrum, your job is to work on your self-refinement.

Religion doesn't have a positive connotation for most people. It's like sitting in *shul* hour after hour, yuch. And it's being punished for not saying the *brachas* and not doing this and not doing that. What I do is I try to make the spiritual world very, very exciting. I think *middos* work is the most exciting thing in the world.

We get together and celebrate. It's really, *mamish*, like a celebration, EMETT meetings, of this relative did this, and I was just quiet. And we celebrate and we sit there and clap. Therapy should be a celebration of what you're doing for your own self-refinement.

You don't think you could have done this without Torah?

Torah gives you the guidelines and the principles. You can get way off track, as we see that people who don't have Torah can go around justifying the most outrageous things, which we see all over. There are so many trips out there and how do you know which one is right? You could go on endless trips. In this new age, you really can't trust your mind to know what direction to take.

Miriam Adahan, 53, is an author and psychologist. She is divorced and resides in Jerusalem. She has four children.

7
A Spiritual
"Evolutionary"

I have this sense that I am living something meaningful basically every day of my life. And I have a sense that I've been able to transfer that to the next generation.

Joan Bieler is the wife of an Orthodox rabbi and a fixture in her observant suburban community. But she had a previous life that was virtually devoid of religion. She wants other frum *Jews to know that—to know how far she came—in hopes that they will be more accepting of those who haven't made the journey.*

Long before she met her husband, Bieler began a spiritual evolution—as opposed to a revolution—which came about when Orthodox Jews reached out to her with compassion and understanding. One of them was a Yeshiva University-educated rabbi who had taken the helm of the Conservative synagogue in Queens where Bieler was a member of a youth social club. The new rabbi had required all club members to take a once-a-week religious class. He opened the first day of class with a question that caught Bieler flat-footed.

He said, "What about you makes you Jewish?" And I still remember that my response to him was that on Saturday night we had bagels. And when I thought about it I couldn't come up with too much of anything else. And that seemed so pathetic to me. And I started going to these classes and I started slowly but surely learning more and more about the religion.

As things went on and I continued with the class, by the time I got to tenth grade, I took biology and geometry, and both those courses had a huge effect on me. The order—the relationship of structure and function in biology and the order in geometry—was very compelling to me. And though most people look at science and math and think that's the antithesis of the spiritual, to me the sense of order I got from studying biology and geometry, if anything, crystalized my belief in a more powerful and higher being and something that organized the universe.

And I really had a strong sense of religion at that point, but it was only emotional. It didn't manifest itself. I had no way of knowing what to do at that point. I was 15, and I didn't know a whole lot about the religion and I didn't have a whole lot of contact with religious people.

That summer, though, two people from the youth group went to something called the Yeshiva University Torah Leadership Seminar, affectionately known as TLS. They had rabbis, YU faculty, who would be faculty at these seminars. There would be retreat weekends, and they got kids with more religious backgrounds, either from day schools or just even kids who weren't in day schools but who were observant, to be advisors. And the kids who went were all kids without backgrounds, generally public school kids.

That summer of '65, two kids from our youth group went, and among the other things that happened that summer, two advisors, staff people, got married at the seminar. And the way people told the story, it rained during the whole day that they were supposed to be married, and then when they decided it was time for the *chupah*, the clouds cleared, the rain stopped, and a rainbow came out over the lake and then they were married.

Well, you can imagine that the kids who came back were, like, totally sold. They had completely fallen in love with everything about seminar and thus about Judaism. And they convinced me, and probably a few other people in the youth group, to go that winter. So my first exposure to this YU seminar was in the winter of 1965. And I remember it being a very, very powerful experience. And I don't know if there exists anything like it today for public school kids, for kids who are unaffiliated.

They had advisors who were great fun who wanted to explain every aspect of the religion, who were never critical about anything that you did. They made it very easy to observe because the environment was just set up for observance.

Every meal was like a wedding, every single meal including break-fast. You'd wash your hands, you'd say *hamotzee* on the bread, you ate and then there would be dancing, just as if it was a wedding, seven days a week, three meals a day. And at the end, everybody would say the *bentshing*, the grace after meals, and it was just a very powerful experience.

There were other kids like myself who came from no background who were searching, and we became friends. And also, there were these advisors to confide in, who were examples because they were both religiously observant themselves and accepting of those of us who had not yet become religiously observant. They were very positive examples.

My hope is that people who know me and who know how religious I am at this point in my life and who don't know me from before, will see where I have come from and therefore be more accepting of people who aren't religious or who are less religious, because more and more, I see the Orthodox community pushing away or not pulling in people who are not religious. I've been saddened by that.

As my high school career went on, I continued to go to these seminars in both summer and winter. I was also very involved in high school in a club that did social work at settlement houses around New York City. And my particular house where I worked was the Lincoln Square neighborhood center, and it was in the neighborhood about which *West Side Story* was made.

But that program took place on Saturday. And as I wanted to observe religion more, I had more and more conflicts within myself as to whether I should go to synagogue or go to the settlement house. At the settlement house, after all, I was doing something very uplifting, socially beneficial, and I really didn't know what to do. Toward my last year in high school, I just was very conflicted. I used to go to synagogue with a pocketbook under my coat and then leave synagogue and go on the bus to the city to go to the settlement house.

And the way I rationalized my way out of this is that I said, "Well, when I leave for college, then I'll be able to be observant." And in August 1967, before I left for college, my parents took me out for my last lobster dinner; lobster was my favorite food. And I left for college, State College of New York at Buffalo.

Once there, she hooked up with the Hillel rabbi and spent Shabbos at his home with his family. It was a first for Bieler.

Previously, I'd had these seminar institutional meals, but this was my first [*Shabbos*] meal with a family in a house. And I really appreciated it very much. And later that year I also spent other *yom tovim* with that family, and each *yontif* was the first *yontif* I had ever spent with a family. I think it had a powerful impact. I had a sense that the family itself, apart from the religion, was very close; but you couldn't really separate it out from the religion, because I had a sense that the religion was part of what made them close. It was just a pleasant feeling in terms of the observance, and I guess that helped me decide that this is the way I want to lead my life.

But I also found it very, very difficult. I remember the first Friday night, that Friday night before I had gone to services, I lit candles in the room after everybody else had gone to the [student] mixer, the first weekend mixer. And I remember feeling like a *marrano*, and I did not have whatever it took to do that again. It was so uncomfortable for me; but not doing it was also uncomfortable for me.

You also have to remember the times. This was '67, '68, and there was a whole lot of anti-war demonstrations and I went to a lot of anti-war rallies and stuff like that. This was all going on on one side of my life. On the other side of my life, I had all these conflicts about religion.

That winter I went to seminar . . . and after lots of very deep late-night discussions with lots of people, I determined that I was going to transfer from Buffalo to Stern College [which is part of Yeshiva University]. I saw that on my own I wasn't going to have the determination to stand apart. I'm a very social person. I'm a people person, and I couldn't stand apart from my friends in the secular environment. And I realized that if I wanted this badly enough—and I had determined that I wanted the religious life badly enough—I was going to have to pull myself out of the environment I was in and put myself into a religious environment.

Her decision to transfer was traumatic for Bieler and also for her parents. She had attended Buffalo "basically for free," thanks to a scholarship and low tuition. Her move to Stern would subject her parents, who were not wealthy, to a greater financial burden. They were not pleased.

Also, they were uncomfortable, I think, with me becoming religious. I mean, as anybody who has kids can tell you, it's very hard when kids turn against your way of doing things, and I'm sure my parents had that kind of difficulty.

When YU accepted me, they accepted me knowing I wasn't *shomer Shabbat*. I explained to them what my difficulties were; I explained to them that I had every intention of becoming *shomer Shabbos* once I went to Stern, and in fact I did, and they accepted me on that basis. I wonder if in this day and age, if they would make the same determination. The week before I went to Stern, I went to somebody's house and that week I was *shomer Shabbos*, and from that day to this I have been *shomer Shabbos*.

In terms of my commitment, from the time I got to Stern there was no turning back. I was totally committed once I got there. I never had a fight with myself, should I get on a bus? Should I smoke a cigarette? From that *Shabbos* on, that was it.

Coming from a secular background, did you suffer culture shock at Stern?

I don't know what Stern is like now, but the religious world was less right wing than it is today. I think my roommates—not everybody in the college—but many of my roommates and a reasonable percentage of the school were involved in politics and other things besides religion. And I was able to find my niche there. So in terms of culture shock, I can tell you the first time I dated anybody . . . I remember talking at these seminars and [hearing] that boys and girls don't touch. And the first time I dated somebody and the guy actually didn't touch me, I came back and I was, like, so shocked. It was such a shock to me that this actually occurred. So, yeah there was culture shock, but it was pleasant.

By that time, I was so starved to be able to observe; I had been for so long unable to do what I had wanted to do, that finally getting the opportunity to do it . . . I think I was just very relieved to not have the pressure to do otherwise.

Her parents adjusted well and even pitched in and bought materials for the family's first succah.

I never force anything on them. I never made them do anything and I also wasn't super extreme. I know people who had their own pots at their parents' houses. I kind of just skirted the issue. I avoided meat and stuff like that. I didn't push them very hard. The first and second year I was at Stern, my mother said she was willing to have me *kasher* the house for Pesach.

She saw that I was in this for good and I probably would marry somebody religious and our kids would be religious. I guess she feared, being a family-oriented person herself, that maybe I wouldn't bring my kids home to her house if her house wasn't kosher, and I think that was her initial motivation for changing the house. And in my third year, after we *kashered* the house for Pesach, she had dishes that she bought, and the house remained kosher after that and has been so ever since.

In addition, my parents have become more observant, though I think initially they had a lot of reservations. They look back now and see how their friends' kids have grown up and things that have happened to their friends' kids and looked back at my life, and I think they're very happy with the way things turned out. They now go to a religious class once a week at their Conservative synagogue. And where initially they found it difficult to spend a whole *Shabbat* with us, or a whole *yontif* with us, now I think they're eager to spend *Shabbat* and *yontif* with us. So they've certainly come a long way.

My brother, who probably had dated non-Jews, ended up marrying a nonreligious Jew, and they agreed to keep their house kosher so that I would be able to come. And since that time, they have now affiliated themselves with an Orthodox synagogue in a suburban New Jersey community. Again, part of my thing in this is that I've never pressured them a whole lot and I've also been very tolerant. And I think that having that attitude has allowed them to have a positive attitude and may someday enable my nieces to become religious.

Do you ever have crises of faith?

I would say that occasionally from time to time I have crises of faith, like everybody else. But I never ever, ever regretted what I did. I think there are always ups and downs in terms of your faith in God and belief in the religion. But having the perspective that I do now, looking back and seeing my kids and seeing my family, and seeing other people's families as well, I can't think of another way of life that could be as fulfilling.

And I'm also very impressed with the fact that observance of both the spirit and the letter of the law enabled me to remain a moral and ethical person. I think sometimes people want to be ethical, they want to do the right thing, but I think that the guidance of the religion makes that more possible.

The only way I can judge the impact of this on my life is to observe the people I left when I took the [other] fork in the road. I have a wonderful family whom I love completely and who are my reasons for living, even though I had to pull out of my career for a long while in order to be with my family. I'm now back in that career, so I don't feel that I've sacrificed a huge amount there.

You know, sometimes the day-to-day things in religious life take up an enormous amount of time. But knowing that you can live your life using the guidance of thousands of years of development of religion behind you, I think that's an enormous stepping stone; it pushes you ahead that much farther. And I can see other people I left when I went my own way who don't have families, who are divorced, who maybe haven't found themseves, who are living lives without meaning. And I have this sense that I am living something meaningful basically every day of my life. And I have a sense that I've been able to transfer that to the next generation.

Orthodoxy has been labeled antifeminist by some. Do you have any problems in this area?

Number one, I think if you demand equality, I think you're going to be in a difficult position. I think that to a certain extent, what the religion teaches is that there are certain benefits in division of labor. I tended, certainly, toward a feminist attitude, and the way I've exercised my feminist attitude is by using the opportunity to learn. My husband very definitely, very strongly believes in women's right to learn every aspect of Torah, and I have been learning all these years. I think that intellectual equality for me has been important.

I understand people who wish that they could have an *aliyah* to the Torah, but it's not a burning need for me. I've sacrificed in order to become religious. I've sacrificed lobster. I sacrificed my long hair. I sacrificed wearing whatever I want to wear, going wherever I wanted to go whenever I wanted to go. And to me, not having an *aliyah* or being the *sheliach tzibbur*, the person who is *davening*, is not all that much of a sacrifice when you consider what you're getting.

I think just like my spiritual evolution was very, very slow, I think there may be a feminist kind of evolution within *halachah*. But I think you have to be patient with that; I don't think it's going to happen in one generation and I don't think it's going to happen in two generations. Nothing in *halachah* goes that fast.

I don't feel so terribly oppressed that I feel rebellious about it. We have a women's *davening* group, a mother-and-daughter *davening* group in school, where occasional Sunday mornings we get together and *daven* together, and a girl can be the leader of the *davening*. There are ways. But I don't think that things will change totally, because I think, as I said, the division of labor in Judaism is very strong. People who have a predilection for doing something that is not defined as their role have to experience some discomfort if they want to stay within the bounds of the religion.

But I think that the spiritual part of it is so much more important than the detail of the day-to-day observance—that if you have to curb yourself on the detail in order to get the bigger picture, that to me is more important. I don't feel superbly frustrated in a general sense. Sometimes in given situations I'll feel frustrated. I think that as things evolve, time will select the right path. But I'm willing to wait. I'm willing to be patient.

Joan Bieler, 45, is a biologist who lives in Silver Spring, Maryland, with her husband and four children.

8
Guess Who Came to Dinner?

I mean, they knew I was Jewish. They didn't have to make a roast pork that night.

There's a darkly humorous scene in the movie Annie Hall *that strikes a chord in many Jews. For Jack Calman, it was art mimicking reality.*

The scene: The Gentile girlfriend of Woody Allen's character, Alvy Singer, has brought him home to break bread with her family, a stereotypical WASP menagerie.

As mounds of trayf *food are dished up, reality suddenly shifts as Alvy, an assimilated Jew, undergoes a bizarre metamorphosis. In the time it takes the camera to cut away and then return, we see him as he now sees himself—or perhaps as his Gentile hosts see him. Alvy's modern Manhattanite is now a frock-coated chasid, complete with a long beard and a bewildered look on his face. The veneer of assimilation has been stripped away, revealing the elemental Jew beneath.*

I lived that. That's exactly what I felt like, and when I saw that scene years later in *Annie Hall*, I thought, Oh my gosh, that's me. How did they know this happened to me? Whenever I feel my Jewishness in the secular world, that scene comes to me all the time. It's amazing.

Calman's Allenesque episode happened more than 20 years ago while he was a 22-year-old graduate student at Harvard. It was his first extended stay outside the Bronx.

I had my first big girlfriend who lived downstairs from me after I left the dorms.

A shiksa*?*

Not only a *shiksa* but a classic, blonde, Episcopal, New England, the works [laughs]. Nice girl [laughs]. Went with her for about a year. So I remember when I dropped the bomb, I said [to my parents], "I have a girlfriend." And they said, "Oh, yeah? She's not Jewish?" So it wasn't too good.

In December, I went home [with her] for the holidays. Her parents lived there [near Harvard]. I never brought her back here [New York]. I knew I could never bring a non-Jewish girl back home, period.

So I went for a plain Sunday-night dinner, and this made an impression on me. The parents said to me as they brought out this roast pork [laughs] . . . I mean, they knew I was Jewish. They didn't have to make a roast pork that night. They were nice people; they were smart people. He was a Harvard professor in the medical school. So they come out with this pink, thick, classic roast pork.

I had seen this stuff before. And the mother says to me, "You do eat this, don't you?" [laughs]. And I said, "Well, not usually, but yeah, sure I'll eat it" [laughs]. I'd had pork in Chinese restaurants, but I'd never had a blatant, 100 percent, full-strength, pink plateful of pork on Sunday night [laughs]. I don't remember if they said grace or not, 'cause that's the only thing I remember from that night [laughs]. I felt like I'd died. That made a big impression on me, 'cause I thought to myself, How am I ever going to be a family with these people?

That was almost at the same time that my father died, he should rest in peace.

Calman displays an old snapshot of a youngster in short pants shaking hands with another kid. It's his father saying good-bye to his best friend shortly before he and his parents bolted their native Romania and came to America. The year was 1926.

They snuck out in the middle of the night, but they made it. When they came to America, a lot of the *frumness* got left behind. The way I figure, [that] they gave it up is very common. All of them wanted to become Americanized.

Calman was born on the Lower East Side of New York but grew up in near poverty in the northeast Bronx in an area that was heavily Italian and Irish but had plenty of Jews too. His father managed dental labora-

tories and then became a proofreader. His mother, who was born in America, helped make ends meet by working as a salesperson and then a school secretary.

They were what I call "unobservant Orthodox," meaning they did not reject the idea of traditional Torah authority, but their daily life was not guided by *halachah*. They went to an Orthodox *shul*. Once or twice a year they went to *shul*, that's it. Major holidays and candles on Friday night, but after that there was TV. They didn't buy *trayf* meat, but there was no [firm distinction between] *milchik* and *fleyshik*. There was really no concept of *halachah* or observance. Judaism was a feeling, if you wanted it, sometimes. There was no learning, no behavioral things, no nothing.

I grew up with an after-school Jewish education. I was Jewish like the Italians were Italian. I didn't think about it too much. I went to Bronx High School of Science, which was 80 percent Jewish, and then City College [of New York], which also was 80 percent Jewish. It was easy to just be the same kind of Jew; it was like having brown hair [laughs].

I had, by choice, one of those Hollywood movie *bar mitzvahs*. They couldn't afford it, first of all, and it wasn't focused on Torah. The big thing was the party, and that's the way I wanted it. I went to *shul* three, four times a week and Saturdays, and Sunday *minyan*, because the rabbi said to and because a good friend went.

I thought that's what you did—the kids go to *shul* and the parents work. I'd come back Saturday and I did whatever they [the parents] did too. That was it. After my *bar mitzvah*, I went to [Sunday *minyan*] maybe six months or a year, and that was the end of my Jewishness.

I went off to high school, but didn't do anything Jewish there. At City College, I had no concept of seeking out anything Jewish. I remember I had a physics teacher in college who was Jewish who said something about *Bereshis* during class and he looked at me hopefully. Blank. It went right over my head that it was even a Jewish reference. And I saw this disappointed look on his face [laughs], and he went on to something else, and I only realized years later what that was.

I got my first shock when I went to graduate school [at Harvard] because now I'd left New York City; it was no longer 80 percent Jewish. It was more like 99 percent non-Jewish.

The first day of classes at Harvard was on Yom Kippur, so I dressed up in a suit and I went to the classes and I didn't write anything. And I felt bad because I think they shouldn't have done it. It was the first idea I had that there was a world out there that didn't pay attention, that didn't care anything that I was Jewish.

Calman's father died soon afterwards, fulfilling a bittersweet prophecy the elder Calman had made decades earlier.

When I was a kid and he would introduce me to other people, he would say, "This is my *kaddishil.*" I didn't know what it meant at the time. It means, "This is the little guy who's gonna say *Kaddish* for me some day." It's an endearing diminutive. I had no idea what it was, until I found out the hard way, many years later. So it connected me way back. *Kaddishil.* I felt like, wham, not only did he die, but I better say *Kaddish* because I'm the *kaddishil.* And that brought me into *shul.* Meanwhile, I had just broken up with my *shiksa* girlfriend.

Around this time, I first found out where the Jewish neighborhood was, about five miles away in Brookline. I started to see that there were Jews out there, some young people too, and it didn't just have to be New York and grandparents. So I sort of liked this a little bit.

Also, I thought there was something a little bit wrong at Harvard. Most of my life was dedicated to using my brains to getting out of the Bronx. And it worked. And then I got to Harvard and I met all of the famous people of the intellectual world there. They'd really made it to the top and I felt smart and good and lucky and proud and important being in their company and learning from them. That experience and education gave me a great professional career that lasts to this day.

Although it was professionally great, many of the people I met there were so unbalanced I couldn't believe it. They were a hundred times more one-track than I had ever been. And this bothered me a little. Not only were they egotistical more than anybody else I had ever met, and some of them had reason, but they thought that because they knew their one thing, they knew everything in the world, which was like the extreme opposite of humility.

They often ignored people; they were just so inflated with themselves. And the part of it that bothered me was that they didn't have a vision of the world. They were just looking in the mirror basically and trying to make themselves great. They were unbalanced in life.

My goal was to get out of the Bronx, be out of poverty, and then be able to do some other things to integrate and have a nice kind of life. That model sort of got shot down at Harvard a little bit by these intellectual snobs.

But I saw that somehow knowing my Jewish stuff was a balancing act against being a total workaholic and against being an intellectual snob and against being a money grubber; that it somehow represented something else in life.

When I got my postdoc at MIT [in oceanography], I moved to this neighborhood where I was saying *Kaddish*. Brookline. And I love it. I eat in the kosher restaurant, different [Jewish] bookstores are in walking distance and I meet Rose who ran the bakery who had a tattoo from World War II; that was my first [adult] contact with the reality from the Holocaust. I see people walking on *Shabbos* a little bit. It was pretty nice. I felt like, well, this is sort of where I belong even though I'm not observant. It was a start for me. I was living in a context.

So I'm starting to think—Brookline, I got a Jewish context, I want to marry a Jewish girl, I'm saying *Kaddish*—there's all this stuff around. I was waking up. I was wondering, what is it in your *neshama* that when you start to think about these things, it turns you on, rather than just passes you by? Because even nonobservant people will speak nostalgically about the *shtetls* or something, but it doesn't influence them at all. I don't know why.

So I'm taking adult ed courses—a Yiddish course, Hebrew calligraphy, things like that—but I didn't have a concept of Torah learning. I'd read paperback books [on Judaism]. It was during this period that I met my original wife.

The Calmans moved to the Washington, DC, area where they settled in a Maryland suburb and joined an egalitarian Conservative synagogue. Their daughter was born shortly after the move.

I became a big *macher* in the *shul*. And the more I learned and the more I got involved, the less I liked it 'cause it just seemed wrong to me.

What eventually bothered me was that nobody was interested in Torah and learning and living Torah. It was all what kind of melody are you going to sing? And what kind of little things are you going to put in for the *bat mitzvah* or *bar mitzvah*? It became like a *bar mitzvah* factory. People would do everything except really study commandments and Torah. And they never observed *Shabbos* the way I thought you're supposed to, at least ideally.

What bothered me the most I think was not that people didn't practice what I thought they should practice. They had what I came to think was the absolutely wrong ideal. That's what got me that I couldn't live with. I mean, I don't mind if you can't live up to an ideal, because that's human nature and I don't blame anybody for any of that. But to pick the right ideal is very important to me.

The more I learned about Torah, the more I saw that Conservative was, in my opinion, wrong. I mean, I used to write the Torah column there for years. Which I thought was good until I realized that I don't know anything. There should be somebody smart writing this, somebody educated. If I'm the most knowledgeable guy here writing about Torah, then I don't belong here. This really bothered me. Then I started to learn the difference between Orthodox and Conservative philosophically, because I couldn't take it anymore.

Their [the Conservatives] ideal seemed to me to do what makes sense to you if you feel like it [laughs]. You could read right there in the Torah that you're not supposed to do something, and not only did they do it, they discounted it [the Torah prohibition]. I thought the whole exercise of Conservative Judaism was to figure out ways to get out of things you don't want to do [laughs].

They'd come to *shul* [on *Shabbos*] and talk about the hockey game they were going to in the afternoon. Or they'd go straight to the mall, this kind of stuff. And I got to the point where I said to some people, "That's fine, but I don't want to hear about it in *shul*." Time after time after time, there was no support for doing anything observant. I could just see that the whole philosophy was wrong. It seemed irreconcilable. I felt like it wasn't even Jewish anymore.

I knew [his community] was not for me anymore. It was just too much into possessions. To me, Orthodox Judaism is an antidote to pomposity—intellectual pomposity and material pomposity, because you have to say, "I'm accepting a higher authority, and this is what's right and I'm supposed to do it, because it says so." Whether I do it or not may be up to me, but the authority is there, and that puts somebody else on top instead of you. That appealed to me greatly. There was a way to keep everything in balance, and humility, and it was nice. I later learned from the Prophet Micah, chapter six, verse eight: "What is good and what does the Lord require from you? That you do justice, love kindness and walk humbly with your God." People need to pay a little more attention to that last part [laughs].

As Calman's embrace of Orthodoxy tightened, he spent more time in a Washington-area community that in some ways resembled Brookline. It's called Kemp Mill, and it has the largest concentration of Orthodox

Jews between Atlanta and Baltimore. Calman, who is divorced and now lives in Kemp Mill, has joint custody of his daughter, who is enrolled in an Orthodox day school.

The biggest shock I got here [in Kemp Mill] was a wonderful shock. Because in my life on the other side of *frumness* I heard mostly bad talk against observant people—they're rigid, they're narrow-minded, they're isolationist, they hate everybody, they cut you right off as soon as you do something wrong, they'll throw stones at you. All kinds of bad talk. And I come here and I meet the nicest people I've ever met. Nobody said anything bad to me.

[Members of] my family [were] afraid that I wouldn't come and eat with them anymore, that I wouldn't do this anymore, wouldn't do that anymore, that I would become their version of what they think an observant Jew is. But it hasn't really been a problem.

Do you eat in their homes? Or do you, for example, insist on separate dishes?

Well, for now, I'm not at that stage yet. I say when I go there [my mother's], I won't eat *trayf* meat or fish and I won't mix milk and meat, but I will eat in her house. I'll eat in her house probably all the time, out of respect for my mother, in spite of some of the difficulties.

I feel like I've come a long way and I hope to go a lot further. My change in lifestyle has only brought me happiness.

How do you handle doubt?

This I addressed long ago. I said to myself, even if God doesn't exist, *chas v'shalom*, the world would be better if people behaved as if He did exist. And I find the same thing with all the *halachahs*. I see they work. My life is better when I do it. That's good enough.

Give me an example.

Well, like *Shabbos*. I used to run around like a nut, no rest in my life. At least now I get a physical rest. In [his previous community] when I got a rest [on *Shabbos*], it wasn't a very pleasant rest, it was very isolationist. So now I moved to a *frum* neighborhood, where I can walk to a nice *shul*, like you're supposed to do, and it's the friendliest, best day of the week all of a sudden.

Not only do I have a nice rest, good friends, pleasant and unhurried meals, but there's a spiritual dimension that simply doesn't exist in the secular world. The conversations are typically about how to lead a morally better life, how to contribute to the community, kindness, and how God's presence influences our behavior. There's also a keen awareness of the damage that can be done by speaking ill of other people and the proper respect that should be shown to nonobservant and even non-Jewish people. The reward is built into the observance. This works.

One aspect of *Yiddishkeit* is to make distinctions not only in yourself, but in the world, which I think is a good thing. Like in ecology today. It used to be that the only distinction was can you make money from it. Now, the distinction is can you make money but at what cost to the environment, say, or to other things. I think that's a Jewish kind of view—tradeoffs and implications and seeing beyond the obvious.

Jack Calman, 46, is a physicist who lives in Silver Spring, Maryland. He is divorced and has one child.

9
A Jew for Judaism

I remember saying to her, "I was born a Jew and I'm gonna die a Jew;
I'm not gonna become a Christian."

*Many Jews leave Judaism without a whimper; they drift silently into a
spiritual void. That wasn't the case with Julius Ciss. He got bush-
whacked. He was lured into another religion that had the trappings of
Judaism. But he didn't have the knowledge or, as he puts it, the "Jewish
backbone" to resist. He became deeply entangled and eventually converted. Before long, he was a rising star in the organization. Even so,
he was never entirely comfortable with what he'd done. He always felt
a little like an imposter—and that gut feeling served him well.*

If you would have told me five years ago that, "Julius, you're going
to be working for a Jewish charitable organization, scraping a meager
living out there trying to work within the Jewish community rescuing
Jewish souls from missionaries," I would have said you're crazy.

Today, basically, I'm an observant Jew and committed to a Jewish
lifestyle, but I was once a Jew for Jesus. Prior to being that I was just an
assimilated Jew.

I was brought up in Toronto, Canada, in a traditional household. My
parents are Holocaust survivors and although I was sent to Hebrew school
after my secular school, I really didn't learn much about Judaism. While
my parents are sincere and sweet, loving people, they weren't very religious and there wasn't a lot of depth in the Judaism in our home.

By the time I completed my *bar mitzvah*, I wasn't interested in pursuing any more Jewish education, and when puberty overran my hor-

mones, I started going out with girls, be they Jewish or non-Jewish. It was through interdating that my odyssey began.

I met a woman, who I will call Mary Beth, during the last week of my fourth year at the Ontario College of Art. Not thinking that such an attractive woman would say yes, I asked her out. To my amazement she accepted. She was a very pretty, tall, vivacious woman with a great sense of humor, a lot of character and personality. I was thrilled and I had a great time with her on my first date.

I quickly asked her out for another date. It was on our second date that she informed me that she was in love with somebody else, so I was a little devastated. I figured, finally the right one comes along and it's the wrong one. I was quite upset until I asked her who this person was that she was in love with. She told me it was Jesus Christ. So I figured no problem, that I can handle.

Little did I know that that basically started the ball rolling, so to speak, with my involvement in Christianity. After that, she worked to salt and pepper every conversation we had with issues that concerned the Christian faith and Jesus and the cross and the death and eternity and heaven and hell and, you name it, she found opportunities to discuss it.

Ciss said he tried to resist her efforts to have him attend church services and Bible study sessions.

I remember saying to her, "I was born a Jew and I'm gonna die a Jew; I'm not gonna become a Christian." I couldn't commit myself to even thinking about such a thing. But she wasn't going to give up. And in her pursuit of trying to find an avenue to reach my soul, she found out about a congregation of Jews who believe in Jesus who met on Friday nights. This is going back to the fall of 1975, and I thought this was interesting, and she urged me to go and try it out.

I went without her and I remember going to this strange service in a rented room in a library. When I walked in they had a few decorations on the wall, none of which looked Christian, but in fact, very Jewish— a Star of David and some Hebrew letters spelling out he word *Yeshua*. They were singing Hebrew songs and the minister up front didn't look like a minister at all. He was wearing a *keepah* and a *tallis* and clearly looked very Jewish. The people in the congregation were also wearing Jewish garb. The men were wearing *kippot* and *talesim*; there was a woman who lit *Shabbat* candles and they recited the *Sh'ma* and sang many Jewish-sounding melodies. The thing looked pretty Jewish to me.

I was aware that they believed in Jesus but it just seemed too Jewish, so Jewish that it made me comfortable. I hadn't really been in a synagogue for a long time, so this was a really nonthreatening type of environment to involve myself in. It was in this environment I found myself learning about Christianity.

The thrust of their message was to convince individuals of their sinful nature and to get them to ask God for forgiveness through the person of Jesus Christ. But in the context of this particular group, they did it in a very Jewish way, referring to Jesus as *Yeshua Hamoshiach*, and they focused on a lot of Jewish themes to try to present this Christian message. They didn't call their religion Christianity. They called it messianic Judaism.

The spiritual leader of this group claimed to have been raised in an Orthodox home, although I doubt that. But 75 percent of the group was Jewish-born. The thrust of these services was to try to get a person to accept Jesus.

What won me over was their use of the Jewish Bible. By using the *Tanach*, they made a case for Jesus being the Jewish Messiah. I had no knowledge of the Bible, really, and very little knowledge of Hebrew, and when they started using various Bible texts to prove that Jesus was the Messiah, I basically went along with the King James version that they were using. And as is the case in Christianity, all their proofs for Jesus' messiahship are based on Bible verses that are either misquoted, mistranslated, or taken out of context from our Scripture.

The hook that got me into the entire movement was their teaching that when the Messiah comes, Jews won't stop being Jewish but they will become more Jewish than ever. If Jesus was the Messiah, than what could be more Jewish than to believe in him.

But not having the Jewish backbone necessary to determine what was or what was not a true Messianic prophesy, I accepted their claims at face value. And based on a gradual accumulation of many of these Bible verses, and the experience of meeting wonderful Hebrew Christians and enjoying it all in the context of a Jewish-style service, I came to the point, after a year, where I decided that Jesus was the Messiah and he died for my sins. I accepted him into my heart.

Ciss underwent a conversion. And over the next several years, his commitment to the cause strengthened. He became a choir leader, taught Sunday school classes for adults and eventually organized a big messianic Jewish music concert in Toronto. (Meanwhile, he broke up with Mary Beth.) He initially tried to hide his involvement with the group from

*his parents, but eventually that facade was dropped. His organizing
efforts on behalf of the concert became public knowledge.*

My father was just devastated when he finally found out about my
new faith. When I came into the house, he didn't want to have anything
to do with me. I asked him why, and he said, "You're not my son anymore." What's interesting is this concert happened at a time when I was
really not so sure I wanted to stay committed to Christianity.

I had an opportunity to accumulate some doubts. As a birthday present,
my mother had given me a 14-volume Soncino *Tanach* with Hebrew
and English and commentary. I started using this *Tanach* in addition to
the Christian sources that I had to present to my classes. I would be
consistently shocked at the discrepancies that would occur when I compared various *pesukim* in the Jewish *Tanach* to the Christian where verses
and words and passages were in some cases totally inconsistent in
translation.

This disturbed me. And I started discovering that there are just too
many inconsistencies. And the more I taught these classes and prepared
my notes, the more I started looking into traditional Jewish sources and
found, in fact, that there were a lot of problems with Christian belief.

*Ciss soon found he had another problem with Christianity—the doc-
trine involving the acceptance of Christ and salvation. He asked his
group's spiritual advisor about it.*

And I said, "So unless these Jews who died in the Holocaust believed
in their hearts and confessed with their mouths that Jesus was the savior, then they're going to hell?" And he said "I'm not saying it, it's the
word of God that's saying it."

So then I asked, "What about Hitler? Supposing Hitler, before he died,
accepted Jesus. Where would he be?" He turned very pale and changed
the topic, because obviously Christianity teaches that whoever accepts
him has to go to heaven. This really disturbed me that the six million
would be burning in hell and Hitler theoretically could be up in heaven
laughing. I had a hard time with that.*

I had a variety of other doubts that I won't go into, but I had reason to
question whether or not I had made the right decision accepting Jesus.
Eventually, it got to the point where I had to say . . . I've got to check out
some alternate sources as to what I believe; maybe I'm making a mistake.

---

*Theologians I spoke with said this view represents an extreme fundamentalist in-
terpretation of Scripture and does not necessarily reflect the outlook of all Christians.

Still, I didn't know exactly which way to direct myself, and even though I was having doubts, I was still committing myself to helping out with the movement. And one of the groups I was helping out was the organization Jews for Jesus.

They had just set up shop here in Toronto, and I was volunteering for them. One Sunday afternoon, I was in the home of the director of Jews for Jesus, helping him out. And while I was there, admiring his bookshelf, my eye caught a book.

I pulled the book off the bookshelf. . . . I was drawn to this book, entitled *Faith Strengthened*, because my faith was weak and I thought maybe this was what the doctor ordered, maybe this is God speaking to me, trying to reach my soul to strengthen my faith and give me the encouragement I need.

As I pulled the book off the shelf, the Jews for Jesus director grabs my hand, almost slaps it, and insists I put the book back on the shelf, that I shouldn't be touching this book. He said Satan uses this book to help stumble believers in Jesus and I should not have anything to do with it.

It was written by Isaac Troki, a Jew in the Middle Ages who was trying to refute Christianity, and it will do me no good spiritually [the director said].

The force with which this person spoke to me and the conviction he had that this was really not for my eyes, was shocking. It did pique my curiosity.

The next day, Ciss bought a copy of the book from the local Jewish bookstore.

I started reading this book, and discovered many of the arguments and some of the contradictions and inconsistencies that I'd already discovered in my own studies, but a lot more well-articulated by Troki. As I explored the book, I decided to examine other books as well, and I was beginning to feel quite queasy that I might have made a big mistake allying myself with Christ.

Ciss appealed to longtime friend, a Jew who had become observant. She then directed him to Rabbi J. Immanuel Schochet, who ironically had been the Toronto Jewish community's chief spokesman against Ciss and his fellow missionaries.

He set aside a whole evening to meet with me. We spent the evening talking about areas of my confusion and my doubt. At the end of the evening, I wasn't able to fully renounce Christian belief, but I clearly walked away with a lot of ammunition for my growing doubt. And it was shortly after that that I was finally able to say to myself that I was no longer able to accept belief in Jesus.

Rabbi Schochet made something very clear to me. He said, "Julius, you've given five years of your life to Christianity; why don't you give five months of your life to Judaism and then decide if you want to go back?" The truth is, that by the time I'd explored just a little bit of Judaism, there was no turning back.

Rabbi Schochet hooked Ciss up with Aish Hatorah, *a Jewish outreach organization that had recently opened a Toronto branch.*

One of the nicest things for me was when I explored *Yiddishkeit* through *Aish,* I was amazed to find Jews who weren't afraid to talk about God in a way that was personal. Unfortunately, I had been brought up in an environment where I just don't remember meeting Jews who talked about God. The only ones who were interested in God were so Orthodox in their appearance I felt alienated in approaching them.

At this point, were you at ground zero in terms of Jewish spirituality? Where were you?

I'd say I was well advanced of where I was as an assimilated Jew. As an assimilated Jew, I had no desire to be interested in things spiritual or to affiliate Jewishly; it wasn't a concern. Now that I walked away from my five-year experience with these Hebrew Christians, I didn't believe in Jesus Christ. But I'd been so exposed to the Bible, to things Jewish via teachings in the *Tanach,* that I was clearly in a position to say I believed in God, and I believed that the Jewish people received the Torah at Mt. Sinai. I just didn't know what to do about being Jewish.

I was invited for *Shabbos* meals with the *Aish* staff, and slowly decided I should go to *shul* as well.

Ciss began attending a modern Orthodox synagogue on Shabbos. *He drove at first. But then he got in the habit of accepting invitations from friends to sleep over at their homes to avoid violating halachic prohibitions against driving on* Shabbos. *He soon became fully* Shabbos-*observant. Meanwhile, he reconciled with his father.*

Now he's very proud of me.

At first, how did it feel to return to the fold?

I didn't come into *Yiddishkeit* for warm emotional reasons. In fact, when I came back to *Yiddishkeit,* I felt more like a Nazi, because there I was, a former enemy of the Jewish people who for five years was involved in a missionary movement whose main focus is the conversion of Jews. My name became mud. The truth was, no matter where I went in the community, people knew who I was, and when I'd walk into a synagogue, people didn't believe I was there for honest reasons. So it took quite a few years before I was accepted as a *ba'al teshuvah*.

Was it difficult to devote yourself to performing the myriad mitzvos that Orthodox Judaism commands, including those that seem counterintuitive?

Yeah. But the more I developed an understanding and a case for the Torah being true, the more I had to say to myself, okay, so some of these things I don't understand; I'll try the best I can. In many cases I'm not claiming I'm perfect in my observance of the *mitzvos*. But wherever possible, I strive to attain the highest ideals. One of the things I realized is, we can't be perfect, we just have to strive. It's a constant uphill battle. There are certain aspects of Jewish observance that are difficult, but I have no bitterness over them. I find ways of utilizing those aspects of *Yiddishkeit* that are difficult and accept them as a means of worship.

I believe that I'm where I belong. I've always had a strong sentimental attachment to the traditional Judaism of years gone by. You know, when I look at pictures of *chasidim* in eastern Europe, the *shtetl* and *Fiddler on the Roof*, all that stuff, I feel a strong emotional pull. There's something in me that makes me feel this is just right. It's where we belong. It's been there since the beginning.

One of the things I felt was missing while I was involved in Christianity was, regardless of how much they made a case for it to be true, it never felt right. There was always a sense that I was being an imposter, always a sense deep down that I felt guilty that I was doing the wrong thing. And the opposite of it is, that in my renewed commitment to Judaism, it feels like I've come home. I have a sense of not only destiny, but tradition—the whole issue of the transmission of our tradition going back to Sinai and the projection of it going forward into infinity. It was a relief to know I had finally gotten back onto the right path.

Julius Ciss, 44, has worked for 20 years as an illustrator for magazines and advertising agencies. He is also a professor at Toronto's Ontario College of Art. He is currently executive director of the Toronto branch of Jews for Judaism, a countermissionary organization. He and his wife, Claire, live in Toronto. They have no children as yet.

10
Frum Before He Knew It

Although it was hard for me to acknowledge at the time that Orthodoxy was the right thing, I think there was a voice in me saying that whatever observance you've seen up until now isn't authentic.

Like many Jews, Lawton Cooper's return to Torah Judaism began in earnest when he first visited Israel. In a sense, though, he didn't have that far to go. Although he was not raised in an observant environment, Cooper already had several of the traits that Yiddishkeit *values. It was basically a matter of nurturing them and learning how to apply them in a new context—not that it was always easy. It wasn't.*

"I think much of it was built into my personality," said Cooper, who had always sought stability and predictability in his life. Yet he also enjoyed a good argument. He prized authenticity. And perhaps most important, he was an idealist and a moral absolutist from day one. "I was always one of those kids who wanted to do the right thing," he said. "I didn't like crossing against the traffic light."

I grew up in Brookline, Massachusetts, which is a very Jewish town. Although I went to public schools, neither I nor any of my friends was what you would call an observant Jew. I had some Orthodox cousins who also lived in Brookline and had a fair amount of contact with them, but I really don't think that that contact had too much of an influence.

However, because of those cousins, my *bar mitzvah* was at the Bostoner *Rebbe*'s New England Chasidic Center in Brookline. And who knows, perhaps that may have planted some seeds; although it did not set me objectively speaking on the way to being more observant.

My father had [religious] training basically up to *bar mitzvah* and maybe a little beyond that, so much of what he had learned he forgot. And I think that both of my parents have very strong gut feelings about being Jewish. But not having the background and not thinking from the point of view of being bound by really strict laws, [they seemed more attracted to] the idea that it's important to have something that's not hypocritical when you're exposing children to religion.

My mother I think had pretty strong feelings against Orthodoxy as she saw a lot of the hypocrisy perhaps on an individual basis. And that's going to be true in any religion; people who on the outside appear to be religious and go through all the rituals and may not be so scrupulous when it comes to business and dealing with other people, and she was very sensitive to that.

Once I became more observant—initially there was a fair amount of emotional struggle in my parents dealing with [the] change—my mother made her kitchen kosher, and I think for her that was really big stuff coming from basically a socialist background, a socialist–Zionist type background.

As far as [the development of] my strong Jewish feelings, I think there were some episodes in my life that happened between then [his *bar mitzvah*] and through college that probably contributed.

One was an organized debate he participated in during his sophomore year of high school. The War of Attrition was underway in the Middle East and anti-Israeli terrorism was rampant. Cooper's debating opponents were two ardent anti-Zionists.

I was feeling almost as if the weight of the future of Israel rested on my shoulders, on my ability to defeat their arguments. And then I was very much affected by the terrorist attack on the Israeli Olympic athletes in Munich in 1972. I remember putting on a black armband; nobody told me to do this. And I drew a Jewish star on it and the Olympic symbol. Kids just thought I was a little bit strange. They'd say, "Are you a radical or something?" But that was without ever having belonged to a Zionist youth group.

I mentioned before about my personality being inclined in the direction of being more observant. I think that I've always been someone who likes stability; I like things being predictable. I wouldn't have always been able to articulate that. My father's very much that way too. I don't need to see things change all the time, not the most basic things in my life.

Cooper may have coveted continuity, but not necessarily tranquility.

I think this is very much one of the things that made me feel comfortable with Orthodox Judaism and learning Torah, learning the Talmud, is that questioning and arguing are very much accepted. The rabbis always say there's no question that Judaism can't accept. And that's one of the signs that it's a true religion, that you can ask all the questions you want; it doesn't mean you're going to get perfect answers to everything, but there's no question that threatens Judaism.

Although I like stability, I like to argue. I think I've always had a sense of—this is something my parents in a psychological way may have put into me—being very sensitive to things that aren't authentic, people that aren't authentic, anything that's not authentic, that pretends to be one thing and really isn't. I think that ties in with the stability issue because truth is stable.

Although I was a good student, I was not the type of person who would go delving into different philosophies and go looking for answers that way. I'm not one of those *ba'alei teshuvah* who went into Zen Buddhism and various Eastern religions looking for an answer. I don't think there's any question that my first choice was to stay within Judaism, although by no means was it a foregone conclusion that I would marry someone Jewish. It was not something that had ever been drummed into my head. It was interesting because there were lots of families where there was absolutely no observance but the kids are told one thing—you shouldn't marry someone who's not Jewish—and that to me smacked of hypocrisy.

By his senior year at college (Harvard), Cooper had become active in Hillel.

What little contact I had with what was then a very small Orthodox group at Harvard was not particularly pleasant. In fact, my senior year I directed the first *shomer Shabbos* play to my knowledge ever at Harvard, sponsored by Hillel. Instead of doing a senior thesis, I decided to direct this play. I encountered a lot of opposition from the Orthodox students who were in the play.

There was one Orthodox Jew who was playing the part of an Eastern Orthodox priest, of all things. And bit by bit, he took out many of the Christian elements from the part he said he really couldn't do, being an observant Jew. I saw that as being very irrational. Why did he take the

part? This I could not understand, what that had to do with being observant. I do now, but I didn't then.

What did this behavior indicate to you at the time?

Obstinancy. Not being willing to be reasonable or to compromise. And
I thought I was reasonable. I tried to negotiate with him over what we
would do, but I found him very uncompromising. I was definitely not
raised to be uncompromising—maybe when it came to basic principles,
but I didn't appreciate the basic principles that underlie his approach.

Although I think I was very much susceptible emotionally to being
attracted to Jewish observance, when it came to anybody that was observant behaving in a way that I saw as being less than exemplary, I would
react against the observance itself. I would react against Judaism, which
is itself not a very rational reaction. I realize now that that was really
essentially a form of religious prejudice.

There was definitely something intimidating about Orthodox Judaism. First of all, not being at all knowledgeable about *Shabbos* and things
like that, one thing I was always sensitive to was being told you can't
do this, you can't do that.

When it came to my senior year, I didn't know what to do. I took the
medical boards, but I didn't know if I wanted to go right on to medical
school. At some point, the idea just came into my head—and this was
probably the most major decision I've made in a gut way, ever—I realized I wanted to go to Israel. It was 1978.

*Cooper searched for a program that would help prepare him for life
in Israel. He chose a Young Judea camp in central New York State, a
semitraditional facility. The session would last eight weeks.*

I remember my arrival at the camp. We had taken a bus from Manhattan, and it was a long, long ride. I remember arriving late at night
and we walked into the dining room, and all of a sudden everybody in
the camp came up to greet us singing [sings] *avenu shalom alechem.*
. . . I'd never had an experience like this before, this feeling of being
really a part of a community of people caring about me just because I
was Jewish. Although I certainly had a sense of belonging at Harvard
Hillel, it had never hit me in an emotional way as that did.

Those eight weeks were very formative. Although I did not become
more observant in any significant way immediately, I think that certainly
cemented my decision to go to Israel. I was at least able to begin my
education in observance. I learned a lot about the *Shabbos* customs, al-

though it didn't affect my private observance. But I learned at least to respect that.

The spiritual side certainly started to develop there; I learned how to say many of the blessings and grace after meals. And then I was placed in a program called WUJS [World Union of Jewish Students] that was my entry into Israel.

Young Judea was a nonthreatening entry into learning more about Judaism. There are some people who are able to go directly into Orthodoxy. I just wasn't one of those people. I think you really have to know yourself. It's interesting hearing myself say this now, since I'd be very uncomfortable today being at the WUJS or a Young Judea camp, certainly on the Sabbath. And yet for me, they [the two programs] are the reason I'm observant today. If my only exposure had been rabbis at the Western Wall waiting to get me to learn at *yeshiva*, I might never have become observant.

[At WUJS] I continued to learn more about Israel and also about Jewish law. It's amazing how much can happen in five months of your life.

By the time the WUJS program was completed, Cooper decided he wanted to spend time on a religious kibbutz.

So clearly something had happened. It had started to sink in. I think that I realized there was something there. There was something that provided a sense of emotional stability, a way of expressing Jewishness, which nothing, including learning Israeli history and wearing black armbands, had ever done. I needed both. What I really wanted was to be an authentically observant Jew, but something was holding me back.

What did being an "authentically observant Jew" mean to you? What did it represent?

I think what it represented was doing the right thing. Although I grew up in a very liberal town in a very liberal state, there was always a very conservative, with a small *c*, side of me that [says] it's important to do the right thing. And although it was hard for me to acknowledge at the time that Orthodoxy was the right thing, I think there was a voice in me saying that whatever observance you've seen up until now isn't authentic. But I couldn't have someone come at me and tell me, "This is what you should do." I had to come at it on my own.

What was right about it?

Once I developed a sense of the concept of a *mitzvah*, that there are certain things that you should do and certain things that you shouldn't do, I realized that traditional Judaism does not allow you to just make up whatever you want. Although you can express yourself emotionally and there is definitely a lot room for individual expression, there are rights and there are wrongs. I was always one of those kids who wanted to do the right thing; I didn't like crossing against the traffic light.

So, in a sense, you were going back to your roots.

Yes. And [it meant] being able to express it in a way that gave me emotional fulfillment.

I went to Jerusalem after having been at WUJS for about a month and a half. That was a very transcendent experience, although there were some negative aspects to it too. I wandered around like I was in a daze and found a youth hostel and then found my way to the Western Wall late Thursday night, long after all the services had ended, and they go on for quite a while.

And I remember standing, oh maybe 100 yards from the wall and watching a lone *chasid* praying at the wall, and looking at him, and I remember writing a little note to myself at the time, wondering what he was feeling, feeling myself like an observer, realizing that this was a very special moment in my life. I was just wondering what was going through his mind, and perhaps being jealous that he was able to feel something that I couldn't.

Cooper ended up staying in Israel for nearly two years, during which he participated in a research program at the Weitzmann Institute and spent two months at an Orthodox kibbutz.

I realized there that I could be comfortable keeping *Shabbat* and I just needed to be in the right environment. When I was out of that environment, whenever I came back to the United States for a brief time and when I was under pressure to do something that would violate the Sabbath, such as drive—when I was under pressure from family—I would give in. It was very hard for me—and possibly because I had some inner doubts myself—hard for me to just say, "No, this is right, this is what I really want to do."

While at Weitzmann, Cooper struggled with the issue of wearing a keepah in public. He remembers a painfully awkward episode in which he wore one to a concert, but kept leaning back in his seat so nobody could see it.

There was something I was very embarrassed about. I'm not sure what held me back at that point.

Cooper would have liked to stay in Israel for good. But he made an emotionally difficult decision to return to the United States to go to

medical school. During medical school, he joined an egalitarian minyan, *which provided a nonthreatening opportunity "to learn more about
observance, certainly about services and how to* daven *and lead prayers
and how to read the Torah. "*

I think this again reflects the idea that I needed to take things
incrementally.

*During this period, Cooper met his future wife. She had been raised
in an Orthodox home, and therefore was uncomfortable with the idea of
an egalitarian* minyan.

I think it says a lot for my wife that she didn't reject me. Many Orthodox women would have immediately dropped me if they realized I
was involved in an egalitarian *minyan*, even though I was pretty much
Sabbath-observant. I certainly didn't drive on a regular basis and didn't
turn on lights, and I kept kosher.

While it's very easy for Orthodox people to reject things like egalitarian *minyans* because they violate Jewish law—in terms of no separation [between the sexes] and women leading services and women singing—nevertheless, I know of myself and others who became more
observant as a result of being involved initially in an egalitarian *minyan*
and eventually went on to be Orthodox.

*Cooper and his wife moved from Boston to Rochester, New York, for
his medical residency. In Rochester, they began attending Orthodox*
shuls, *although once Cooper decided to try a nearby Conservative synagogue, a large, nationally known institution.*

At that point I probably was still not too uncomfortable with mixed
seating. What really turned me off was the fact that it seemed so cold,
having been in a very, very warm Orthodox *shul*. The [experience of]
going to this place where virtually nobody came up to talk to me and I
didn't have any sense of people really wanting me to join the synagogue
or being curious as to who I was or what my background was, contrasted
so sharply with my experience in both of the Orthodox *shuls* in Rochester. The rabbis and many of the congregants were very open, invited
us for meals, and were very interested in us personally.

People got us involved immediately in communal activities, and that
certainly was another important factor. It's one thing to keep the rituals. It's another thing to actually be part of the community and have a
sense of communal responsibilty, that other people's religious lives may
depend on what you do. There's an expression—*kol Yisroel areyvim zeh
la zeh*—all Jews are responsible for one another. I was starting to have

a sense of that and a feeling of what it's like to be an adult Orthodox Jew in the whole sense of the word.

In Rochester, Cooper began participating in a regular Talmud shiur.

As a resident [physician], I would often nod off in the middle of the *shiur* and pretend I had heard what the rabbi said. But he was very understanding. I never had a sense from him that he was personally insulted about the fact that I fell asleep in front of him. I know many people who would be. He was doing it *leshaym shemayim*, purely for the sake of Heaven.

His ego was not involved at all, and I think that had a really powerful influence on me. It made me realize how despite the fact that from the outside, Orthodox Jews can seem to be cold, strange, tied up in ritual and uncompromising, once one starts to get through the surface, then in fact one finds people who are very principled and caring.

The difference between learning Torah and learning secular subjects, or taking a course in Bible criticism in college, is that it's not purely an intellectual experience, although surely Gemara is a very intellectual experience and a great intellectual challenge at times.

But it brings together one's personal emotional commitment to Judaism with one's desire to delve intellectually into the depths of Judaism. And the more one learns, the more one knows how little one knows, that the Torah is infinite and the greatest rabbis only begin to scratch the surface. And when one has that realization, that no matter how far one goes there's always room to grow, then you realize that—provided you don't become discouraged, which it's certainly very easy to become at first—but if you keep pushing ahead, then you realize that your life will never be empty.

What was your family's reaction to your new lifestyle?

As I've said, I'm an argumentative person, and inappropriately got into a number of heated discussions with my parents. But I think the very positive and encouraging thing to someone who is becoming more observant and is concerned about the reaction of family is, however negative the reaction is, with the years it tends to mellow.

First of all, people get used to it, to people being observant, it's just human nature. Second of all, once parents start to see grandchildren growing up and they see them firmly committed to being Jewish and to raising their own Jewish families, God willing, and then they contrast that to other relatives' children who may have married people who aren't Jewish or certainly have very little Jewish content in their lives.

As people get older they tend to get more religious, even if they don't become more observant. They become much more emotionally attached to their religion. And that certainly happened with my parents. It was my father who got me to put on *tefillin* on a regular basis during medical school.

Cooper now wears a keepah *at work, having decided to do so five years ago when he interviewed for his present job.*

One thing I said to myself when I came down for the interview for that job was, I'm definitely going to wear a *keepah* for this job, and if I don't get the job because of the *keepah*, it wasn't meant to be. I had a physician colleague who belonged to our *shul* in Rochester—and I really admired him for this—who began wearing his *keepah* after going out into practice, wearing it at work. And really it wasn't in me to start doing that.

When the opportunity came to start wearing it, I realized that I really needed to seize this opportunity. Wearing the *keepah* while seeing patients has gotten me into some very interesting conversations that I would never have gotten into before, especially with a name like Lawton Cooper.

How do you handle doubt and crises of faith?

Being plagued by doubt is not foreign to Orthodox Jews. In fact, one should question things. There is a tradition of arguing with God, and I think that's really a very appealing thing to people who are considering being more observant and look at Orthodoxy as being blind faith. They put it in the same box as fundamentalist Islam or born-again Christianity. It really isn't. It very much encourages questioning.

I think to me the greatest challenge is not crises of faith, but things becoming rote. When I think back to my days in Young Judea and WUJS and the egalitarian *minyan*, there were sparks of enthusiasm that I had then that I don't have today. Or if I have them, they're just less common. The single greatest challenge is finding those sparks.

What has been the overall impact on your life of your return to Torah Judaism?

It feels like knowing exactly where I'm headed, knowing that when it comes to life decisions—where to live, what to do on weekends—many of those decisions are made for me by dint of being an Orthodox Jew, feeling that sense of belonging and security.

It's very easy to take all of that for granted. But I think that is certainly what it boils down to—feeling that even though for many, many areas of life, the greatness of Judaism is that it does accept grayness, nevertheless I'm already starting from a base. It means having a map, having directions.

I see many Jewish people who are very happy, well-adjusted people who have very little Jewish observance in their lives. But having become observant, it's hard to imagine what it would be like to steer through all the stresses of life, of earning a living, all the increasing tendency in society toward people becoming numb to bloodshed and immorality. It's hard for me to imagine how I would deal with that. I don't think I ever really realized how complex life is until I became observant.

How so?

When I look at many of my nonobservant colleagues at work, Jewish and non-Jewish, in many ways their lives are really pretty simple. You have to ask yourself, what are people's ultimate goals in life? And I think if one looks at the higher goals that secular society holds—being able to achieve the most in education or seeing that your children get it and living a comfortable lifestyle, and nice vacations and a nice home . . . Even before I became observant, I was quite unmaterialistic, now even more so. I realize that the goals I have for myself and my family and my children, grandchildren, are so different from those of my colleagues. I have a sense of, when it comes to big decisions, what my priorities are.

Lawton Cooper, 39, is a physician. He lives in Silver Spring, Maryland, with his wife and three children.

11
The Searcher

I remember hearing the melodies of Friday-night *davening* and they filled
me. . . . It felt like I was a pitcher being filled with water.

*Jay Eisenberg grew up in the San Fernando Valley in California, which
is not exactly a hotbed of* Yiddishkeit. *So he took his spirituality where
he could find it, and it wasn't in shul. He found it in a Baptist church. He
had fallen in with a group of non-Jewish high school kids who invited him
along on a church-sponsored skiing trip. "They kind of got me hooked,"
said Eisenberg. "They convinced me that* Yoshka *was* Moshiach *and that
this was part of my completion and fulfillment as a Jew. I bought it hook,
line, and sinker and I truly believed it for a couple of years."*

*When his parents found out, they forbade him to return to the church,
and he complied. Thus ended what seemed to be nothing more than an
embarrassing youthful indiscretion. In retrospect, it was much more than
that.*

The reason I think it's important is that you could see the seeds of
probably ultimately what brought me back [to *Yiddishkeit*], which is that
I was a very spiritual person from the start. I needed something. I was
looking for something. When I went on this trip and they started talking
about God, something that as a modern secular Jew was missing in my
life, I felt myself very emotionally drawn to it. It didn't take much to
convince me. I wanted to be convinced. Still, the feeling didn't hold.
There was still something missing.

Eisenberg joined a secular Jewish fraternity at UCLA. During Succos
of his freshman year, a rabbi in a black hat and a black coat showed up

uninvited at the frat house carrying a lulav *and an* esrog, *items Eisenberg had never seen before. When the rabbi offered to* bentsh lulav *with the fraternity brothers, the president of the house asked him to leave. The rabbi then cut a deal with him: He'd arm wrestle the strongest guy in the house. If the rabbi lost, he'd leave without a word. If he won, they'd all* bentsh lulav.

It wasn't even a contest. The rabbi beat him a second. He took a couple *keepot* out of his pocket and he lined us all up and we all *bentsh*, repeating after him, *baruch atah Hashem* . . . [laughs]. I remember that the whole incident was really neat and it touched me deeply. It really did. But I didn't really know at the time how much it would mean to me later on. If you had said to me at the time that some day I'd be the one walking door-to-door in my neighborhood on Succos looking for Jews with whom to *bentsh lulav*, I'd have thought you were insane.

That winter he met his wife-to-be, Sandy. On their first date, he sipped lobster bisque, one of his favorite foods.

I remember Sandy proposing that we go to synagogue one night. Granted, it was a Conservative synagogue, but what do I want to go to synagogue for? But I was of a mind that if she had asked me to swim naked across Niagara Falls, I probably would have done it. So I consented.

The next Friday night I took Sandy to her parents' *shul*, and I remember sitting there and I could hardly read the words. I was 19 years old. Six years had gone by [since his *bar mitzvah*] and I think it was the first time [since then] I'd opened up a *siddur*. But I remember hearing the melodies of Friday night *davening* and they filled me the way . . . it felt like I was a pitcher being filled with water; I could just feel these melodies coming into me. I had an incredible emotional high. I felt [I was] finally at a place where I was at home and I wanted to get more *Yiddishkeit*.

We decided to get engaged and married. We decided we wanted to keep a Jewish home, but we didn't know what that meant. I wasn't a particularly religious person. God wasn't particularly important to me at that point in my life, but God wasn't that important to Sandy either. We did have a strong sense of Jewish pride, however, and the one thing we felt strongly about was that we wanted our children to grow up as Jews. We knew that assimilation and intermarriage were rampant and we knew that we had to do something to ensure the Jewish future of our children. To me, this meant celebrating holidays, lighting *Shabbos* candles, singing Jewish songs. To Sandy, it meant something altogether different. That's when she hit me with a bombshell. About two months before we got married, she said, "Jay, how would you feel about keeping kosher?"

I said, "What are you, nuts?" [laughs]. I said, "You want to go to *shul* on Friday night, fine. You want to keep Judaism alive in our home, fine. But keeping kosher? You expect me to give up lobster bisque?" She said, "You know something, my friend keeps kosher, could we at least try it?" Her friend had told her that the one thing about keeping kosher is that every time you sit down and eat a meal, you reaffirm your Jewish identity. It's a very powerful concept if you think about it. So I said, "Okay, fine." We decided to keep kosher in the home but not out of the home.

We got married at a Conservative *shul* and we started to make a Jewish home for the sake of an identity and Jewish feeling, but it was not particularly based on religious belief. Three months later, we took a delayed honeymoon that turned out to be a major turning point. We went for three weeks to *Eretz Yisroel*. I remember being on the plane, and not even knowing why, but the moment the wheels of the plane touched the ground at Ben Gurion [Airport], my eyes welled up with tears, and I had an incredible feeling of emotion. I know now that it was the *kedusha* of the land touching my *neshama*.

It was just a very emotional thing. I remember the whole time I was there I kept my head covered. It was the first time I had ever done so outside of a synagogue. Part of it was the Jewish pride thing. I figured I'm in Israel, I'm going to wear a *keepah* and no one's gonna stop me because this is my land, my people. I didn't know what I was pursuing at the time. But being in Israel—being at the *Kotel* at *ma'ariv* and being in *Chevron* at the Cave of Machpela, being at *Kever Rochel*, being in these places I remembered learning about in *cheder*—but when I learned about them in *cheder* they didn't seem real to me. I never made the connection that what I'm learning here is history.

It always seemed like a bunch of stories, and even the people who taught in Hebrew school when I was a kid gave modern-day rationalizations and explanations. This was the way I was raised as a Jew, not to believe in miracles, not to believe in anything spiritual.

Being in a place where I could see with my own eyes things that I had previously thought to be mythology had a very profound effect. It was a very spiritual experience for me. At that point, I still wasn't talking to God. But I began to feel that there's something here that's more than just the Jewish identity thing and boy it's neat to be a Jew because we have all these neat songs and these fun holidays. There's something more here, there's something more substantive.

I returned from Israel more committed to Judaism than before, and I think I resolved that I was gonna look into it a little more. It's funny; you make those resolutions and then you settle back into your life as usual. Well, God in his infinite wisdom wasn't going to allow me to rest easy. Unfortunately, my father-in-law, *alev hashalom*, who was a lovely, lovely man, passed away in May 1975. And all of a sudden, I had to take responsibility in a way I'd never taken responsibility before.

Maishe didn't have any sons to say *Kaddish* for him. He had a couple daughters. I got permission from my parents, and I became his *Kaddish*. I started going to *shul* every day. We lived down the street from a Conservative synagogue that had an Orthodox weekday *minyan*, a bunch of older men who put on *tefillin* every day. I got my father-in-law's *tefillin* from Sandy's mother and I started putting them on; they taught me how to put them on. I started to become involved in a way I never thought I was going to become involved.

I began to learn how to *daven*. It was more growth in terms of becoming familiar with ritual than anything else. It wasn't so much an emotional impact as it was being with these people. I had a lot of questions and I got a lot of answers. This was more [about] becoming more knowledgeable, which is important too.

Over the next several years, the Eisenbergs' religious growth continued and then plateaued. The Friday-night routine was candles, Kiddush, hamotzee, *eating,* bentshing, *services . . . and then TV. "No matter what was going on," said Eisenberg, "we had to be back from* shul *in time to watch* Dallas. *And then, about six years after they were married, their first child, Adam, was born.*

I watched this child come out. And I saw in front of my eyes a miracle, an absolute miracle, and I was blown away by it. And I remember, after the excitement, after the commotion, after the joy of seeing my son, when things finally settled down and he was in my wife's arms, I remember taking a walk around the hospital and I remember talking to God for the first time in my life as a Jew. I was very thankful, and I remember saying to God, "I know that you're there because I know that what I just saw today could not have been an accident."

At that point, I started to have a relationship with God. I went out and bought myself a *chumash* and I started to read the Torah in preparation for *shul*. I started to pay close attention to the rabbi's *d'var Torah* on Saturday. I started going to a weekly Torah class. This was in a Conservative synagogue, but I started learning a little bit about my religion.

This 11-year period [from his marriage until his son was about five] was a time of real growth in terms of learning more about our religion. Any time a holiday came up, we would study about it and we would add a little more to what we did, but we didn't stop working on those days.

I made a very important decision when I interviewed for a job in 1979. I told the personnel manager that I would prefer not to work on Saturday, and I didn't work on Saturday. I wasn't *shomer Shabbos*—we still went to the mall—but I didn't do anything that had to do with earning a living. After all, the Written Torah forbids "work" on *Shabbos*. I thought I was obeying that commandment.

The family relocated to Southern California in 1986 because of a job opportunity. Once there, Eisenberg became involved with Chabad *after a pair of incidents. First, he heard a Conservative rabbi give a talk on "Jewish unity," which had a "harsh, negative message" that didn't sit well with him. Next, he and his family were asked to leave another Conservative synagogue on* Shabbos *because his kids were making too much noise. He immediately dropped off his wife and kids and drove to a nearby* Chabad House *where he heard the rabbi talk about the need for Jews to have unconditional love for each other.*

I'm saying to myself, here's a Jewish unity talk and here's a Jewish unity talk, and I never went anyplace other than *Chabad* after that. I couldn't follow the *davening*. I didn't necessarily like the *mechitzah*. I don't know what these people were about, but I knew that there's something here that's *emes* and this is where I belong. All I know is that I liked what I heard and I saw that these people are for real, these are the people I want to be around.

So I started going there every *Shabbos* and I started to go to the weekly *parshat hashavuah* class at the rabbi's house on Wednesday night. And I started to add a couple books to my Jewish library. I started to learn about my religion. And we started to have a *chasidus* class on Saturday morning and I started to go to that. I started to learn about souls and other worlds and a whole spiritual realm that I never knew were part of Judaism.

I began to see the truth in *Yiddishkeit*. But there was one more event that was going to kick this from third gear into fourth. I have to tell you that at this point, we still weren't overly observant and I still had my doubts and my questions about God and Torah.

I remember having a discussion with a friend of mine, David Joseph. He said, "Jay, just remember one thing: If you accept that God gave the Torah at Sinai, if you accept that the Torah is divine, and comes from God—and I'm talking about the oral law and the written law—then everything else makes sense. You have to follow it. It all fits together. If you don't then it doesn't." And those words kind of stuck in my head for a while.

Not long afterwards, Eisenberg and his wife attended a lecture on the "hidden codes" in the Torah, which are believed by some to prove conclusively that the Torah is the revealed word of God. Eisenberg became a believer.

All of a sudden, I was faced with what to me was undeniable, indisputable, unquestionable proof that the Torah was divine, not something that was written by Moshe Rabbenu or by committee, as I'd been told previously. David Joseph's words came back to me.

So I decided at that point that I needed to become totally *frum*. I needed to become *shomer Shabbos*, I needed to become totally kosher, I needed to become everything.

My wife was sitting beside me at that lecture, and she didn't have the same conclusion. She thought it was interesting [laughs], but she didn't have the same conclusion. I was about to create for us the toughest year in our marriage without realizing it. I never anticipated what was about to happen.

All of a sudden I was ready to take on every *mitzvah*; I was ready to go full blast. And Sandy wasn't ready. She wasn't nearly ready. And everything became an argument. She wanted me to go pick up the kids on *Shabbos*, I didn't want to get in the car; that became an argument. When she cooked something on Friday night and I discovered it had nonkosher wine, I didn't want to eat it and, "Now my cooking isn't good enough for you." That became an argument. Everything became a big argument. When I wanted to put on *tzitzis*, she didn't like the way I looked in *tzitzis*. It was just back and forth and went on and on and on and on.

Another thing. She was very, very disturbed about the whole issue of the *Rebbe*. She thought that this thing with the *Rebbe* was like Catholics with the Pope and she couldn't understand it. We got close to separating.

They were counseled by friends, including the Lubavitch sheliach in the community, who urged Eisenberg not to push his wife.

He said try to select *mitzvos* that didn't affect the other members of the family and go along with other things. He kept saying over and over and over, "As long as you're moving in the right direction, you'll get there. You don't have to take on everything all at once. It's okay to say to God, 'I know that I'm supposed to do this or I'm not supposed to do this but I can't do it yet.'"

I'll tell you something; I'm a believer that the most important word in the vocabulary of a *ba'al teshuvah* is "yet." Because that little word resolves all of the conflicts, all the conflicts of how do I justify violating Torah? How do I justify not keeping a *mitzvah*? It's not the Conservative way of doing things where you invalidate the *mitzvah*; that's how you justify it, by saying it doesn't apply anymore. What you say to God is, "I know I should be doing this, but I can't do it yet." And that's an honest approach. It allows you to move forward.

Around this time, the Eisenbergs attended the wedding—in Crown Heights—of the sister of the local sheliach. *Everyone in the family was treated warmly, including Sandy. Even the* Rebbe *himself seemed to pitch in. During a* farbrengen, *he waved and smiled at the Eisenberg children.*

And that seemed to be somewhat of a turning point. We had another difficult year, mind you, but then things started to go back the other way. Sandy had a whole different understanding of who the *Rebbe* was, and it touched her very deeply, and me as well.

I started to really lay off Sandy and the kids. A funny thing that happened is that as soon as I started doing that, she started to move in my direction. She decided to take on *Shabbos* then she decided to take on *yomim tovim*. Then she decided to re-*kasher* the kitchen.

She was hesitant to take on the mitzvah *of taharas hamishpachah. But that too changed.*

When that aspect of your relationship is forbidden at that point in time, you realize that now you're relating to each other on a level where there're no ulterior motives and there's no hidden agenda. It had a profound impact on our marriage and our family's growth in *Yiddishkeit*. This was about three years ago.

What's interesting is that Sandy still hadn't gotten to the point where she accepted that the Torah is divine. Everything she was doing, she was doing for her family because she saw the benefits of living a religious life. She saw how it brought our family together, she saw the difference between her children and children in a secular environment. By this time, the kids are back in Orthodox schools, which was also something she had initiated.

During a weekend retreat, Sandy became convinced that the Torah was God-given.

She was very touched by Rabbi Tauber, Ezriel Tauber, and his story of how he and his family survived the Holocaust. I remember her saying, "After what this man has gone through, who am I not to believe in God?" I was more moved by the practical stuff. She was more moved by the emotional stuff.

Eisenberg, however, had another hurdle to clear, and he did so with the help of a Gentile co-worker.

I used to wear my *keepah* everywhere except at work. One day, Steve Hamilton, a Gentile, who I have wonderful respect for, was standing at the window early in the morning. He saw me get out of my car and reach on my head and take the *keepah* and put it in my pocket.

I go to my office and he comes storming into my office and says, "What's wrong with you?" And I said, "What do you mean 'what's wrong with you?'" He said, "Why do you take that," whatever he called it, "why do you take that off your head?" I said, "Well, it's work and I don't want to wear it at work." And he said, "You should be ashamed of yourself."

He said, "You're a Jew, right? Do you believe that it's important to be a Jew?" And I said, "Of course." He said, "If that's what you are, you should be proud of it." Here's a *goy* telling me this [laughs]. God sends messengers in many forms. So I thought about it for 48 hours and got the courage to put a *keepah* on my head and keep it on while I was in the office. For about 24 hours people would come by, [and ask] was it a holiday or what? And I dealt with the questions, and that was it.

What about family members? How have they reacted?

Oy. This is a big problem [laughs]. My mother and father, who are divorced, are not religious. My brother is very, very much against Judaism. My sister, I don't think she even understands. I tell you . . . we made a lot of mistakes with our family. The biggest was when Sandy and I started to become more religious, I began to resent my parents for not giving me more religious experience as a child and I became very judgmental and very condescending and I have to tell you I wasn't very nice about it.

When we became *Chabadniks*, we began to realize that our judgmentalism was wrong and we began to just basically accept them the way they are. But by then it was way too late. The damage had been done and they no longer trusted us. Plus, their frame of reference doesn't allow them to understand that we live in a world of absolutes. Any time I try to explain with the most patience and love that I can, it ends up in a big argument.

That aside, what has been the overall impact Yiddishkeit *on your life?*

In no particular order, it has meant being able to cope with difficulties when you realize that everything that happens comes from God and God is good. It's an incredibly powerful weapon for battling depression. I never get down like I used to. *Shalom bayis* has strengthened our marriage in ways that I never dreamed possible.

And just the whole issue of knowing who I am and that there's a purpose here. I'm 42 years old and I'm not going through a midlife crisis. I don't understand what a midlife crisis is. People get to the point where they're 42 years old and say, "Gee what does my life mean?" Well, I know what my life means. My life means a connection to God. It means bringing holiness into the physical world. It's got purpose, lasting purpose. It literally means everything.

Jay (Eliyahu) Eisenberg, 42, is a partner in a business that markets and distributes collectible postage stamps. He and his wife live in Agoura Hills, California, with their three children.

12
Never Say Never

My parents used to tell me about a *pintela Yid,* and up until that time, it was just a nice little expression. But what I've learned . . . is that there really is such a thing as a *pintela Yid.*

Steve Eisenberg used to laugh at Jewish rituals and vowed "never, ever, ever, ever, ever" to keep Shabbos. *He stopped laughing and learned not to say "never" after visiting Israel and later hearing the stories of Jews who paid with their lives for keeping their faith. He became* frum *during high school, and it made for lonely times. But he persevered with the help of some friends. Before long, he was reaching out to other Jewish kids who were as estranged from their heritage as he once was.*

Eisenberg deepened his commitment to outreach several years later after a traumatic experience—one of his closest pals married a Gentile. "Religiously, I felt like I had let her down," he said, "because I could have done more. I should have been more proactive." And now he is. When he's not trading stocks on Wall Street, Eisenberg helps disaffected Jews stave off intermarriage by helping them reconnect with their roots. And when his efforts work he feels renewed. "Every time I see a Jew return to Yiddishkeit," *Eisenberg said, "I see God."*

When I was 17 I went to Israel on a summer program. It was a modern Orthodox tour, and I was very, very Zionistic. Had I known how religious it was, I would never have gone. But over those ensuing six weeks, *Shabbos,* for the first time, began Friday night and ended Saturday night. You *bentshed* and you washed, not only when Uncle Morris would cut the *challah* at a wedding or a *bar mitzvah,* but you did that every time you had bread. And the whole system, the whole *mitzvah* system, started getting plugged in.

Now, the idea of why would this God need me to do this, this and this, I still didn't get. But all of a sudden, I had the clarity which I never seemed to have gotten before. These were part of a bigger system. Up until that point, either you were the 47th Street brand of Orthodox Jew or you were the suburban Bloomingdale's Jew. For the first time I was able to see people who had synthesized both worlds.

After returning home to West Orange, New Jersey, he got involved with NCSY (National Conference of Synagogue Youth) at his parents' urging. In the meanwhile, his first cousin Sherril, who had become frum, was emerging as "a tremendous catalyst" in his life. "She was like the intellectual lighthouse in the family in terms of Yiddishkeit," said Eisenberg. "I thought she was crazy but I knew intellectually and emotionally she was right." During a havdalah service at an NCSY-sponsored shabbaton, he experienced what he called "a breakthrough, a spiritual watershed. It was something someone said that just got to me, where I just said, 'I'm going to do it. I'm going to do this.' I stopped fighting."

I guess it was a Holocaust type of story, what people did and didn't do for their *Yiddishkeit* and *mesiras nefesh*, what they have given to observe their *Shabbos*. And here I was, with all the freedom and choice in the world and I owed it to them to be able to carry on the *Shabbat* which they fought for and our people fought for for thousands of years. The following *Shabbat* I didn't drive, and once I broke through that, that was a major obstacle. But *tefillin* came I think the following year.

So here you are a suddenly frum *guy at the ripe old age of 17. What was it like in high school?*

High school was very heavily secular Jewish. I was very isolated, very alone. You know, Friday night, the big social night, and basketball games and proms, seasonal parties; and I couldn't relate to my secular peers, and certainly not to my non-Jewish friends.

It was a very lonely period. It was very interesting, because on one hand, my parents only wanted me to be very Jewish and be involved in synagogue life and not be the rebellious Hebrew school kid that I was. On the other hand, I couldn't be too *frum*. It was like, what is it exactly that you want me to be? And my friends thought I was . . . it was totally absurd, it was crazy. Someone our age taking on these things? They couldn't relate to it in any way.

Fortunately, I had two or three friends from my community, from the *shul*, who had supported me. I would go there for *Shabbos* lunch and those were amazing experiences. We had a youth director and his wife, Michael and Dorri Witkes, and they invited me for *Shabbos* lunch or Friday night dinner, and just seeing the father bless the children; there was just a very special *Shabbos* atmosphere. The whole thing just felt right. There was a feeling in the home, there was a peacefulness.

I came from a beautiful, functional family and there was tremendous love and all that, but this was something very special. It was a glow in the air.

My father passed away [during his junior year in high school], and at that point I was already fully observant. At that point, I borrowed the spiritual deposits I had made during the previous 12 months. And that's what really helped me grow to a different level.

In other words, fortunately I started this route before my father passed away and it helped get me through this very difficult time because I had this structure. I didn't have to start figuring out the world. My father passed away at 41 years of age. But because I had *Hashem*'s assistance in my life—I knew that I didn't understand why *Hashem* took a 41-year-old father and left three relatively young children—but I believed in something higher, that there was a purpose, there was a mission, there was a plan. So that helped me tremendously during this dark period of my life.

While he was nearing graduation from high school, Eisenberg was commended for his religious accomplishments by a family friend and Orthodox community leader, Murray Laulicht. But Laulicht also told him he'd only scratched the surface of Yiddishkeit. *He urged him to take his Jewish learning and living to a new level.*

I remember feeling very resentful. How dare he say these things? I had worked so hard. And I was looking at Brandeis and Rutgers and other secular colleges. And the idea, the notion of going to a religious institution like YU [Yeshiva University]—though a lot of my NCSY advisors were pushing this on me for two years—was very scary. In other words, I would do the stuff, but the idea of being an Orthodox Jew scared me; if that makes any sense at all.

Why did it scare you?

Again, because of the notion that I would have to leave secular society, that I would have to put a beard on, that I would have to go behind the ghetto walls of Flatbush. That was basically the only *Yiddishkeit* I could relate to.

You had no religious community to relate to in West Orange?

We had a modern Orthodox community. Unfortunately the community wasn't as welcoming as it could have been. Unfortunately, I could count on my fingers how many families in my community welcomed me into their homes for *Shabbos*, and I would have given anything to be invited.

You can sit in classes for hours and hours and hours, but the true living laboratory of *Yiddishkeit* is really the role model, by living it. I know the power of the *Shabbos* experience. It has to come from the heart, the Torah experience, it has to ring true. It has to touch you in a personal way, otherwise it doesn't sustain itself.

Eisenberg ended up going to YU, where he greatly expanded his knowledge of Judaism and where he became "socialized frum."

I learned the ropes, the camps, the community, the lingo, the expressions that *frum* people threw out all the time, that had been very intimidating to me. I had tremendous insecurities. I had always felt like an outsider . . . that it really wasn't me. YU helped me in the process of, this Torah is as much mine even though I didn't grow up with it. It's as much mine as someone who grew up *FFB*.

Eisenberg went to business school and then landed a job with an investment banking firm on Wall Street. This is where he met his first totally assimilated Jews—people who didn't know Purim from Rosh Hashanah.

There was a cathartic moment. It was the epiphany that really changed the course of my adult life, I believe. One of my closest friends told me, "Steve, I have good news and I have bad news." I said, "What's the good news?" "The good news is I'm engaged." "What's the bad?" "The person's not Jewish; but what are you gonna do? I love him, blah, blah, blah, and I want you to be an usher at the wedding, we have to sit down and plan this." And I'm going, "Wait a minute, whoa, whoa."

And this was one of the toughest moments of my adult life on a social, emotional, and religious level. In the firm, I became a racist because I wasn't going to attend the wedding. On a social level, here's one of my closest friends and it just ripped me up that I could not be a part of this happy moment for her.

Religiously, I felt like I had let her down because I could have done more. I should have invited her more for *Shabbos*, I should have been

ubavitch. I got hooked up with Rabbi Simon Jacobson, and that basi-
ally redefined everything I believed in my *Yiddishkeit*. Was I *frum* up
ntil that point? Yes. But the depth and the understanding that I have
or Judaism now is in a whole different place on every possible level. In
ther words, I never understood why does God need me to do a lot of
nese rituals.

What I learned from the [Lubavitch] *Rebbe* and from Simon Jacob-
on's classes, for instance, is that the word *mitzvah* is translated as
ommandment and actually the root word means connection. And the
pposite of a *mitzvah*, God forbid, is an *averah*, which comes from the
vord *aver*, which means to pass over. When one does a *mitzvah*, you're
connecting to something deeper than the act itself; you're connecting
with *Hashem* and something deep within yourself.

When you don't do a *mitzvah*, God forbid, you're involved in an
averah and what you're doing is passing over an opportunity to connect, and that is a very different understanding of Judaism than what I
had. Nobody wants to be commanded; everybody wants to be connected.

I would say I'm more observant than I've ever been in my life, but
I'm also, and this is key, more accepting of secular and nonpracticing
Jews than I've ever been before in my life. *Chasidus* has taught me what
do we know and how do we know the value of a *mitzvah*. Yes, every
Jew should be a practicing Torah Jew, but it may be that for this person
to have a kosher meal, that's equal to me keeping *Shabbos* all year.

I used to say, "I'll never ever, ever, ever, ever keep *Shabbos*." Always. "Never ever, ever." I've learned not to say never ever. And I have
dozens of friends of mine that I've brought to different programs and
who are now *shomer Shabbos*, and every one of them said, "never, never,
never." Where does this come from? We don't know the effect it has,
because we don't see. Only *Hashem* sees the spiritual CAT scan of a
human being.

Most people when they say they don't want to be an Orthodox Jew,
. . . nobody wants a day where you can't drive and you can't play
racketball, but every person wants meaning in his life. If you could show
a person that *Shabbos* isn't just a day of not driving and not playing
racketball and not going to the mall with your kids, but a day of getting
in touch with yourself and your family and friends. When they see that
Shabbos is pro, not anti, all of a sudden they say, "Wait a minute, this is
not the *Shabbos* that I don't believe in." People say Club Med is so great,

more proactive. It was very difficult wearing your reli
that setting. I felt very, very religiously needy and I fel
felt guilty.

And then one *Shabbos* in this time period I happened
Rabbi Ephraim Buchwald's beginner's service at Lincol
gogue [in Manhattan]. And as I looked around the room
Rabbi Buchwald, it really was a flash. I realized that I
my friend back to the Jewish people, but I looked arou
and I saw the eclectic nature of the participants. And I list
Buchwald's message on the vibrancy of *Yiddishkeit*, hov
to our generation.

And I said, you know, if he talks to me, then I know he
friends of mine and peers at work and people that I know or
And I started, slowly at first, bringing these friends of m
Buchwald's beginner's service. And I can't say they've all b
but it made them grow, it took them to a different place.
questioning who they were and what they were and what
believed.

I realized that the great spiritual pandemic that's annihilat
can Jewry was really by intellectual default. These peopl
making a conscious decision; it [the case for embracing Ju
was never presented to them.

My parents used to tell me about a *pintela Yid*, and up unti
it was just a nice little expression. But what I've learned c
past 10 years or so is that there really is such a thing as a *pi*
Because I've seen friends literally at the end of a *Shabbat* m
the table saying, "Steve, you know I don't know if I could
come Orthodox, but you know I do love *Shabbat*" or "I w
to learn more" or "I'd like to have my son go to Hebrew sc
"I'd like to marry a Jew." And that's been my raison d'être fo
10 years.

One of the reasons I'm so involved in the *kiruv* movemen
everytime I see a Jew return to *Yiddishkeit*, I see God. And th
me the faith to know that no matter what I experience and see, t
and suffering I see and have experienced personally, is that I kn
too is part of a plan. Do I understand it? No. But Moshe Rabben
the same questions.

The last blast-off for me spiritually has been the last six, sevei
since I've really gotten involved in an intellectual way with C

no cars, no money, no technology. I say to them, "I can relate to that; I have that once a week."

Steve Eisenberg, 37, is managing director of Ehrenkrantz King Nussbaum, Inc., a money management firm in Manhattan. He is single and lives in Manhattan.

13
Born Again

I wanted to be as far away from being Jewish as I possibly could.

Arthur Filson* became an observant Jew with the help of a born-again Christian whose proselytizing efforts backfired. What may be even more remarkable than that is that he rediscovered Judaism at all, given his background. Filson hated being a Jew.

He grew up in an overwhelmingly Gentile community in Chicago, where his Jewishness was a source of intense embarrassment. When his buddies played Nazi, he played right along with them.

He somehow wound up in Hebrew school. But on the day of his bar mitzvah, *the terms of a Mephistophelean pact he had made with his parents kicked in. It is the same pact many Jewish parents tacitly make with their kids. The terms: Finish your performance, and you're free to abandon Jewish education.*

In this case, both sides lived up to their ends of the bargain. Filson, however, did more than just abandon his Jewish education. He basically quit Judaism.

I memorized my *bar mitzvah,* and I think I did a good job. And the *cholent* was not even cold on Saturday afternoon and I was gone. Out the door. And from that point on, I denied being a Jew, not only to everybody else, but to myself. I wanted to be as far away from being Jewish as I possibly could.

---

*In order to protect the privacy of the narrator, his name has been changed at his request and some details of the story have been altered.

Why?

I had a distaste about it because of feelings of embarrassment I had about my parents. It might have stemmed from the fact that my parents had been married for 20 years by the time I was born. They'd tried unsuccessfully to have children for that long. So they were older and a result, there were things about what they did and who they were that were embarrassing to me.

As I look back on it now, they were things that I would have been tremendously proud of at this stage, but I was embarrassed by it. My parents were actually proud of being Jewish, and that was then a big embarrassment for me. It was almost like part of the rebellion; to get away from them was to get away from Judaism. It's part and parcel of the same thing. I don't know that I can really separate it.

I went to a high school where there were maybe three or four Jewish kids in my whole class out of a hundred. There was just complete assimilation by me at that point. Gentile girls is all I went out with.

How were your folks coping with this?

Basically ignoring it, for a variety of reasons. My mother had a serious illness at that time and my father had a heart attack. They were dealing with their own things. My younger sister went through some very serious problems then. So everybody was kind of dealing with their own things. I was left on my own, more or less. We didn't have Friday night dinners anymore; nobody went to *shul* anymore.

If anything, my parents would try to go to *shul* on *yontif*, and then just Rosh Hashanah and Yom Kippur. I wasn't even doing that. I would say that from the time I was 17 or 18 until I was probably 26 or 27, I was never in *shul*.

I worked my way through college in a rock 'n' roll band from 1968 to 1972 and got into some very, very negative things, even for our secular society, and so far away from anything Jewish, that I was not even recognizable as a Jew. When you're in a band in that particular kind of culture, you're in a very fast culture, so anything and everything is available to you.

Even if you didn't do drugs or do those kinds of things, just being involved in that culture put you in a situation where your values shifted.

My father would constantly want to give me some Jewish influence, so he would send me articles from the Jewish newspapaper or articles about Jews in magazines. When I was in college, he would send them to me and I would just throw them away. I didn't want anybody to be able to associate anything Jewish with me. I didn't want anybody to know I was Jewish, and if I could have changed it, I would have changed it. It was a very self-hating time in my life. As a result, I tried . . . emulating people that had characteristics as far from anything Jewish as possible.

Filson went on graduate school and got an MBA.

By the time I was 28, I had a very successful accounting practice, and it was in that particular practice that I met a person named Bill Wilkerson. Bill Wilkerson was and is a born-again Christian. He would not classify himself as a born-again, but as a Christian. He was the kind of person who had, has, tremendous integrity about what he's doing and tremendous commitment about what he's doing. He's a person who really walks the talk.

He is absolutely doing what he believes he should be doing, and as a result, he was a highly credible person because he's living the kind of life that's he's talking about. So he became a client of mine and through that relationship we became friends. In fact, we're still friends 17 years later.

He was very evangelical at the time [when they first met], and was trying to convert everybody he came across, especially if he came across a nice young Jewish man. He gave me a Bible and I read it. It was both the Old Testament and the New Testament. I read through the *chumash,* read through Psalms; *Mishlei,* Proverbs; and then through the new stuff, their stuff, a couple times actually, over a six-month period. And he asked me, he said, "So don't you believe now? Now that you've read this, hasn't the light come on?"

And I said, "You know, it's really too important a decision and I don't want to make it without going back and learning what I think I should have learned when I was younger but didn't because I hated Hebrew school so much that I was basically turned off."

So I kind of realized that at the age of 28, I had not learned what I should have learned. I kind of had this feeling that since I was born Jewish, there must be something there for me. So I decided that what I needed to do was to go look for it. And I said to him, "I can't tell you. I've got to go back and I have to learn what I should have learned." That's what I'm in the process of doing right now, 17 years later.

Take me through the process.

It was a scary concept. I was frightened of believing in Jesus. It must have been because of something my parents said when I was growing up or some things I learned.

He contacted the rabbi with the Conservative synagogue his parents had attended.

His name was Isaac Berliner, and at the time he must have been about 50 years old. And he was absolutely tremendous. He welcomed me with the most warmth and the most openness. I started going to services on *Shabbos* with my mother. And that was a very good experience. At first I didn't have a clue as to what was going on, [but] gradually I developed a real affinity for that service.

At the time, Filson was married to a non-Jewish woman and they had two small children. His wife did not oppose his efforts, although she was understandably skeptical.

I once said I'd like our kids to be raised Jewish and she said, "Why? You don't even believe in it." And I said I think that there's some value in being brought up in a minority. It teaches you strength.

My daughter [his second child], I named when she was born. I was going to a Conservative *shul* at that point, but not very often. I was learning a little bit, and I got called for an *aliyah*. And I couldn't even read the *brachas* on the Torah, in Hebrew or in transliteration. It had to be told to me in order for me to say them.

The embarrassment Filson suffered that day helped motivate him to delve more deeply into his heritage. He is a perfectionist who detests feeling incompetent.

What do competent people want to do when they feel incompetent? Not be incompetent. There are two ways to do that. One is to run away and never come back and continue to be competent in your secular life and never deal with it. And the other is to sit down and start working at it. Well, I had encouragement from Rabbi Berliner to sit down and learn. Taking a *siddur*, he said, "You know you can do this," and he worked with me, and I started *davening* early in the morning and started working on my Hebrew again and I basically relearned Hebrew. I wanted very much to participate and unless I developed a level of competence, I couldn't participate.

In order for me to develop self-respect, I had to get in a position where I could lead. Without being able to be in that position, it was too much of an ego strain for me to continue.

It sounds like a clear line for me, but it was not. I went to *shul* for, I would say, three or four years with my mother and never did anything. Maybe I got to the point where finally they would call me for *hagbaha* or *galillah*, and I felt I was comfortable doing that.

Aside from your ego, what was pushing you?

I was very successful in business. I had my own firm at that point. I had two beautiful kids. I had a beautiful wife and it was great. So I didn't go into it because I was lacking anything in that regard. I went into it more. . . . I was kind of being pushed. I was being pushed by this born-again Christian. And in order for me to give an answer, I had to know more.

In the late 1970s and early 1980s, Filson got involved with the Anti-Defamation League. And then he did tax work for a group that was establishing an Orthodox day school in his community. This brought him in contact with frum Jews for the first time in his life, and the experience was positive. He found them to be open, caring and accepting—even though his marital situation was known. "It was really an eye-opening experience for me," said Filson, whose Jewish learning soon intensified.

It was probably not until five years ago [that] I really took on the *mitzvos.* And I didn't take them on all at once; I don't think it's wise to take them on all at once. I've seen people who've done that and sort of blown themselves out. I was very slow and very circumspect in what I did. The *mitzvos* I took on, I took on for particular reasons.

Now, what happened to me is that through all this period I was changing. I [had been] taking things on, but I was taking them on intellectually. I was not taking them on experientially. And one of my teachers, Rabbi Yitzchak Gorofsky—who was the executive director of one of the Orthodox day schools here—he and I had been learning together probably about four years. And he said, "This is all well and good, but you've gotta start doing some things. You know, I mean take on a *mitzvah* and start doing it." And it was very hard for me.

At that point I was going to *shul* with my mother still. I was driving, and we had learned about the forbiddenness of driving on *Shabbos*, and learned about *kibud av'v'ame,* and it was a very difficult time for me. But I gave up going with my mother and started walking to *shul.* I started going to an Orthodox *shul.*

After Rabbi Gorofsky left to take another position, Filson began learning with Rabbi Yisroel Pincus. The two went to Israel in the early 1990s. "That was a big leap for me," said Filson, who resolved to ratchet up his commitment to Judaism once he returned to the states. He said he would begin by wearing a yarmulka *to Jewish communal gatherings— smaller ones, presumably—where kosher food was being served.*

When I got back, there was the big ADL meeting, and there were like 600 people going to this dinner and they were having kosher food. And I was going, and I called Rabbi Pincus and I said, "The first thing I'm gonna have to do is wear it in front of 600 people. I don't know if I'm ready to do that." He said, "No, no, look at it this way. If you did it by small meetings, how many meetings would it take you to get up to 600 people?" I said, "Oh, you're right [laughs]," and I did it. It was a major step. I was already keeping kosher at that point and was *shomer Shabbos* after we got back.

[Earlier] in the summer, when I started keeping *Shabbos*, I made myself wear my *yarmulka* from the time I left the house until I'd get to *shul*. That was a big step, but I'd walk on the back streets to get there [laughs]. Then it progressed to wearing a *tallis*, and now it's not *Shabbos* for me unless I walk down the street wearing my *tallis*.

Do you wear a keepah *at work?*

No I don't wear a *keepah* at work. I have a lot of non-Jewish clients, and I'm really less concerned about them. I have a lot of nonreligious Jewish clients, and I'm scared about what their reaction would be and I'm also scared about what the reaction would be with my partners.

What do your partners think?

My partners think I've gone off the deep end. I have two partners and I'm very close to them; actually I have three now, but at the time I had two, and I'm very close to both of them. One of my partners was born in a very, very secular Jewish family and really has never learned anything. One of my partners learned a lot and knows a great deal but doesn't practice. The partner that never learned anything, he's even said as recently as a few weeks ago that he doesn't know me anymore. He and I went to graduate school together.

Filson said that after giving it much thought, he declined to attend that partner's recent remarriage—to a non-Jew—because it would have conflicted with Shabbos.

He was very upset at the time. We still have some rough edges over that. *Frumkeit* definitely has created some barriers in my life, most of them very difficult to deal with. We have him [the partner] over for *Shabbos* and we include them and he's learned a tremendous amount [laughs], but he's still not accepting.

I'm a very intense person, and tend to do things 110 percent when I do things. And that's the way I've taken on *Yiddishkeit* also. See, everybody's perception is that I've taken on *Yiddishkeit* very suddenly.

What they didn't know is there were 12 years before that that I learned. It was really slow and methodical and that's where I went through the agony.

To stop doing things that I was doing that were wrong was the first level. And then to pick up the positive things, that was the most perceptible change, but it was not the deepest change by any means. At this point . . . the change was going from being self-hating to be self-loving for the same reason, because I'm Jewish.

Filson was divorced in the early 1980s. His ex-wife had cited his workaholism—not religious differences—as a prime reason for the breakup of their marriage.

I couldn't understand what she was saying. She was saying that I wasn't giving her what she needed. And I counted off, "Well, you've got a great house and you have a condo at the lake and you have a maid and a housekeeper, two cars. What more do you want?" It took me five years at least to understand what she was talking about, if I even did then, in terms of time commitment. If she wanted me home Friday night early so we could do something together, sorry, I got to work, I can't come.

Well, if *Hashem* says you gotta be home before it gets dark [laughs] . . . at that point, if you have some *yiras Hashem*, you're home. I think one thing that *Yiddishkeit* really brings is *Shabbos*. *Shabbos*, above everything else, really brings home family.

Were there any other behaviors you found particularly hard to change?

This is a very personal thing; I've never really told it to anybody. While I was in the transition phase, before I had really taken on the *mitzvos*, I was divorced and I was dating and I was active sexually. I was living by myself, and I would go out with a woman, and get involved with her, like Friday night, and I would go to *shul* on Saturday.

And I would say to myself, what am I doing? I mean, this is like absolutely ridiculous. And I think it was really the *Yiddishkeit* that kept me moving in the right direction.

I would confront myself—this happened a few times—and then the behavior stopped. I got tired of confronting myself with that issue. *Trayf* food was not as hard as that. Harder than that was going to events and not eating. And that's what I do now. I still have to go to events. I still have to go to lunches with clients and things like that, and they don't have a lot of kosher restaurants in [my community.] It's a difficult thing.

So basically I don't eat or I'll eat just fruit that I can peel myself, and that's been a transition too.

Did you have any difficulty with the concept of belief in God?

I had a very strong sense that God was in my life all the time and he was watching everything I was doing—and that I needed to start changing my behavior to develop and enhance the relationship I had with him. I kind of knew what I needed to do way before I ever did it; it was gaining the willpower to just do it.

Has frumkeit *affected your professional life?*

I have made a lot of changes in the way I conduct my practice. I was always very good at what I did, but I was always doing it for my own ego, not my clients. My clients were just necessary evils to being able to prove how wonderful I was.

That's changed to where I really see myself as being a *klee* for *Hashem* to work in people's lives in helping them with their problems. I see myself in a different role. I really see myself as . . . *Hashem* [having] given the tools he has given me for a particular purpose.

I've changed my billing practices really drastically. In the past when I wouldn't know what to charge, I would guesstimate [on hourly charges], and generally resolved doubts in my favor. Now, I try to be very precise.

Have you reconciled the fact that you are a religious Jew, yet your children are not Jewish?

They're not reconciled. It's a very emotional issue. They come to us for the holidays and they like doing that. My parents come. I have a sister who's in Israel and she has three children and one or all of them come. I have another sister, a younger sister, who has also married a non-Jew, and she will come sometimes and sometimes not, kind of the way I had been when I rejected everything. The kids also come for *Shabbos.*

Have you asked the kids to convert?

No. My kids at this point believe that they are half Jewish. I have not disabused them of that notion. I have been terrible in talking to my kids openly and honestly about this issue. I'm avoiding it. We have a good relationship and I just don't want to talk about it because I don't want to bring anything up that's going to be a barrier.

Do either of them show any interest in Yiddishkeit?

My son, definitely not. My son is only interested in cars, period. My daughter has shown some interest. She's 14, and she's a lot more conversational than my son is, about all issues. She asks about it. We talk about it and we talk about religion in general.

What has been the impact of Yiddishkeit *on your life?*

Before *Yiddishkeit* I had a lot of money which I ended up losing through various kinds of investments and it was a very painful time because I *was* my financial statement. If my financial statement was going up, I felt good about myself. If my financial statement went down, I felt bad about myself. And now [laughs] it's external to me. Where I am now is with my learning and where I am with my practice of *Yiddishkeit,* and it's just changed my entire emphasis; *Shabbos* more than any other single thing.

I remember going through some very, very difficult times professionally. And I remember when those things were going on, bad things would always happen on Friday. What that ended up doing was making my *Shabboses* so great [laughs]. Because what I would do is, I would put myself totally in a different space for *Shabbos.* In order to do that, I had to get myself really, really into it on *Shabbos.* My *kavanah* on Shabbos was really intense, and it just made for some incredible *Shabboses.* So it was really an incredible time. *Shabbos,* I think more than anything else, saved my life. It literally saved my life. *Yiddishkeit* literally saved my life.

Arthur Filson, 46, is an accountant who lives in the Chicago area. He has remarried.

14
Abba Knows Best

In some way, I really wanted to retain my Jewishness. I couldn't handle
the idea that I would never have a *Shabbos* table or *Shabbos zemiros*.

Chani Frankel grew up during the 1970s in a Reform household in a
mostly Gentile neighborhood on Long Island. Yiddishkeit wasn't even
a blip on her spiritual radar screen, although she sensed early on that
the Judaism she had been exposed to was somehow lacking. She eventually developed a "gaping need" for meaning in her life and for "a sense
of connection to time or history." That link was forged through a series
of incidents and episodes that took place over two decades. At one time,
she might have seen them as a hash of unconnected, random events. But
when she looks back now, she sees a grand design.*

The first turning point I had was as early as four years old. My father
called me over . . . and he said he had something important to tell me.
And I went over and like out of nowhere, he put his hands on my face,
and he just looked at me and said, "I have something really important to
tell you and you have to remember it for your whole life."

And he said, "There's a God and he's good and he loves you." And
he said, "You're a Jew and it makes you different than almost everybody else in the world. And you have a special relationship to God and
sometimes people don't like Jews. But you're never ever to be afraid of
that and you're always to trust that there is a God and he is good and he

---

*The name of the narrator has been changed at her request to protect her privacy.

loves you." And then he just sent me back to play. And it was really a major moment. I felt like he sort of infused something into me.

That "something" resurfaced about eight years later at an inopportune time.

On the day of my *bas mitzvah*, I remember going outside and pacing around the pool in our backyard and getting very, very sad. My parents had spent thousands of dollars on one of these big American *bas mitzvahs* in a wedding hall, and my mom saw that I was sort of teary-eyed and she called me in. And she was, like, "what's wrong?" And I remember telling her that, "They never taught me what the words mean. They just taught me the letters and how to read them, but they never taught me what anything means, and so it doesn't mean anything."

The truth was [laughs] my mom was really upset with me. It wasn't a moment she wanted a critique on Reform Judaism and their methodology [laughs], thousands of dollars later. Right after my *bas mitzvah*, that was it for synagogue.

But I was always concerned with this concept of God, knowing that I was different. I didn't feel there was a bridge between my spiritual intuition that there is a God and my intellectual feeling that, yeah, that's really stupid, there can't be a God. There's so much suffering, there's so much evil, I just don't think there's a God.

Thirsting for new cultural experiences, she enrolled in a university near Atlanta. But when the South soon lost its allure—something having to do with KKK national headquarters being located nearby— Frankel set out in search of more exotic cultures. She enrolled in a program in which students live and study aboard an ocean liner as it circumnavigates the globe. As it turns out, the ship was disabled when it ran aground between Turkey and Alexandria. Frankel finished her remaining two months of study in Israel.

That was a moment, in retrospect, that was created so that I should get to Israel. At the moment I wasn't thinking anything of the sort. I found Jerusalem to be very mystical and magical because the architecture . . . it was so foreign and different. I remember going to the *Kotel* and praying to God, saying, "I hope that you're well, that you stay well and that your presence stays in the world. That you help us to understand you. But I don't know what to say to you."

Anyway, that trip ended and I went back to [the Georgia university], and I took a class on the Holocaust, and that was an extremely pivotal thing in my life. I think the thing that was so traumatic was seeing in history the legacy of anti-Semitism, particularly in Germany and particularly among brilliant philosophical thinkers.

And I remember reading *Night* by Elie Wiesel, and taking on in my mind that I was him, pretending that when he would talk about his father, I'd feel as if it was my father. It took over a dimension in my life the way I'd never experienced before, and for days and weeks, I only ate, like, stale bread and potato soup.

I got very depressed. I actually dropped some difficult courses. I started hating non-Jews, thinking they were all horrible. And we had a man come to speak to us [in the Holocaust class], a survivor of the Holocaust.

History came alive, horrifically, a short time later when the Holocaust survivor's wife was slain in a suspected Klan ambush, according to Frankel, who was emotionally overwhelmed by the experience. Later, during an impromptu soul-searching session which took place while she was jogging in a downpour, Frankel came to the realization that it was time to abandon the prison of fear and depression she had constructed for herself.

I had to go back into the quote, real world, unquote, and live my life six million times more effectively and emotionally—that when I cry, I cry for the six million. When I laugh, I laugh for the six million. And when I eat something delicious, I appreciate it for those who couldn't. It was very cathartic, and I healed emotionally.

Frankel returned to the oceangoing education program, this time with a more overtly Jewish perspective. "In each country, I was able to find some synagogue or some Jewish writings," she said. "My attitude was starting to change significantly." When she returned stateside, she transferred to the State University of New York, where she adopted the cause of Soviet Jewry. During her junior year, she went back to Israel.

That's when it first started to be a religious experience for me. I don't know why. But I wound up having this attraction to Jerusalem because I was now in Tel Aviv. I had only experienced Jerusalem, and I didn't find in Tel Aviv that same sort of mystical feeling on *Shabbos* or anything. So I started having *Shabbos* dinner with my friends, and then we'd go out afterwards. But I would end up going down to Jerusalem more and more. And I really started becoming a Zionist.

Frankel considered making aliyah, *but her mother convinced her not to. During graduate school, she took her fourth trip to Israel.*

I was traveling with a friend who was a Mormon. And I was trying to show him that it was really a beautiful culture and everybody was going to accept him even though he was Christian. And nobody would even host us.

I remember it was around Pesach time and we were told we could eat by these people in the Old City. The host told me, you sit here and have your friend sit there. And I was, like, really upset, what are you doing? And during the meal, we were singing *zemiros* and it was really moving. He [the host] lived right above the *Kotel*. And he leaned over to me and he said, "If you spend any more time with this guy you will never ever have a *Shabbos* table in your life, you will never have *zemiros* like this, you will never have Jewish children." And I burst into tears. That was it for me.

He touched some sort of spark inside that Judaism was really important to me. In some way, I really wanted to retain my Jewishness. I couldn't handle the idea that I would never have a *Shabbos* table or *Shabbos zemiros*. It was a strange thing because the friend that I was traveling with was someone who was so familiar to me, and here this Jewish stranger was more familiar in some deep way, and I felt extraordinarily confused.

Still confused, she returned stateside and enrolled in a university in California, where she continued studying philosophy—and found it lacking.

What I found is that there is a ceiling on secular knowledge in a secular university precisely because they had no absolutes. All the philosophers could only speak about their ideas relatively because they had no concept of a God or of an absolute reality external to one's thinking. And so I saw there was a ceiling, and I wasn't getting any of the answers . . . [to] all the questions that were plaguing me my entire life.

There was one particular case, where I'd been dating out in Los Angeles. I was now out there about three years. And I was dating this man from Holland who was the most ethical, kind, decent human being I'd ever dated. And he wanted to get married. And I couldn't. And I didn't know why. He said we could raise the kids Jewish, and I didn't even really know what it meant.

Then, when it was Easter, he got these bunnies from his parents, chocolate bunnies from Holland. And he said, "Won't it be cute when they send those things for our kids?" I said, "Wait, you said we'd raise the kids Jewish." And he said, "We will, but *they're* not Jewish [his parents]. They'll send things for their holidays." And I said, "Well that won't work, that's not raising them Jewish."

Meanwhile, her parents had begun learning about their long-lost
Yiddishkeit *through the Lubavitchers. They informed her, in the stron-*
gest of terms, that it would be unwise for her to continue the relation-
ship with the young man.

It affected me. And I did wind up breaking up with him. And at that
point, that's when I said, you know what? It's not Zionism. It's not some
ethereal thing. What is Judaism? Am I a bigot? Or is there something
real to this? I realized I had to start making some decisions. I couldn't
just randomly say I'm a Jew. It's like, what is it to be a Jew?

She got a partial answer when she accepted her girlfriend's offer to
attend a program for singles in Los Angeles sponsored by a well-known
Jewish outreach organization.

You would *shmooze* with people and ask these obvious ethical questions, and at the end, the teachers would stand up and give a *d'var Torah*
for five minutes. I had never heard of a *d'var Torah*. But I craved those
divrei Torah; I couldn't wait. And after these meetings, I'd go up to these
teachers, [and say] "Tell me more. Where did you get that? That's really
fascinating."

And so they funneled me into Torah learning. And that's where I just
said, wow, intellectually. Like, wow, there was no longer a ceiling on
knowledge because I was introduced to the Jewish concept of God, of
an absolute reality external to us. And why we need that in order to define the way we are going to live.

How did you bridge the gap between thinking Jewishly and actually
doing mitzvos?

This was a very hard gap for me to bridge. It was very slow. I just
kept going to the classes. The more I started to get involved intellectually, people would start to invite me for *Shabbos*, and the more I'd go
for *Shabbos*, the more I loved *Shabbos*. *Shabbos* was the bridge. You
know what I really loved? The *bracha*, the *yehi ratzon bracha* that the
women say, just touched me so deeply, even if I would go out dancing
on Friday night after a *Shabbos* meal at my friends' house, I still wanted
to light those candles and say that prayer.

And it took two-and-a-half years of back and forth struggle. And I
remember once I got very, very turned off because I was learning with
all women and I was getting really to the center of the community, and
we started learning *The Path of the Just*, and here was all this intimidating [fire and brimstone] stuff. I hated it, and I was turned off, and I said
forget this.

I didn't completely go off. But I did start learning with a Reform rabbi in L.A. It was very convenient and it was very nice, and they sang on *Shabbos*, and they drove to the *shul*, but I didn't find the same type of passion for the truth and the same love of Torah and the same drive to get answers philosophically that I found in the Orthodox community.

After speaking with some of her Orthodox friends, she decided to learn in a yeshiva *in Israel. There, she immersed herself in a "totally Torah environment."*

I felt that I learned more in three weeks there than I had learned in six years of college and graduate school. This idea of an absolute just opened up a whole world of learning to me. Our Jewish heritage was so phenomenal. It was so respectful of the mind, and it filled such a cavity in me.

Do you ever find that frumkeit *and* feminism *are philosophically incompatible?*

I wouldn't say that it's all so smooth for me. I have serious issues, still. *Tznius* is difficult. However, I think one of the greatest hardships that a woman has to go through now in secular society is what the social and sexual revolution of the '60s did to her, because I have come to believe that fundamentally men and woman are different. And if a feminist takes issue with that, why is the book *Men are from Mars, Women are from Venus* so popular? Because it's even becoming popular in secular literature, that men and woman think differently, feel differently, need differently.

I don't feel in any way that I'm not respected or that I'm put down. I feel very elevated and I'm not looked at as an object. Like the way women dress in secular society; they have to recognize that their self-esteem is coming from their physical appearance. That's why they don't want to age, that's why they don't want to get fat. It doesn't matter how much money they earn or how brilliant they are. It doesn't matter; if they don't look good, they're not gonna be wanted in secular society. That's not how it is here.

Are you ever plagued by doubt? If so, how do you handle it?

I definitely have a lot of doubt. But one of the brilliant things about Judaism . . . I mean *Yisroel* means "struggle with *Hashem*." I am always in doubt of . . . does it have to be exactly like this? Should I hold by this rabbi or that rabbi? The essence of Orthodox Judaism is we believe that the Torah is absolute. However, we have *machlokeses* all over the place. Different rabbis are holding differently, and everybody says, oh it's so black and white to be an Orthodox Jew, and it's easy because you just have these rules. Well, the further inside you get to Orthodox Judaism, you see that you're allowed to have doubt. You're allowed to work with it and struggle with it and grow through it.

Overall, what impact has Yiddishkeit *had on your life?*

I had this gaping need for meaning and a sense of connection to time or history. I think that being an Orthodox Jew has connected me to the Creator. So many Americans say, yeah, I believe in God, but they don't know what the heck they're talking about. They've never pursued what that meant.

I feel like I've pursued that and I have a connection to history and a purpose in life. My life is so enriched because the one thing that America doesn't really give people is a spiritual dimension, and I believe innately we're supposed to develop that. We need to develop that to be whole and healthy.

Chani Frankel, 31, is an educator. She and her husband currently live in Jerusalem and have one child.

15
The Return Flight

Hashem . . . gave me something when I needed it. He gave me something to link me to a past I really had no connection with.

It seems appropriate that Miriam Garfinkle's spiritual journey began on an airplane. The plane was bound for Poland, the first stop on the "March of the Living," a program in which Jewish students visit the concentration camps and then escape to Israel so their souls can recuperate.

A resident of Orange County, California, an overwhelmingly Gentile area, Garfinkle had never had contact with observant Jews. "I had never seen one or met one," she said.

She soon would. In April 1990, she found herself at JFK Airport in New York, one of hundreds of assimilated teenagers belonging to the B'nai B'rith Youth Organization. However, due to a seating mixup, Garfinkle was unable to sit with her group. The only seats available on that plane were in the section reserved for another group—a group vastly different from hers. They were yarmulka-*clad students from a Talmudic academy in New York.*

[There was an empty] seat between me and this religious guy. It was as if *Hashem* had created a separation [laughs]. For 10 hours he and his friends argued with me about Torah, about God and about religiosity.
  What was the nature of the argument?
  What is God to you? Why have any Judaism if it's not religious Judaism? What does your Judaism mean to you and where does it fit into your life? And why does it have to fit into your life? Why don't you fit your life into Judaism?

And I really didn't have answers for him. He said, "What does the Torah say?" And I said, "I have no clue." And he said, "You've never read it?" And I said "No." I was really embarrassed. I didn't know who Rashi was. When you grow up in a Conservative or Reform lifestyle, you're not even given the tools to make your own choice. He made me realize how ignorant I was.

The entire March was amazing. More than 3,000 kids, more than 5,000 people, and day after day, I would find him [the *yeshiva* student] to talk to. I hung out with [the *yeshiva* students]. I really wanted to see how they lived. I wanted to be like them. I'd never seen anyone have that kind of *kavanah* or that kind of belief in anything. And I wanted to know what their God was all about.

I would see them make *brachot* on food and I thought that was amazing. It took food to a completely different level I'd never even considered. There were all these things that I'd never considered, and I just wanted to know all I could.

When I was at Auschwitz, I went into Block 27. And downstairs there was a tape running of movies the Germans had been making. On this one there was a man talking and someone translating. What he said was: If there are any Jews left in the world, and if they knew nothing about him and why he died and who he was and the kind of things religious Jews did in Europe, then Hitler won. We had a responsibility to learn about our Jewish history and our Jewish heritage and we had a responsibility to him. If we didn't fulfill it, it would be like walking on his grave. He would have died for nothing.

I thought about that for a long time. And I thought about a lot of the things I saw in Poland. I realized that if every American Jew became like me, then five generations down the line Hitler would have won. We would have done it to ourselves.

Whether or not I was going to become religious . . . I didn't think I could keep *Shabbos* and everything else. But I at least had to educate myself. I had to make an educated decision. So I made a promise to myself; one, I would teach people about the Holocaust, and two, I would learn.

But there was a lot of uncertainty, too. I was really scared because at first I felt that maybe it was a cult or maybe I just misunderstood.

A cult?

Yeah [laughs]. How come I was the only kid out of 350 who thought these people were just amazing? Why was I so attracted to them, the family values and the interpersonal values? Maybe because I had a difficult childhood or maybe because of my family. And then I realized that it really wasn't [just] that.

You went from the camps straight to Israel?

It was like going from death to life. There was this unbelievable surge that you belong to the Jewish people, and that this land is yours. Whether you believe it's because six million people died or because *Hashem* promised it to the Jews. Whatever it is, *Hakadosh Boruch Hu* promised the Jews *Eretz Yisroel* [voice breaking] and Torah. It's yours, you're part of it; it's part of your soul.

It really changed my life. I realized that to know yourself and to know God . . . are the two things you really have to know, and everything will come afterwards. It gave me this calm, this easiness and this ability to just go forward. I gained my belief in *Hashem* in Israel.

I don't know that I didn't believe in God before that, but I didn't know exactly where I fit in. Now, I made a definite decision that being Jewish wasn't a sideline issue, something to put at the bottom of your emotional resume. It had to take the foreground in my life.

She returned to Orange County, alien turf for any Jew, much less an observant one. She was one of only eight Jewish students in her 3,000-pupil high school.

If I didn't fit into high school before the march, I certainly didn't fit in afterwards. Before I went on the march I had people throw firecrackers at my hair, put swastikas on my locker, and throw pennies at my feet. When I was a freshman and a sophomore, I didn't want to go to high school because it was blatant anti-Semitism. I felt victimized and abused; I was never going to fit in [there]. It wasn't a question of living with *goyim*, it was a question of living with people that hated me because I was Jewish.

She helped establish a multi-cultural student union and worked with the school administration on a hate-crime education program. Although she eventually gained the grudging respect of many of her peers, school was mostly an unpleasant experience. In fact, life in general in Orange County was a struggle for her. She was unable to find people her age who were engaged in intellectual and spiritual pursuits, Jewish or otherwise.

I was very lonely. Emotionally, I had no peer group at all. I was really into something [far beyond] geometry in high school. I was trying to find my spiritual self. I knew what I was doing was right, it's just that sometimes it's hard to remind yourself when it's really difficult to do.

People thought I was really strange. At times I thought I was crazy. Imagine trying to keep kosher when you don't really know the laws. You're living in your parents' house, using paper plates for a year-and-a-half, trying to keep *Shabbat* in El Toro [her hometown]. I listened to my parents mow the lawn underneath my window on Saturday, and it drove me crazy. I didn't know what to do.

How did your parents react?

It was very difficult for them, I think, just because it created a new tension where there was already tension. When a 15-year-old walks back into your house and says, basically, I'm rejecting the values you gave me and I'm rejecting you because you're not a religious Jew, that's really difficult. I think my parents thought I was nuts.

[Meanwhile] I was still writing letters to [the *yeshiva* student she had met on the march]. He would write me these you're-doing-okay letters. He was my *rav*, my best friend, and my confidant. I can never thank him enough. I needed someone to be my sounding board and say it's okay, you're not going crazy.

After her junior year in high school, Garfinkle was about to leave to spend the summer in Israel when she was approached by a Gentile coworker.

She knew I was going to Israel, and she said, "Miriam, I want to give you a Jewish star that my [great-]aunt gave to me." I thought it was going to be some little trinket or something. [But when] she said, "Here, this is for you," and plunked it down on the desk, I was absolutely awestruck.

Garfinkle describes the necklace as a Jewish star medallion made up of a series of triangles, each containing a tiny hand-sculpted symbol of one of the 12 tribes of Israel.

I really felt like it was a sign from *Hashem*. Her great-aunt [who had no living Jewish relatives] had told her niece, "Please give this to another Jew." That's all she really told me.

When Garfinkle was in Israel, a man offered her 15,000 shekels (then about $5,000) for the necklace. When she refused his offer, he advised her to immediately take the piece to the museum. He was convinced it was a collector's item.

The next day we went to the museum and his [hunch] was confirmed. It was a very, very rare item that was made, I believe, approximately 300 years ago in Europe. When I got back and told my friend the story, she said that [members of] her family swallowed it during the Holocaust when they were in the camps, and that's how they got it out. And she [the great-aunt] said she had to find a religious Jew to give it to; [her niece] spent five years [looking] and she finally gave it to me.

I didn't have candlesticks or a *Kiddush* cup or anything that had been passed down from generation to generation. I got something from somebody else's family. It was sort of strange because to me it was almost like my family line started with me and her family line stopped with her great-aunt and I had to make the link. I had to make my family into hers and hers into mine.

Since then, she has collected several ritual objects, including her great-grandmother's candlesticks from Russia.

But [the necklace] by far is the most meaningful because I believe that it came from *Hashem*. I really believe He gave me something when I needed it. He gave me something to link me to a past I really had no connection with. I've worn it every single day now for four-and-a-half years.

Miriam Garfinkle, 21, has since attended Stern College and studied at the Nishmat Advanced Center for Women's Learning in Jerusalem. She coordinated the Jerusalem Fellowships program for Aish Hatorah and is currently working on a photographic book on the Jewish communities in Judea, Samaria, and Gaza.

16
Seeing Is Believing

I saw something about these people that struck very much to the bottom of my heart.

David Gelber's* view of Judaism was badly skewed for years. His first Jewish memories are of overt anti-Semitism in his native Russia. Once he left his homeland, he came into contact with Jews who were fully emancipated—both from tyranny and from any meaningful contact with their heritage. Many of them were self-centered, materialistic, and unhappy. Gelber was one of them. "I felt very empty inside," he said. The "something" he found to fill that void was the product of many influences over the years, but one episode stands out. It began with what seemed to be a chance meeting on a street in the north of England.

My first encounter with *Yiddishkeit* was when somebody in school [in Russia] called me a *zhid*, which is a derogatory name for a Jew. I was about eight years old. My grandmother, whom I stayed after school with at the time, told me to be proud that I am Jewish in a very unique way that I cannot say in English. It rhymes in Russian.

I always knew that I was Jewish, and somehow because of my parents and grandparents, always felt proud to be one. The only thing I knew about *Yiddishkeit* is that every Pesach we were invited to my grandparents house where we ate *matzoh*, chicken soup and *matzoh* balls. Nobody ever explained to me what any of that meant, except that it was a

---

*The name of the narrator has been changed at his request to protect his privacy.

Jewish holiday. It was the only Jewish holiday we ever celebrated. I had no idea there were any others.

My parents decided to emigrate to the United States when I was 15. On the way to America we had to go through Italy. When we were there, there were Christian missionaries who were proselytizing and they showed me movies about Israel and talked to me about God. I wasn't about to become Christian because I was aware of the Christian persecution of Jews, but some of the ideas that they mentioned were very interesting. They mentioned, for example, that a person could test if *Hashem* is there by asking for things and seeing if that will come true. That's a dangerous proposition sometimes, but also a way to get connected to *Hashem*.

So that brought me to *davening*. I had actually begun to talk to *Hashem* and ask him for things that I thought I needed and my family needed. It had nothing to do with the Jewish way of *davening*. I created my own form a little bit. So I asked *Hashem* for things and . . . I was answered many times, *boruch Hashem*.

So I came to America and I went to a Jewish day school in [the Washington, DC, area], but I didn't pick up much *Yiddishkeit* because I was more interested in learning English and generally establishing myself in my new country. To me, it was just a way to go to a private school. But in any case, I continued my experiment with *Hashem*, if I can call it that, and I saw many great things that I thought came out of it. And I believe it was not an accident.

For example, my sister was in an accident, and every day I would *daven* that she would be well, and she was unharmed. My mother, *boruch Hashem*, was saved from an illness. I *davened* for us to be adjusted to America and to be able to live here normally, and that also came through, thank God.

After I graduated from the day school I got in the business called Amway. And in that business they stressed belief in God from a Christian point of view, but they did stress it sometimes in a general point of view. And they brought some scriptural verses which I thought rang true. And again I think that pushed me a little further.

At that time I felt that since *Hashem* has done so much for me, I felt maybe it was a good idea that I should give something back. I was now about 18 and started to go to the University of Maryland for an engineering degree and at same time I was working in a machine shop as a machinist—usually Friday night and Saturday, as a matter of fact.

I thought that I knew about *Shabbos*. I just knew there was such a thing because as I passed Orthodox *shuls* I would see people walking and I could see they weren't driving. And from somewhere I heard the idea of not working on *Shabbos*. So I thought that's what I'm going to do. I said that's how I'm going to thank *Hashem*; I'm not gonna work on *Shabbos*. I told my boss I will not work, and he said okay, you can work on Sunday.

After doing that for about two months, he said, "Well, I don't have any work on Sunday any more, so you'll have to work at McDonald's if you don't work on *Shabbos*." Without having any other job and without good proofs or understanding of why I was doing what I was doing, I started working on Saturday again.

After graduating from college, Gelber made another attempt to keep Shabbos, *during which he'd walk to an Orthodox* shul *near his parents' home. The attempt was short-lived. It ended when he began driving his grandfather—who was too old to drive himself—to another* shul, *this one Conservative. There, Gelber began to learn a few things—for example, that there are important Jewish holidays in addition to just Rosh Hashanah, Yom Kippur and Pesach.*

After this, I started working as a computer programmer, and I was making good money. I thought I could satisfy myself by trying to look for material pleasures. I bought a new car. I had a new apartment. I had a girlfriend—Jewish, but the previous one was not. I was going to different restaurants, I was traveling to foreign countries.

But I felt very empty inside; I felt very unhappy. I didn't feel fulfilled. I felt like I was wasting my life somehow. At the same time I felt that, in general, in America, life is very empty and people don't have friends— I'm not talking about *frum* people—but generally they go home and work very hard and come home and watch television; a very empty existence.

But when I went to a *frum shul* I saw people I was very impressed with. I was impressed with the way they carried themselves. They weren't arrogant. I felt warmth. I felt a sense of fulfillment and a sense of happiness a little bit there. I was invited for lunch a few times. I felt they had a day off [*Shabbos*] when they could really relax instead of like everybody else, running around like chickens without their heads all the time.

I felt there was some meaning, some holidays that people celebrated, and in America the only thing that's a celebration of a holiday is going shopping for a sale—that's the celebration of every holiday, going for a sale to the local mall.

Gelber thought a change of career might help, but that never happened. He then traveled throughout Europe, occasionally stopping to visit synagogues.

Everywhere I met Jews. I was looking for happiness, that's what I was looking for. And everytime I saw these Jews they were not happy. They weren't *frum* Jews, and I saw no meaning in their lives. It was not there.

Gelber had planned to visit London, but he was unable to find a ship that was going there when he wanted to. Instead, on a whim, he grabbed the next available ship. It wasn't headed anywhere near London. It was bound for Newcastle upon Tyne, near the Scottish border, more than 200 miles north of London.

This was a coincidence. It was a luxury boat and I thought this is like the dream of my life to have all these restaurants there and casinos and everything. But I was very bored there somehow. I danced with some Swedish woman, thinking that that would be fun. And I thought being there would be fun, but it was still empty and it was sort of boring to me all of a sudden.

I got to Newscastle and spent a couple of days there. I was on my way out to hitchhike down to London. And I remember, on my way I saw a *frum* Jew in black hat and the whole *frum* outfit walking down [the street] with his wife. It occurred to me that I have not been to a *shul* in Newcastle yet.

I ran after him and said, "Can you show me a *shul* here? I haven't seen one yet." He said, "Yeah, I'm walking there, you can come along." We walked across the bridge from Newcastle to Gateshead, which happens to be what they call "the Jerusalem of Europe." And I told him my story and we started talking and he invited me for dinner at his house.

It happened that it was the beginning of Succos. And even though usually he doesn't go to Newcastle, that day he had to do some shopping. He told me he'd introduce me to some rabbi from New York who lived now in Gateshead. When I met the rabbi in *shul*, he told me, "Look it's Succos. Why don't you stay for a week and see how we live?"

So I gladly agreed. I think maybe I heard the name [Succos] and knew it was a Jewish holiday. Besides that, what it really involved, I really didn't know. So he put me up with a beautiful family with ten children, this rabbi, and I lived there a week. When I went to *shul*, and went dancing in the *shul* and stayed with the family, I was struck by their hospitality and by them accepting me in jeans or whatever, dirty clothes maybe—somebody off the street, inviting me in their house for a whole week and feeding me and letting me live there without having any idea who I was.

I saw something about these people that struck very much to the bottom of my heart. I saw that they weren't just nice on the outside, like so many people in America are, but truly nice on the inside as well, and they backed that up with deeds. I saw they were happy.

I saw incredible harmony between the husband and wife in the home, not just on *Shabbos*, but throughout the week. I saw how ten children— to me they were like angels—how they behaved . . . the whole thing.

They told me that nothing happens by chance. And all of a sudden, when I realized where I was and how the whole events sort of led me to that point, it struck me that that may be true. I was almost in a trance from everything that happened. And I tell you, when I saw the family and I saw everything, I thought this is the kind of life that I would like to live. I really thought that is something that could bring happiness to a person.

The person that I lived with, Rabbi K., gave me a *yarmulka*, and now for three years ever since that, I've never taken a *yarmulka* off my head. I still have that *yarmulka* with me.

Gelber read some books about Judaism, but he wanted to learn more. On the recommendation of one of the rabbis he met in England, he enrolled in the Ohr Somayach Yeshiva *in Jerusalem, where he would learn for two weeks.*

On the way to *Ohr Somayach* I met on the bus the rabbi who I was supposed to have my appointment with at the *yeshiva*. Every step of the way, I was sort of guided by the hand.

I started listening to lectures by Rabbi Cardoza there [at *Ohr Somayach*], and was incredibly impressed because the ideas seemed very true. I'd never heard of anything in my life that seemed so true to me intuitively as well as intellectually.

In any case, I was struggling with the idea that all of this that had happened to me so far was just chance, just an occurrence that could happen to anybody. But the powerful combination of all my prayers along the way until now that came true, as well as the coincidences that came together, was such that I couldn't discount it as mere chance. I simply could not.

Tell me more about the two weeks in Ohr Somayach.

I thought that I had found a way to approach life. I found a . . . wisdom, an incredible wisdom that was all there, that all I needed to live a productive, meaningful life that will lead to something, that will produce something positive, was there. Before, I was always interested in learning about wisdom. But you know, it was a piece here, a piece there, you don't know who is right, who is wrong. It seemed like here was one system that made sense, one system that encompassed everything, that contained not only intellectual depth but emotional depth, the goodness of a person. . . . It was a wholesome approach.

Was it difficult to begin performing mitzvos *after having viewed Judaism strictly in spiritual and intellectual terms?*

It wasn't really a gap. I saw a few more proofs about Torah being *min hashamayim*, and after that idea sunk deeply into my mind, I was in such awe that *Hashem* existed, that basically the only struggle was to keep normal and not jump into doing everything at once. If it says it in the Torah and I know the Torah comes from *Hashem*, that's what we should do. The amount of things I've been given leads me to cast doubt aside, with a little bit of effort, of course.

What has been the overall impact of Yiddishkeit *on your life?*

I think I have a much greater sense of purpose and I'm still working on that in terms of finding out what *Hashem* wants me to do. There's a lack of this desperate emptiness and feeling that life is going for nothing, is being wasted, and at end of my life I'll say what was this all about?

David Gelber, 32, lives in the Ohr Somayach *community in Monsey, New York, where he learns Torah part-time and teaches English and math at a local* cheder. *He is single.*

17
A Messenger Who
Forgot the Message

I couldn't understand how a beautiful girl, a professional, working in downtown Manhattan, looking totally "normal" and intelligent. . . . How she could possibly want to be involved with prayers? What could it mean to her?

Not long ago, Asya Gorokhovsky was approached by a coworker—a Jew and fellow Russian native—who was also a cynic when it came to religion. He asked her whether she became observant because of miracles she had witnessed. "No miracles," she said. "Just plain Jewish education. The myriad miracles that I see now every day are the consequence of my belief, not the prerequisite." But those miracles had precursors— events that were "extraordinary," "mystical," and perplexing in their own right, even if they weren't quite miraculous. "It was as if something was going on," said Gorokhovsky, "that would prepare me for the future."

One day after we bought a house, I was unpacking boxes of books. My kids were "helping" me, and there was total disarray on the floor. As I was standing on a chair putting a book on a shelf, I heard the voice of my 4-year-old daughter: "Mama, when I grow up, I will know this book very well." And I look down, and I see my daughter holding a book, and the title is *The Guide for the Jewish Homemaker*.

I was stunned. Those words were so strange, as if somebody had put them into her mouth. I never knew we had that book. I had no idea what it was about except that it was something Jewish. Why did she pick up that particular book? It was probably the only Jewish book we had. I had no knowledge of anything related to Judaism. She could have asked, "What is this book about?" Or, "Mama, could you read it to us?" But what did she mean by saying, "When I grow up, I will know this book very well?" That phrase continues to haunt me even now as it is realizing itself as prophecy.

Growing up in Russia, Gorokhovsky knew she was Jewish, but she had no idea what that meant. Her father was a colonel in the military. Occasionally, he or his wife would let slip with a Yiddishism, *but they never taught her anything about her faith. Jews were usually spoken of in euphemisms—when they were discussed at all. When her parents would refer to someone as "one of us," she could tell by the tone of their voices that there was more to being Jewish than she knew at the time.*

I was totally ignorant. I thought Jews were like Gypsies, that the only distinction [was] that you can tell Jews by their looks and by their names, and maybe some peculiarities in their character. That's all I knew about *Yiddishkeit.* There were very few Jews in the Siberian town where I lived; it's called Tumen.

It's like I was a messenger who forgot the message. I mourned all my Jewish friends who intermarried, not being able to explain why. I just had a gut feeling that it was a betrayal. It's still an enigma to me that I felt that way. I think it's imbedded in me.

My mother said that her great-grandfather had a synagogue, and all she remembers him doing is sitting there and reading books. Now I understand that he was learning [Torah]. She says nothing else interested him. He would be, like, completely out of this world. "And to this day," she said, "you take after him."

The only effort that I remember from my father ended in vain when he said, "I want to tell you about Jewish history." And I was thrilled. I went to my best friend, who was a *goy,* and I said, "Irena, my father's going to tell me about Jewish history. Do you want to join me?" And she said of course. So I rushed back to my father and I said, "Irena is going to join us. Isn't that wonderful?" My father got pale. And he said forget about it. And that was the last time I heard any reference about Judaism from him. He died in 1971 when I was 16.

At the age of 25, Gorokhovsky came to America with her mother, settled in New York, and became a computer programmer. The next year, 1981, she married a transplanted Jew from Moscow who had a Lubavitch background, but the home they made together was fully nonobservant. Nevertheless, her Jewish consciousness was being raised by terms—such as kosher, Shabbos, Yom Kippur *and* Torah—*that she was now hearing for the first time in her life.*

I didn't understand what they meant. The word *Shabbos*, let's say. I had a colleague at Citibank, Jay Bloom, and he was religious. And I would say, "Jay, what are you doing this weekend?" And he would say, "Well, tomorrow's *Shabbos.*" And after a pause he started enumerating a million things that he was going to do on Sunday. I was mystified. Tomorrow is just *Shabbos* and that's it? He referred to a whole day with just one word, and was so elaborate about Sunday. What could it possibly mean? I was embarrassed to ask.

Around this time, Gorokhovsky had a dialogue with her inquisitive young daughter, the one who had discovered The Jewish Homemaker.

She asked, "Where does Babushka [grandma] come from?" I said, "From her mother." "And Babushka's mother?" "From Babushka's grandmother." "And Babushka's grandmother? "From Babushka'grandmother's grandmother." By this time she realized she wasn't getting anywhere, so she paused and asked, "Where does the first man come from?"

That caught me off guard. What was I, the daughter of a Communist, supposed to say? I was agonizing because I could pronounce neither what I had been taught nor what all of a sudden was emerging from some unknown depth within me. I really felt a fierce struggle inside when I heard myself saying, "God. God created the first man." I was trembling and I had to turn away. I was too embarrassed to look at my daughter. This was my first "action."

My first steps to observance grew out of guilt, not conviction. I felt sorry for my religious colleagues imagining how painful it must be for them seeing Jews who did not care. I wanted to please and comfort them.

Like the time Rosh Hashanah was approaching. I knew it was some kind of Jewish holiday, so I told Jay, who was by then my supervisor, that I was taking off the first day. He said, "Asya, the holiday is two days." And I said to myself, he should be happy I'm taking one day. What's the difference, one day or two? I took the first day off, and of course, I didn't know of any *shuls.* For me, marking a holiday was not showing up at work.

So the second day I woke up and realized I couldn't go to work. Something stopped me. Jay's words were on my mind. I called in sick. But the following day, the first thing in the morning I rushed to him and said triumphantly, "Jay, I wasn't here yesterday!" I was so proud of myself, so brave. That was my first sweet taste of observing a *mitzvah*. I knew I had done something right.

It was also from Jay that I heard one of the most powerful phrases in my life. My kids were five and six. It was August, and he asked me an innocent question: "So what's doing with the kids? Are they going to kindergarten, something like that?" "Yeah," I said, "I signed them up at a public school around the corner." And then he said—he said it almost to himself—"Why don't you send them to a *yeshiva* so that they'll know who they are?"

And that froze me completely. I thought, what can he possibly mean by that? They have to find out from somebody else who they are? Their mother doesn't know who they are? This is ridiculous. In public school they won't be able to know who they are? I have to send them somewhere? This phrase was like a time bomb. It would be haunting me for years. Only much later could I understand what he meant. But at that time, I was embarrassed to ask.

A few months later, in 1989, somebody handed Gorokhovsky a flyer on a street corner in lower Manhattan.

It said, "Give 45 minutes of your lunch for 3,500 years of your heritage." And that phrase also pierced through me. My whole experience of coming back is through phrases I've heard or read that somehow would stick in my mind and make me think and analyze and agonize over them.

So I started learning about my heritage [with Rabbi Yitschak Rudomin of now-defunct Sinai Heritage Centers of New York]. I came for secular culture; that's what I wanted. I wanted stories about Israel. I wanted something modern. I had no desire to be involved in religion.

In fact, even two years after these lectures . . . I asked one of the students, "How do you like these lectures?" And she said "I enjoy them very much; they were very entertaining at first. But I would like to learn some prayers." And that was another shock, another phrase that would haunt me. I looked at her, like, are you crazy? You look pretty intelligent. What are you talking about prayers? This is something ancient. This is something stupid, God forbid.

I couldn't understand how a beautiful girl, a professional, working in downtown Manhattan, looking totally "normal" [laughs] and intelligent. . . . How she could possibly want to be involved with prayers? What could it mean to her?

When did you finally figure out what it meant to her?

I got completely hooked when after a couple more years of these lectures. . . . You know when you have a double vision and then you focus and then you have one picture? When I started going to these lectures, I had double vision on Judaism. I thought secular Jewish heritage had nothing to do with religion. I can choose if I want to be involved in this or in that. At that time I wanted to be involved in secular Jewish things.

That meant folk dancing, Jewish history, Jewish anecdotes, or Jewish language. At one point, with all the knowledge I got from Rabbi Rudomin after all these lectures, somehow my vision got focused and the two things became one. I realized that Judaism is praying and learning and *mitzvos* and history and culture and Yiddish and Hebrew and dancing and singing and this and that, and it's all one.

Physically, all of a sudden those two visions combined into one, and that also shocked me because it came as a very sharp point. It came instantly. It wasn't gradual. All of a sudden, I saw clearly. All of a sudden you can't segregate it, you can't separate it. One cannot exist without the other.

Then you realized you had to do mitzvos, *and so forth?*

Yes. But I had to be diplomatic with my husband. There was a gap between us. I had to be discreet with him. I could not reveal to him my real goal. And my real goal, I realized, was I wanted to be religious in the fullest, fullest sense. Doing everything, the maximum. But I couldn't tell him that; he would be scared away. It would be too sharp for him without the knowledge I had. I had to educate him. I had to trick him. I had to be discreet. I was relating what I had learned in the rabbi's lectures.

The Gorokhovsky children had been attending a local Talmud Torah. *But it became apparent that they needed a more intensive approach to Jewish education if it was to have a meaningful impact on them. The turning point came one day when the children, who were being watched by a babysitter, refused to attend the Talmud Torah after public school and instead stayed home and watched TV. They were nine and eight, respectively, at the time.*

I was very upset they didn't go, but I realized that it was the actual proof of the words of Rabbi Rudomin that Talmud Torah doesn't work to the interest of the kids. Only full Jewish education works. I realized I had to take another step.

Gorokhovsky and her husband agreed that it was time to look for a yeshiva *for their children. "The point is," she said, "that my husband had the same* pintela Yid *inside him that I had. He agreed with me very quickly and went along with me. It just took a few years of gradually becoming observant, gradually becoming* kosher, *gradually becoming* shomer Shabbos. "

I was looking for a modern Orthodox *yeshiva* because I felt the transition [to *frumkeit*] would be smoother. I knew the only way to be a Jew was to be Orthodox. I didn't want to be a part-time Jew or pick-and-chose Jew, but I realized that it would take time. While we were visting one *yeshiva*, standing in a hallway and observing, all the adults that I saw in the school had beards.

I remember saying, "I think this place is too religious for us; all the teachers here are rabbis." Before my husband could respond, I heard a protesting voice from somewhere near my knees. It was my son, who was nine at the time. He said, in Russian, "Momma, a rabbi *is* a teacher." I felt ashamed. Even at that point I was ignorant. To me, a rabbi was an ancient piece of rock.

The children were enrolled in a modern Orthodox yeshiva.

This gave us a boost. Our transition, which had already been happening, began to skyrocket. We realized we had to break off from the old world; we had to start all over again. It's as if we boarded a train and left everything behind us. The train had been moving slowly, but now it was accelerating. We had to find new friends and new spiritual surroundings. Even to this day, we feel sorry about the people we left behind who never woke up. We feel pity for them. We realize that since somebody woke us up, it's also our duty to try to wake other people up. That's why we're involved in *kiruv*. We became connectors.

But there's been conflict with my mother. She sees *tzitzis* on my son and starts crying. It's as if she is in mourning. She thinks that she took me out of Russia to bring us to this advanced country, and it all went down the drain. Instead of becoming very modern and successful we were brainwashed and became stupid and ancient.

In her eyes we're sinking down and this is a very traumatic experience for all of us. Because she lost her whole family in the war, she feels there is no reason for her to praise God. He never did anything good for her.

But my daughter once said, "I feel sorry for Grandma that she's not religious, that she doesn't understand how interesting it is. I'm so happy I'm religious because then you have something to accomplish in life."

And that's exactly how I feel. I have a purpose in life, a goal. Every day I'm accomplishing something.

Asya Gorokhovsky, 40, is a computer programmer who lives in Brooklyn with her husband and their two children. She is heavily involved in outreach efforts, particularly those aimed at Russian Jews.

18
Upward Bound

My *neshama* was hungry for something—alternative values in connection with God, in connection with my religion that [were] not superficial.

Howard Hoffman suspects that his link to Yiddishkeit *was forged before he was born. But that connection was soon stretched to the breaking point, as it is for many young American Jews. His early Jewish education consisted mostly of hiding from teachers and swapping baseball cards during Hebrew school. Before long, though, his connection with Judaism was strengthened thanks to his recently widowed grandmother and a kindly rabbi. But he needed more.*

Over the next few decades, he conducted a restless, rebellious search for authentic spiritual sustenance—something to grab his soul, red meat for his psyche. His odyssey took him deep into leftist politics and into mountaineering and wilderness survival training. It even took him into Israel in wartime. Hoffman eventually found his way to a rebbe *who nurtured him for 12 years and helped him, as he put it, imbibe "Torah Judaism in the most authentic way." But he did more than that for his student. In a heroic gesture that changed Hoffman forever, the old man who had taught him how to be a Jew offered his waning life so that Hoffman's desperately ill infant son would live.*

My own sense is that being born in 1947 I was a *gilgul neshoma* of a Holocaust victim. Various books . . . bear this out, that many of the souls born right after the war were reincarnated souls from the Holocaust—a feeling [I had] since I was a very little boy because the people who

I grew up with did not exactly follow anywhere near the same path that I did.

My love of the Jewish people and of the land of Israel was nurtured at an early age by my mother, Lillian. She stimulated in my soul an unconditional caring for the land and people of Israel that has stayed with me the rest of my life and has superseded any denominational identification. She was a guiding light for 30 years of the movement to free Soviet Jews. I developed a pride and assertiveness in my Jewish identity through the many demonstrations we participated in on behalf of Soviet Jewry and Israel. As a young kid seeing that really made an impression on me. It was a big part of my childhood.

I grew up in Denver. My father was a liquor store owner. He spent Friday nights working. That's how we got together; we worked in the liquor store together and went out to dinner—no *kashrut*, no *Shabbos*, barely Rosh Hashanah and Yom Kippur.

I was going to *cheder* three times a week besides *Shabbos* services and I hated every second of it. And most of my Hebrew school education was spent standing on the toilets so that my teacher could not see that we were trading baseball cards over the partitions in the bathrooms. Finally when my friend and I in the sixth grade drew up a plan to dynamite the *shul*, they threw me out of [Hebrew] school. The synagogue that I went to [in conjunction with Hebrew school] was an Orthodox synagogue with Reform congregants in terms of practice. Nobody really thought Jewish education was important in their lives.

When Hoffman was in seventh grade, the family switched shuls *to be closer to his grandmother on* Shabbos *and on holidays following the death of her husband.*

That changed my whole outlook. It [the new *shul*] had a wonderful rabbi, a warm, loving person, a man by the name of Rabbi Adelman. And I started to go on *Shabbos* voluntarily, to each *shala shudis*, to study *Pirkei Avot*. Nearly all the students who attended these sessions came from Conservative homes and then became committed Orthodox Jews. I continued to have quality Jewish learning in this class through my high school years.

What exactly did you like about that shul*?*

One was the warmth of the rabbi and the kindness that he showed. Second was the voluntary approach. Third was the older European men with songs and a lot of warmth at the *shala shudis*. It was not like going to Hebrew school where we drove the teacher crazy and she would drive you crazy and nobody wanted to be there.

Another key player in Hoffman's turnabout was his recently widowed grandmother.

[She] had come from a chasidic family in Europe, although she never told me about it. My grandmother loved *Shabbos*. She made *Shabbos* lunch for me every *Shabbos*, which had not happened before. This was new to me. I would sit with her and go over line by line each *sedra* and *Shabbos davening*.

So I got the benefit of this wonderful *Shabbos* experience. I would go to her house, and of course she would have a lot of stories, but also a lot of *emunah*, simple faith, and she was a good cook. Our whole [home] life was tumultuous and dominated by work. Going to my grandmother's house was very peaceful and quiet and beautiful and definitely something different from what I had at home or I had in my neighborhood, which was suburban America, Jewish suburban America. It was shallow in terms of any study or traditions.

I [was] not in any Orthodox framework yet at all. I had not changed my dress. I did not wear a *keepah* or *tzitzit*. But I spent my *Shabboses* this way. That was the difference. I was [still] really into sports, and my high school was typically upwardly mobile, first-generation American. Really on the make, highly competitive. It was fun and pressured at the same time. My high school was mostly Jews and everyone wanted to be a doctor or whatever. I already realized that that was not for me. I was forming an alternative value system.

I [had] already started to do a lot of mountaineering instruction. In high school I helped start the Colorado Outward Bound school. It was the beginning of the Outward Bound school movement. It was significant.

As part of this experience you spend three days alone in the forest without any food, without any sleeping bag. Only later did I come to find out that it was a program that was started by a Holocaust survivor as a way to teach compassion in Western education. It had a very big influence in my life because here again was more of a cooperative model, a wilderness model that had a strong spiritual component in it. When I would be alone, I would have communication with God, talking, praying, having some kind of dialogue.

My *davening* experiences were mixed. A lot of it was superficial, but on the other hand, I learned a lot of technical ritual skills, like saying *maftir*, that are important to me to this day.

The next stage was when I went to Dartmouth College. It was startling to me because at Dartmouth when I wore my *yarmulka* on *Yom Tov*, all the other Jews would scatter. I encountered a lot of Jewish self-hatred and closet Jews. A small group of us ran a Hebrew school, and I [got] my first quality exposure to Jewish learning from Rabbi Jacob Neusner. He was the professor of Judaism there.

I quickly decided that I wanted to major in religion more than anything else. I was very much engaged in studying Buddhism, Hinduism, all the full range. I think that I first met Zalman Schachter and Shlomo Carlebach at that time. [Both were well-known Jewish outreach workers, who first took their message to college campuses in the 1950s.]

The Hebrew school you helped run; what age group did it serve?

Full range, up through high school; mostly elementary up to *bar mitzvah*. It was important and it was good for me. It started a lifelong commitment to Jewish education. I saw that that was my talent and that was what I wanted to do, *chinuch*. My name is *Chanoch*. I was still into fraternity life and sports and somewhat on the fringes of life at Dartmouth. I drifted towards people who were different, like foreign students and inner-city black students. My roommate was the son of a Moslem imam from Lebanon, and that further exposed me to alternative value systems.

What was happening with you spiritually?

As far as real contact with a real God, I had not had any experiences. Real spirituality was, as far as I could tell, mostly missing from American life where I was living. Already it was apparent to me that it was much easier to find a Zen master than a spiritual rabbi who could touch my soul.

At the same time [1966] I did start getting involved politically. Vietnam was heating up, and I am getting angrier and more deeply involved in the political movement against Vietnam. I saw clearly that losing the war in Vietnam was a window of opportunity for people who wanted to question the American experience.

Hoffman was becoming alienated, not only from the American political establishment, but also from the "Animal House" atmosphere on the Dartmouth campus. During his junior year, he was scheduled to travel to France, where he'd already spent time training for the liquor business. Neusner, the Judaism professor, suggested that he go to Israel instead. So he went. "It was a critical move toward pursuing the path of spiritual development rather than economic achievement," he said. He studied at Hebrew University while he awaited the start of the 1967 war.

That changed me forever. I was digging trenches and I was digging bomb shelters and I was delivering mail. When the war started I was walking along the partition within the Old City in *Yerushalayim*, and the whole world exploded in front of me. I just kept thinking, why are they trying to kill me?

It was just an incredible experience all around—the Jewish people, the emotion. . . . The embassy, of course, asked all the American Jews to leave and go back to America. Most people were really quite frightened and it felt like there was a ring around Israel; we were very vulnerable. It felt ominous and it was not clear at all that we were going to win. So the decision to stay and not go home was a major decision on my part.

Why did you stay?

It's a very emotional question. I did not feel that there was any other option.

Right after the war I read everything that Elie Wiesel wrote, and that had a big impact. And I experienced *Shabbos* in *Yerushalayim*. *Shabbos* really meant something to me. I had studied Talmud and Tanach in Hebrew University and I really loved it. So I would say that it created a real spiritual hunger in me for more and more learning, and a different kind of learning, not a Western academic type of learning, but a depth-of-Torah learning.

Coming back to Dartmouth [after the war] was a major culture shock. [What] had an impact on me was the maturity of the average Israeli student at the time. They had all been through the army already. It really changed my whole outlook on learning and education. I felt alienated and got more involved in leftist politics. Vietnam was exploding.

Hoffman graduated from Dartmouth with a degree in religion cum laude. He was accepted into graduate programs at Harvard, Columbia, and the Jewish Theological Seminary (JTS).

My *neshoma* was hungry for something—alternative values in connection with God, in connection with my religion that [were] not superficial.

I chose not to go to JTS became it became apparent to me that there was a good degree of hypocrisy concerning observance at JTS that would be corrosive to one's Jewish identity and if I went there it would be damaging to my *Yiddishkeit*. While it would train me professionally, it could destroy me spiritually.

He rejected not only JTS, but also Harvard, Columbia, and the rest of the big-name schools. He instead chose to get his masters in teaching at Antioch College, which was located in an inner-city Philadelphia neighborhood that was plagued by violent crime.

It was exactly what I wanted, actually. It was real. It was not middle class. I learned to be a teacher there. My Jewish life was mostly on hold, but I started to live in the real world. I got my teaching certificate. I did a whole outdoor program with the [street] gang kids there.

Jewishly, I had been reading a lot of *Yiddish* literature, and those books were vivifying my Jewish imagination. [They] were giving me some meat that I wanted. I longed to go back to Israel.

In 1970, Hoffman returned to Israel, where he taught in two kibbutzim *and had contact mostly with secular Jews. His spiritual life floundered somewhat as result. He returned to America later that year when his draft board called, but he managed to flunk his Army physical. In the meantime, he continued his mountaineering and also visited communes to investigate "this whole counterculture thing." He wasn't overly impressed.*

I started looking around for something meaningfully Jewish. Conventional Jewish observance had become empty for me. In my search for a Jewish experience with integrity I ended up with Rabbi [Shloime] Twerski who was from a big chasidic family of *rebbes* that go back 18 generations.

As Hoffman found out more than a decade later, his family and the Twerski family go way back. Members of Hoffman's grandmother's family were chasidim *in a town that was wiped out by the Ukranian Nazis. One of their* rebbes, *as it turns out, was a member of the Twerski family. He was the Trisker Maggid.*

So if you want to say that it was an accident that I came back to this, maybe so, but it is an awfully strange coincidence.

He [Rabbi Shloime Twerski] had just left an Orthodox congregation in West Denver and he decided to form a group called TRI [Talmudic Research Institute], and I was one of his first students. There were only four students.

What was TRI?

This was an attempt to offer something that was meaningfully Jewish to American Jewry. He started out with a small group in the basement of his house. He had a unique background in the sense that he had the full intensive *yeshiva* education, and at the same time he had also gotten his degree in philosophy at the University of Chicago.

He was able, for me, to synthesize both worlds—not just an enclosed ghetto approach, not the superficial approach of conventional Judaism, but a really genuine approach to Jewish learning and Western education. That was what I needed. I needed someone who could synthesize the best of both worlds.

He had a tremendous capacity to create an environment in his home for *yom tovim* and *Shabbos*; it did not feel like we were on the same planet. This was like the counterculture that I was looking for—this whole chasidic approach to being able to see the soul as unique. He could talk to a whole group and you always felt that he was only talking to you.

[He could] make each person feel absolutely important and of infinite value. That was his talent and that is what I needed. I did not need any kind of social Judaism or cookie-cutter Orthodoxy. This is what I needed and this is what I got.

I spent 12 years with him studying and living close to him and imbibing Torah Judaism in the most authentic way. For me it was water for my soul.

I was still in and out somewhat halachically, but I was definitely on my way to keeping *Shabbos*. At the same time, however, I was dating, at various times during those 12 years, non-Jewish women. I was not finding many Orthodox women who would even go out with me. I was still fairly unconventional. Politically, it did not seem to mix. It was pretty hard to fit into the regular Orthodox world, yet I fit perfectly into Rabbi Twerski's environment.

At one point I had to clearly bite the bullet. Getting married was definitely a problem for someone coming into Judaism from the direction that I was coming in from. I did a bunch of my own work and one thing and another and ended up deciding [that] a non-Jewish woman was out of the question.

Hoffman got married in 1977 to a woman from a Reform background. In the meantime, he started his own business, which involved working with delinquent youth. But before that, he returned to Israel immediately following the Yom Kippur War of 1973.

A lot of my students that I had had two years prior had been killed. That had a profound effect on me as well. By this time I had probably read a thousand books on the Holocaust. That's probably exaggerated, but close to it. I'd done some writing, some poetry, etc., a lot of stuff on the Holocaust, and it just was real sobering.

Meanwhile, his sense of spirituality was heightened during several side trips in Israel, including at least one through the Sinai.

I just walked into the Sinai sight unseen, assuming good things would happen to me. It was very desolate in those days and amazing things happpened to me there. I wouldn't call them miraculous, but they were certainly extraordinary.

I climbed Mount Sinai for the first time with a retired, 65-year-old, four-foot-tall retired toymaker from Warsaw via Manhattan. Here I was a mountaineer and I couldn't keep up with this little guy. His whole dream in life was climbing Mount Sinai. We climbed before dawn; it was a great experience for me. Very moving.

One of the most significant meetings I had was above Nazareth. I met an old priest, a 96-year-old priest who had come there to die in the hills of Galilee. I spent a lot of time talking to him and it struck me that I'd grown up with a paucity of spiritual models. And here was a real spiritual man and I considered him very wise and very successful.

Even my rabbi, Rabbi Twerski, was considered a failure by many in the community because he didn't have a big salary and he didn't have a big *shul*. And here was a person I considered a total success, based on my spiritual criteria. I realized at that moment how twisted the whole American societal hierarchy of success was. I think in my own mind during this whole period, as I was starting my business, I was really debating what criteria of success I wanted to apply to my own life. That was a very difficult inner debate.

A big event happened when our son was six months old [in the early '80s.] This is the pivot point of the whole story. We were out on a hike in Moab, Utah, and he got a pulmonary edema and it was misdiagnosed, and it turned out to be a very rare blood disorder. In the computer, there were 11 cases of this and eight of them died and the other two besides my son were vegetables.

We were, to say the least, in desperate condition, in the intensive care unit of the hospital. We had moved out of our house into the hospital, 24-hour watch. He was on transfusions and dialysis. At that same time, Rabbi Twerski, who had cancer, came and he did very powerful things—

vidui and all kinds of different machinations to try to save my son's life. It was between Rosh Hashanah and Yom Kippur this happened.

At one point, he said, "Well, I don't know what else to do." We had done a second *pidyon haben* and changed the [baby's] name and did a bunch of other things. And he said, "Well, I'm gonna buy your son from you. He gets better, you'll get him back. In the meantime he can have the *z'chus* of being my son." So that's what he did. He paid the money— I still have the money, a $20 bill—and he bought my son from me.

So we're blowing the *shofar* at the hospital and we're praying night and day. This is where I learned to *daven*; this really broke through a lot of barriers spiritually for me. And at that point he [Twerski] started getting worse and worse and my son started getting better and better. So the day before Shmini Atzeres, my son comes home from the hospital and the rabbi passes away.

The proximal problem my son had was both kidneys were totally blocked. They opened up [without surgery]. At the same time, Rabbi Twerski died of a blocked kidney, on sundown of Simchas Torah, right when Moshe [had] died. That was pretty powerful for me. It certainly changed my life in a very intensive way, more than all the other things combined.

Even on *musaf* of Rosh Hashanah when he [Twerski] couldn't even stand anymore himself, he stood the whole *musaf*, which at our *shul* is three, four hours, to *daven* for my son. He led the *tzibbur* in *musaf*. So that was a major event. That intensified my spiritual life about a hundred times.

[When] he passed away, my image was that my Judaism would not survive his death, because I was so dependent on him to create these environments for me. So I started a process of intensified study. His [Twerski's] idea was to renew *bais medrash* learning as opposed to institutionalized competitive *yeshiva* learning. I started my own outreach really.

I decided if I got my main sustenance from Torah, than my business would be a tangential part of my life rather than being a cause of fear and anxiety. It [his preoccupation with his business] was corrosive to me. I didn't like what it did to me. It mainly made me feel miserable, even though things always worked out fine. It wasn't giving up on earning money; it was giving up on that being the center of my life. And I think my wife was very grateful when I made that change as well. So that was a big shift for me, when I kind of gave up business success as a major goal.

In the mid-1980s, Hoffman became education director of a chavura in Denver that had been formed by a group of middle class professionals in conjunction with Rabbi Twerski. "They had no label," said Hoffman. "They weren't Reform, Conservative, or Orthodox. They were just a group of Jews who wanted to learn authentic Judaism, and this was ideal for where I was at as a teacher."

A couple of years ago, I decided that I wanted my main thing to be teaching Torah. The business now was going to be squeezed in betweeen teaching Torah. I contacted Rabbi Carlebach about a program for getting *smicha* because his position was as close [as possible] to mine as far as what he did with Torah in terms of reaching out to people. It really moved me.

Did you have any trouble shifting from Judaism's spiritual–intellectual realm to the performance of mitzvot?

A lot of people would ask *Rav* Twerski a question [about performing a *mitzvah*] and he would say, "Forget it, you're not ready for that yet. Get the big stuff and then you'll go to that." And so he took a very gradualist approach, which really worked for me, which was a constant dialogue between study and action. I never felt any pressure either from him or from the community or even from myself to go faster. I neglected a lot of details for a long time, so my development as a halachic Jew took a good number of years.

Has your increased observance affected your marriage?

It's a point of tension and that has always been somewhat difficult. I consider it a major accomplishment [that we've been able to] accommodate our differences in spirtuality and outlook in approach to Torah and sustain our marriage and sustain our family. It took a lot of work and maturity, a lot of ability to accept differences and not try to stamp them out. With the other kind of philosophy our marriage would not have lasted. We have evolved into a lifestyle of constant growth and complete commitment to Torah and *mitzvot*. An important part of that has been my wife's leadership of the Jewish Women's Resource Center of Denver.

Overall, what has been the impact of Yiddishkeit *on your life?*

The Torah has given me the opportunity to perceive and develop my *neshama* and live according to its dictates rather than the pressures of my environment and inner desires. It also has given me a framework for my family life and my cultural life that constantly challenges me to grow and live a life of *simcha*.

Howard (Hanoch) Hoffman, 49, is a rabbi, a businessman, and a psychodrama therapist. He teaches shiurim *at least twice a day. He and his wife live in Denver, Colorado. They have three sons.*

19
A One-Way Ticket

There were thoughts and ideas and emotions . . . that touched my soul so deeply, and my heart, . . . that just pierced through me. And I realized that this is a whole part of my being that [had] not [been] dealt with.

Many people return to Judaism because they're searching for meaning in life. They feel spiritually unfulfilled or confused. Some are in emotional pain. And then there's Andy Kaufman. Back in 1980, he was a contented, well-adjusted college graduate with a bright future in medicine—and little interest in his heritage. He wasn't searching for anything, except perhaps a brief adventure overseas until it was time to return home and start medical school. So he loaded his backpack with philosophy books and clean underwear and headed off for Israel, which he'd heard was a fun country. The plan was to hang out there for a while and then travel through Europe by rail. He never made it to Europe.

When I came to Jerusalem, Israel was affecting me. I was meeting all these people, and I was touched by the fact that the whole country was Jewish. It was that cultural connection you had with a Jew, you know? Even though they were all different shapes and colors and sizes, it was a very interesting experience. You could have a deep conversation with anybody. It was just amazing.

During the trip, Kaufman bumped into a high school classmate from suburban New Jersey. They used to cut school together to listen to David Bowie albums.

We decided to stop off at this place called *Yad Vashem*. I didn't even know that much about the Holocaust; I knew that it existed. So we went there with a few other people and some other people we picked up, and they were nice young people. And they happened not to be Jewish, and I couldn't even tell. It didn't make a difference to me; it never did in the past.

We went through this *Yad Vashem*, and I had never seen these picures, I had never read these things. I was a typical American Jew who knows nothing. And I read every single caption. And it was very interesting. When I came out, I couldn't even talk. I went off in a corner and I cried for 15 minutes.

I was oblivious to anything around me. And we came out in the sun and it was a beautiful, shiny Jerusalem day. It was in March; you know how the sun shines over there, it's just so beautiful. And I came out of the darkness and I was thinking to myself, Why am I here? All those people were killed and I'm here in Jerusalem in the beautiful sun, and it struck me—I'm here but I could have been there. And I thought about it.

And the other people came out and looked at me, "What did you think?" I couldn't even talk. And one of he guys said to me, a nice guy, "Didn't you think it was a little overdone?" And I looked at him, I was shocked. And I said to him, "No, I thought they should bring out the smell of burning flesh when you look at the pictures to give you a better feeling" [laughs]. And I looked at the guy, and just curled back. And he said, "What do you mean?" To him it was just pictures on the wall.

So we decided to go toward the Old City, and quickly [with] the beautiful day and the Israeli girls . . . I got back into the mood of having a good time. And we're crossing the street to walk into the Old City by the Jaffa Gate, and my friend looks up and says, "Look, it's David M."

Every community has a David M. This one was valedictorian of Kaufman's high school and the top student in Hebrew school. ["I was the worst," Kaufman said of his Hebrew school career]. David M. had gone on to graduate with honors from Yale and attend the London School of Economics. When Kaufman and his pal bumped into him, he was taking a year off before going to Harvard Law School.

We said, "What are you doing here?" And he said, of all things, "I'm studying at this *yeshiva*." Now, I'd heard of *yeshiva* before, but it had certain connotations to me that [meant] it was totally not something of interest to me. I figured that's a place where total losers go. I'd met very few people who wore a *keepah* outside synagogue in my life, and if they did, I wasn't so impressed with them. We used to beat up the kids who wore the *keepahs*. It was not for me.

And here was David M., a guy I had respected, who had an impeccable background. And he says, "Yeah, they have this program and you could stay there for free and you could take some classes while you're there." And he said, "It's not glassy-eyed Jesus-freaky," which was the expression he used. He knew what we thought. He said it was a very interesting place. I said, "Well, if you're there, maybe I'll check it out." It was the perfect introduction for me.

Because if it was someone who didn't have his impeccable credentials, there's no way I would have set foot in the place. So we walked around and we hung out together and we went down to the Western Wall. I'd heard about it, but I don't think I had any magical experience at the wall the first time.

Having nothing better to do, Kaufman and his friend followed David M. to his dorm room at the yeshiva.

And there happened to be a few guys sitting there, and some of them had *keepot* on their heads, and they had these strings hanging out from their sides, *tzitzis,* and they looked normal and everything. But all of a sudden, I had this overwhelming urge to run.

I said to myself, what are you afraid of? I mean, if this is some sort of cult or weird place, it's a *Jewish* cult. I could have walked into the Moonies. [But] I said they're not gonna get me because I'm not looking to be mooned. This is a Jewish one, so what's the difference? It's your own people. So I overcame that urge to run.

I looked around the room and I stopped each kid and I said, "Where are you from? What were you doing before you got here?" I don't know what they thought of this. Each one was from a good university and they all looked sort of like with-it type of people, intelligent. They looked like a quality group of guys. I was, like . . . what are they doing here? It's incongruous. They seem normal, but they're wearing *keepot.* It can't be, something's wrong. They didn't look like a bunch of brainwashed guys. It was like, what is wrong with this picture?

Kaufman had a little time to kill before heading down to the beach at Sharmel Sheik *to check out the Scandinavian women. So he followed David M. to a class, and he wasn't particularly impressed with what he first saw.*

Another rabbi comes in for another class, and he had a trimmed beard and he looked like a sharp guy. I never saw a rabbi like that. My idea of rabbis were real losers, like they couldn't get a job doing anything else. This guy, he looked like a cool rabbi. That was an oxymoron. Cool rabbi? Right. I was a real bigot.

So the guy comes in and he sits down and starts taking attendance, and then he comes to me and I said, "Oh, I'm just sitting in," and the rabbi says, "so am I." And a couple guys laughed. I didn't know what they were laughing at; maybe he's a substitute teacher. Maybe he's just sitting in.

So he goes into this story: He said there was a man who lived in the last generation and his name was the *Chofetz Chaim*. I never heard those words before. It could have been the Bloobity Bloop.

He was an extremely pious, humble, great man. On top of that he was an unbelievable genius. He wrote great works that today are very influential to us. And he was an extremely kind and considerate and giving person. So there was a man who said, "Look, I want to meet this man." So he asked around, "Where does he live?" And he was directed to this small town called Radin.

He said, "What do you mean? This is where the great *Chofetz Chaim* lives? He should live in a great metropolis. How could he live in such a small place? Where does he live?"

Sure enough, they pointed to this one-room shack of a home. And he said, "What is this, a practical joke? The *Chofetz Chaim* lives here?" So he goes and knocks on the door and someone opens the door and he sees this bare room, no furniture. It's got a table, a little couch, chairs, nothing on the windows, nothing on the walls, bare, right? And this old, old man is leaning over some books and he says to this man, "So this is the great and wise *Chofetz Chaim*?" The old man looks up and he says to him, "He's not so great, but I'm the one they call the *Chofetz Chaim*."

So the traveler says, "You? Where are your things?" And the *Chofetz Chaim* turns to the man and says, "Where are yours? Me, I'm just passing through." And the rabbi who's giving the class turns to me and says, "So am I. We're all just passing through." The timing was beautiful. And I went, ahhhh, very good [laughs]. It really nailed me. He gave a class in something; I don't even know what happened after that.

We hung out for dinner and met some other people and I found it was a very stimulating group, very engaging. It was not what I expected. So I said, "I'm going to *Sharmel Sheik* and I'm going to come back in three weeks," and that's what I did. I hung out on the beach with all the Scandinavians. I was back in Jerusalem in five days including travel and everything. I went nuts [at the beach]. I couldn't connect with anybody. It was totally boring.

I came back to Jerusalem, and in the rain, back to this place, *Aish Hatorah*, you know, "Sign me up. I'll go to classes." I spent a week, and during that week it was probably the most stimulating, engaging, energizing, growth experience week I have ever had in my whole life.

You got so much in one week, you thought, what do these guys have? They were discussing things that I knew I wanted to learn more about and I wanted to incorporate into my life and be able to say to my grandchildren some day. You knew you would use these ideas. These are values, things you don't hear other places. They had such insight and such clarity. It had psychology, it had philosophy, but it was so much more practical.

In a university setting you were learning facts that didn't pertain to you. But this was stuff that was equally as brilliant and clear and scientific, but it applied to other areas of our lives—relationships and self-growth and improving your character traits and touching parts of yourself and learning more about yourself.

One of his instructors was Rabbi Zelig Pliskin, a man with a long red beard and an encylopedic knowledge of major psychological works. He is renowned for his teachings in interpersonal relationships.

I never saw a professor like this. And they had other teachers who were equally . . . really different and brilliant and funny and entertaining. It was a collection of really talented, unusual people. And the students themselves were also very impressive.

I remember going up to Rabbi Pliskin and saying to him: "Look, you're teaching very interesting ideas of psychology and and philosophy, and I think there's a lot I have to learn from you, but can I ask you a question? What does this have to do with Judaism?" And he looked at me [as if to say] "what?" I said, "What does it have to do with Judaism? Judaism is a bunch of Bible stories that are antiquated and basically irrelevant. I'm Jewish, I've been to Hebrew school."

And he laughed and looked at me and said, "What are you talking about? Everything I'm telling you is from Jewish sources." And he showed me—this is from Maimonides and this is from 100 years ago from different thinkers and this is from 2,000 years ago and this is from the Torah and this is from the Talmud and this is from 3,000 years ago. I never heard of the sources, and I said, "Wow, this is one of the greatest-kept secrets there is in the world."

I remember, the first day I got there, I met this rabbi. I later became very close with. And he was an Israeli, sort of hulky bulky type of man, like a linebacker. Again, [laughs] it totally didn't fit my image of a rabbi at all. But he was a really brilliant guy.

And he told me, "We can give you room and board, but you have some obligations. You have to go to three or four classes a day. And the other thing is you have to ask questions."

Now in university, they don't tell you you have to ask questions. That's not part of the learning process in university. In university they say I'm gonna tell you and whoever gives it back to me the best, the way I like, gets the prize, right? It's not a place of a true intellectual endeavor.

I got so much out of a week or two, so I decided to go for the three-month program. I called my parents and told them I'm changing my plans and I don't think I want to spend so much time in Europe, and I think I'll spend a few months here. And my mother said, "Oh that's interesting. Great, you want to explore your Judaism, wonderful." I was the Renaissance man, I was interested in this and this and this.

So I spent a couple months there. And I looked at a couple friends and we all realized there's so much here that we're just beginning. The question is, do we believe this stuff, is it true? I mean this is serious stuff. You know, they're claiming that God spoke at Sinai. They had whole classes on it. What do you mean, God wrote the book? Every word? Every letter? It's extreme, isn't it? [laughs].

So I decided—and I wasn't alone—that we all wanted to maybe go back to the states and arrange our affairs and take a year off and come back and really get into it. We knew that you need to give it some time; there's too much here to learn and it's too valuable and you don't know where you're going to take it.

Kaufman decided to defer medical school for a year and return to Aish Hatorah.

My parents freaked out. They were convinced I was in some sort of mind-manipulating environment, and they were very nervous. Actually, I never used my brain more in my life, not even close. The university was a joke compared to this, and I was a good student. It was a whole different experience. You felt energized; you would go in and study and it lifted you up.

Before returning to Aish, *Kaufman spent a short time at his parents' home in Fairlawn, New Jersey.*

I was wearing *tzitzis*, I was wearing a *keepah*, I wanted to keep *Shabbat*, I ate kosher, and everybody thought I was nuts. They were probably partially right. I did not have it well-balanced, integrated in me. But I knew clearly that there was something of great value here. And I didn't know how far I would take it or how observant I would be or how long it was going to last, but I knew I was right, that I had to go back. I felt that I had a bit of a responsibility, like I had bridged two completely different worlds.

I felt I really had to . . . work it out better so I could speak to people [and tell them] what it's about. I had to be a spokesman because I realized that there are millions and millions of Jews out there and they don't have a clue. And I was one of them.

He returned to Jerusalem. And after almost a year of "learning and growing" in Torah, he made a difficult decision. He would not pursue a medical career.

I didn't know exactly what I wanted to do, but I didn't want to do that. I think they, my folks, were resigned to it. So I stayed. And I got involved with working with students and sharing what I'd gotten with them and so on. There was always a sense of . . . you have a responsibility, there's a big problem out there. And I knew it very well. There was something of great value in our people and nobody knows about it. They were going down the tubes fast, and we're losing it.

I had decided at some point that this stuff was real, that it was true, that it really made more sense that there was a God and he did give the Torah. I worked on it, and it wasn't a simple thing. The decision was made in a rational type of way, in a thinking way, in an analytical way. It was a constant growth and decision-making process.

There was a lot of struggle and conflict in terms of integrating some of the ideas in terms of observance. When you get into the details, it's a long haul until you can incorporate those ideas into your lifestyle.

But eventually you changed. You felt more comfortable with it because you were doing it and because you went through the ideas so many times. It wasn't just an emotional high, it was based on things that you were learning, insights you were getting.

Among the political–social issues Kaufman had to work through was Orthodoxy and its relationship to feminism.

One thing was for sure, I had an interest in relationships between men and woman. That's something that fascinated me before I went to Israel. And I was really interested in the Jewish viewpoint about love, sex and marriage, dating and marriage, whatever.

Most of the rap that people have with Orthodoxy is a misconception; they don't know anything about it. They're ignorant about other aspects and they're ignorant about the aspect concerning women also. And they look at it in a very superficial way because our society is a very superficial society, it's very concerned with image. And most people think Judaism, like the church, is centered around the synagogue. That's the perception of what Judaism is all about, and that's totally not true. Judaism is centered in the home and it's very internal and the woman's role is very crucial and very central and very important and as important as the man's.

Kaufman got married in 1984 to a ba'alat teshuvah *from New Jersey he'd met in Jerusalem. He got his* smicha *from* Aish Hatorah *after having attended the* yeshiva *for five-and-a-half years.*

What really blew me away was I spent years in one room, the *bais midrash*, and I never felt closed-in or bored for one minute, and I had grown so much. That was a real testament [laughs] to the power of this Torah.

I was a happy person; I had everything going for me. I wasn't a depressed person. But I was living on a plane of existence that wasn't deep. The joy or feelings that I had, it was sort of like from my nose up; I wasn't feeling deeply. [But in *Yiddishkeit*], there were thoughts and ideas and emotions and things that touched my soul so deeply, and my heart, that just pierced through me. And I realized that this is a whole part of my being that [had] not [been] dealt with.

Rabbi Andy (Chanan) Kaufman, 36, is executive director of the Jerusalem Fellowship Program at Aish Hatorah. *He and his wife live in Monsey, New Yersey, and they have six children.*

20
The Incredible
Expanding Man

I felt like I was part of a Rod Serling movie. I felt like I was getting smaller
and smaller until I felt like I was going to become like a speck.

*Bert King has a jaunty mustache and a thing for loud sport coats. He is
a world-class kibbitzer and a shmoozer with a funny story or a clever
saying to fit every occasion. But he takes his Judaism seriously. King
has a deep and abiding faith in God and a love of Jewish learning. He
didn't always. For years, he was thoroughly assimilated and seemed to
be wandering aimlessly through life. "I felt," he remembers, "like I was
a ship at sea with just a sail and no rudder, and wherever the wind put
me I went." But he began to get his bearings in the early 1960s after he
and his family moved from Nashville to Norfolk. His next-door neighbor unwittingly helped point the way.*

I . . . lived next door to a psychologist, and his wife was an artist. We
were the best of friends and we did everything together. I had four children, he had four children and he was a member of country clubs and
his family owned a large furniture business. He was a very wealthy man.
They were not Jews. They were Episcopalian.

One evening he had us over at his house. He was a huge man, about
6-foot-6. And he said, "You know, we've done so many things together,
we've talked about so many things, we've philosophized and so forth,
but we never talk about religion."

And he said to me, "I'd like to know, just what do you think about Jesus?"

And I told him, "I don't think anything about Jesus. Nothing comes into my mind." So he said, "Well, you have to have some opinion, anything whatsoever, because you live in a Christian society, you helped me put up my Christmas tree, you know there is such a thing as Christianity and Jesus. Give me any idea." I said, "Well, whatever Jesus was, and possibly he was a very learned man, . . . but no matter what he was, he was no God and no son of God."

And he came over to me and he put his arm around me and he held me real tight and he said: "You know, there are so many members of our congregation that feel the same way as you do. They don't think that Jesus is God or the son of God. And if they could feel that way, you could feel that way, and you could become an Episcopalian too."

And then he squeezed me real tight and he said: "And then we'd be like brothers." And I knew what he meant by brothers because I knew he was a very wealthy man. He had a lot of connections and so forth and he could be a big help to me.

He was very serious . . . then he said—and these are the words that actually changed my whole life—"It would really be easy for you because you're certainly not a Jew."

And I felt like I was part of a Rod Serling movie. I felt like I was getting smaller and smaller until I felt like I was going to become like a speck. And when I left there I felt so disheveled and I said to myself, well, what else could he think? I mean, what he said was true.

I didn't have any association with Jewish people, I didn't go out of my way to be with Jewish people, I didn't go to *shul*, I didn't observe holidays, I didn't keep kosher, I didn't do anything.

And I felt very bad and I went home that night and I couldn't sleep. When I got up in the morning, I had my mind made up. I had my daughter going to a nonsectarian school, but I did notice that she was coming home with Easter baskets and she would sing Christmas songs and I took her out of that school and I put her in the Hebrew Academy in Norfolk.

This was, I guess 1961 and or 1962, and I put her in the academy and I said, "Well, my job is done, I've done all I could." But I'll never forget the day my daughter came home and she said, "Daddy, you know what this coming Wednesday or Thursday is?" I said, "What is it?" She said, "It's Rosh Hashanah." I said, "It is?" She said, "Yeah, you know what that is?" I said, "No, what is that?" She said, "That's the birthday of the world."

And when she said that, I said . . . what are they teaching that child down in that school? I mean this is ridiculous. I knew the world is billions of years old and this is the birthday of the world?

So I went down and I started talking to this Rabbi Borenstein and he told me to come to certain classes. Little by little I got into it and the main thing is that I finally had some identity in knowing I was Jewish. If you realize how far I was from any *Yiddishkeit*—I was anti-Semitic at one time. I didn't want anything to do with Jews.

I didn't see what the benefits were of being a Jew. In my family nobody had anything ever to do with anything of a religious nature. In fact, in high school [in Washington, DC] I made a point of going to school on Yom Kippur so that nobody would know that I was Jewish. I didn't know anything about what being Jewish was except that we had lox and bagels on Sunday.

I was 31 years old before I met a practicing Jew. I was working for a firm in Nashville [a custom-made clothing store], and I had a tailor working for me, and this was my first real experience in *Yiddishkeit*.

Whenever anybody would come into the store they'd go to the back to see Sam [the tailor], and he'd give them money, no matter who it was. It really didn't make a difference if they were old, white, black, green, or anything. He'd give everybody money. And one day I was in the store, and . . . a little fellow came in . . . and I said, "Sam's not here." And he said, "what about you?"

I said, "Oh, I don't deal with this stuff; I've got a wife and two kids and I don't have time to be involved." I said, "Sam, he's got a lot of money, he can do things like this." I said, "I don't do this." So he left.

A little while later, Sam came in and I told him, "One of your friends was looking for you." He said, "What did you give him?" I said, "I didn't give him anything." He said, "What did he look like?" I said he was short and wearing a brown suit and a dark brown hat. This was in August. He [Sam] rushed out of the store and he was gone for two hours. And when he came back—and this was an older man, he could have been my grandfather—he was really sweating. He came up to me and even though he was older than me, he'd call me Mr. King.

He said, "Mr. King, anytime somebody comes in here and he needs something," he said, "you give it to him." He said, "You don't have to worry, I'll give it back to you." He said, "But I just want to tell you one thing. Don't think in your mind that you're doing them a favor. They're doing you a favor." And I'll never forget the impact that had on me because in my whole life I had never come up with anything like this. I mean everything I knew in my life was you looked out for yourself first and this idea of charity and so forth. . . . Here was a man who was out practicing what he believed in.

And when Passover came around—and I'd never had anything to do with Passover—he brought *matzoh brei* with all kinds of jams and jellies into the store and he said, "I'll feed you and I'll feed your family. Just don't eat any *chometz*." I never even knew what *chometz* was.

King was transferred to the Norfolk branch of the clothing store, where he began to follow Sam's example and give to the needy.

Business wasn't so good, and they let me go. And there was a man who used to come into Norfolk, and he was collecting for a *yeshiva*. I didn't even know what a *yeshiva* was. I knew the man and I knew the way Norfolk was. And I knew that if he didn't get any money, he wasn't going to have any place to sleep.

I got a call from my tailor [not Sam]. He said, "The *shnorrer* is here." I said, "What do you mean?" He said, "The guy who always comes in here and you give him five dollars is looking for you." And this was a man [the tailor] I had worked with for eight years. I said, "Well, give him five dollars and I'll pay you back." And he said—and this was a man who was in the Holocaust—"No, I can't do that. You're out of work and I work very hard for my money and I'm afraid if I give him the money I'll never see it again. I can't do that. I can't give him the five dollars."

After some arm-twisting, King arranged for another tailor to pay the man. He eventually reimbursed that tailor.

Believe it or not, that five dollars was food money and I mean it was something I had to extricate from my life and from my whole family's life to take care of this guy. It was comparable to me giving $500 today. And, of course, the businessmen down in Norfolk thought I was a meshuggah for giving, you know, five dollars like that . . . and I noticed things changing in my life.

There was a fellow who was married to my second cousin and he had a lot of physical problems. And he had a job which I thought was the hardest job in the world. He would get up in the morning and go into North Carolina [from Norfolk] and sell encyclopedias. With four children, I can't imagine how anybody could do a job like that. And this guy had a back problem, and his children were sick. Nothing was going good for him.

And I said, "Hymie, how do you manage to make it every day? How do you get up?" He said, "Well, I have help." I said, "What, the guys working out in the field?" He said: "No. When I get up in the morning, I put on *tallis* and I put on *tefillin* and I ask *Hashem* to help me. I only have to make one book sale a week, that's all I need and I know I'm going to make that sale every week."

And I looked at him and I said, "Well gee, I'd like to get involved with that." And he said, "It's not a game. It's not something you can pick up and drop down. If you really want to be committed to it, I'll show you." And he did. And I really thank God that I ran across Hymie.

In the early 1970s, King moved to the Washington area and settled in Kemp Mill, a suburban Maryland community that has the largest concentration of observant Jews between Baltimore and Atlanta. King— who is retired, divorced, and lives alone—is fully immersed in the religious life of his community. A mainstay at one of the neighborhood's Orthodox synagogues, he is forever rushing off to daven, *pay a* shiva *call, share in a* simcha *or participate in a Torah study group, where he is known for asking lots and lots of questions. Three of his four children live in Israel and one lives in New York. All of them are* frum.

There's a great feeling of closeness in the neighborhood and great camaraderie with the men my age; we feel we're here for each other. I like to feel that I'm very close to the young people too. In fact, I feel very close to everybody in *shul*. I like the fact that when I go to somebody's wedding I know that I probably went to their *bris* too. I feel like I'm part of something. I know I'm sharing something.

I go to a *kollel* with [some very learned people] and I think of the line in *Hallel*, that "*Hashem* lifted me out of the dunghill and had me sit with princes." And that's the way I feel—who am I to be with these people? I get this kick out of it.

After reading the *chumash* again year after year, I still find things I never saw before. You realize that you're not reading something by Longfellow or Shakespeare; if you really have the right idea, you're reading what *Hashem* said that this is the way to live, and what could be more important than that? You realize that everything else . . . what value does it have?

What's the old expression, who is a rich man? A man who is content.

If that's the case, I'm a multimillionaire. Here I am [living] a block and a half away from a *shul*. I have an 1984 car with 43,000 miles on it 'cause I never get a chance to go anywhere, which I don't really care about. And I'm very happy with my life. I know I'm very selfish in saying this, but I only like to associate with people who think the way I do. When I meet somebody who is materialistic, or trying to gain power for whatever reason, I just stay away from them. I think the people around here are genuine; everybody seems to be very straightforward and honest.

I've got a cousin, a first cousin, who's very brilliant; he's got several doctorates. In fact when they brought rocks back from the moon, they gave them to him to analyze. And he [once] lived in the most abject poverty you can imagine.

When he was telling me about that, he said, "You know where I came from, and . . . the main thing is I feel very good about myself because I did all this by myself. I pulled myself up by my bootstraps." And I just looked at him and I kept thinking that if he doesn't realize what part *Hashem* has played in his life, then he's lost the whole thing.

And that's the way it is with all my relatives. In fact my own brother, I'm not as close with him as I'd like to be. I mean I love him and I want everything good for him, but it's, how do you say . . . I'm listening to AM and he's playing FM. I mean we're in two different spheres. He thinks the whole [*Yiddishkeit*] thing is madness.

The bottom line, the very bottom line is that you have to be aware. And if you're not aware, you might as well be a tree. And the fact that I'm involved in *Yiddishkeit*, the fact that I'm living in this community, the fact that my children are in Israel. . . . I'm very aware of everything around me and I can see purpose to my life and I can see basically why I was born. I really think that my life is going to count.

Even to this extent—this may sound very absurd to you—but if I should die tonight, I would say that I lived a very full life, that *Hashem* was very good to me. Even though if you knew one ten-thousandth of the tribulations I've had in my life, you'd say, boy that guy really had everything thrown at him—physically, emotionally, economically, every way you can imagine. But I still believe that *Hashem* has treated me very well and everything was for a learning purpose.

Have you ever heard the expression that it's better to give than receive? I say it's better to be in a *position* to give than to receive. The one thing I pray for all the time is, "*Hashem*, just put me in a position where I can give." I don't want to receive anything from anybody. I just want to be in a position where people will come to me or I'll be in a position where I can do something for somebody else.

Bert King, 65, is retired and lives in the Kemp Mill neighborhood of Silver Spring, Maryland.

21
Taking It to the Streets

It was a total experience . . . that wasn't drug-induced. It was natural. . . .
There was a connection to the past, it made me feel good in the present
and gave me goals for the future.

*Yosef Langer has completed a momentous spiritual journey, but in a
sense he's right back where he started—on the streets. Back when he
was a pseudohippie/merchant seaman, a Gentile woman asked him a
question about the Hebrew alphabet, but he couldn't answer because
he knew nothing about it. He was embarrassed enough to decide to look
into his heritage. He found a mentor. And then he found his way to a
Chabad House and then a yeshiva and finally the rabbinate. Since then,
he's been reaching out to lost Jews wherever he can find them—including Grateful Dead concerts. His main venue today, however, is the streets
of San Francisco, where he tools around on a specially outfitted motorcycle. He calls it his "mitzvah bike."*

I grew up in public schools [in Oakland, CA] and went to an ultra-
California Reform synagogue. It was known that the rabbi indulged in
ham and eggs on his Sunday breakfast. My grandparents were from the
old country, and I believe [they] were the instruments who planted the
spark of my tradition in me. They made sure that at my *bris* that I was
given a Hebrew name, *Yosef*. My English name at birth was Gary.

I had a conveyor belt *bar mitzvah* and basically took my goods and
ran away after that, tried to disassociate myself from Judaism. Anyone
that would ask me what religion I am, I would meekly tell them Jewish.
And when they would tell me, "Oh, you don't look Jewish," it was the

158

biggest compliment anyone could give me. I was blonde and blue-eyed and people said I looked like Paul Newman. That was like a big star in my cap, if someone told me I didn't look Jewish.

So anyway, in '68–'69, I was searching in different religions and philosophies trying to refine myself, pick up some of the pieces I had broken during the sixties—psychological, spiritual, social pieces. I was eating naturally, exercising, the whole scene. I [became] a merchant seaman. I went to college, San Jose State, because there wasn't enough partying at San Francisco State. I graduated from college, but I didn't know who I was and where I wanted to go. I was studying Bible up in the Unity Church in Oakland.

What is the Unity Church?

They're into metaphysics and there's a whole mix of young and old, black and white. It was a real typical religious open liberal scene in Oakland at that time.

So a woman by the name of Elsie asked me about the infinity of the *aleph bet*, the Jewish alphabet. I had long forgotten the Jewish alphabet, let alone the infinity of the alphabet, which I understood after I started exploring it, is basically that every passage in the Torah is infinite and by definition, each letter is infinite and there are indeed volumes just on the letter *aleph*, volumes of explanation. So I felt embarrassed. I didn't know about the alphabet, let alone the infinity of it.

So he decided to learn. A rabbi directed him to a learned Jewish philanthropist, Mayer Goldberg.

I rode my bike to his house and had a tie-dyed T-shirt on and [laughs] an Afro hairdo and knocked on his door and said, "Rabbi Laderman told me to come to you about learning the infinity of the *aleph bais.*" So he smiled, and said, "Come in *boychik.*" And he sat me down and said, "That's typical of American push-button spirituality." He said, "The way it is in Judaism is that you have to take one step and then another step and then build a plateau and maybe fall back a step or two, but you have a foundation underneath you." And he proceeded to teach me, within six weeks, the *aleph bais* again, and opened up the narrow image of Judaism that I had had.

What was that image?

In my meeting with him he suggested I go to *yeshiva* on the East Coast in Brooklyn, and it represented a very restrictive, narrow path, dark and gloomy, and I couldn't picture myself—being a golden boy from California, from this liberal haven over here, this never-never land, being thrust into the dark clutches of Brooklyn, very narrow, very restrictive.

Mayer told me, "The sea's no place for a nice Jewish boy." And I knew I wanted to be more Jewish. So I went down and lived in the *Chabad* House in Los Angeles, and learned how to *daven*. I cooked in the kitchen—because I was a cook by trade through the Merchant Marines—and basically that was my first introduction to day-to-day, moment-to-moment living Judaism.

It was a total experience . . . that wasn't drug-induced. It was natural. . . . There was a connection to the past; it made me feel good in the present and gave me goals for the future, family orientation, the possibility of helping others.

The *Chabad* House only takes you to a certain level. And so . . . after three, four months there, the rabbi would tell me, "On your way to wherever, stop in Brooklyn and experience the chasidic community there and the *Rebbe* and the *yeshiva*." I'd never been to a *yeshiva* before.

Langer took the rabbi's advice and went to Brooklyn. It was 1970.

I was one of the first *BT*s to enter Crown Heights. There was maybe a dozen of us, and we were a new breed. We were bringing a new culture.

Despite an initial bout of culture shock, Langer and Crown Heights adjusted to each other. A neighborhood grocer opened up his home to Langer, who spent numerous Shabbos *dinners there, along with other newcomers.*

I was studying in *yeshiva*, but I wasn't the typical student. I had never really developed good study habits. However I knew that I liked to serve people and make people feel comfortable when they would come into the *yeshiva*. So after two-and-a-half years they asked me to manage the kitchen.

In Crown Heights, Langer met his wife, who had come from a Conservative home in Flatbush.

I saw in Judaism . . . I realized that one didn't have to be a social butterfly, which I was all my life. I wasn't in touch with who I was. I was just clinging to whoever I could cling to. But now as I sat there I realized that I could give more to the rest of the world by being who I am and not necessarily hanging on the street corner or hanging in other circles, in Gentile circles. But I felt more compassion, more ability to give now, being an observant Jew than when I was growing up on the streets of Oakland. And it was because of the perspective that the *Rebbe* gave me. I saw his compassion for the whole world.

My whole existence prior to coming to Judaism was . . . very detached from my soul. And when you're detached from your soul, . . . it leaves you insecure and you cling to anything that will make you feel good at the moment, whether it's a party or going to a bar or all the cheap thrills that societies cling to because they're detached from their God-given soul.

As I got more and more immersed in the structure of Judaism, which was enhanced and opened up through the philosophy of *Chasidut*, this really gave me an anchor of who I am and where I'm going. I realized that through not knowing who you are and what to do with your life, this leads to chaos; this is what the world looks at often as being free.

In the mid-1970s, Langer received his rabbinic ordination and then became a Lubavitch sheliach.

One of the golden threads of *Chabad* philosophy is to be a lamplighter and take what you have and take it out into the streets and light up the world.

Toward that end, Langer began reaching out to disaffected Jews in some unusual places, such as Grateful Dead concerts. His gimmick was a handout with a Grateful Dead motif. It was the work of a Deadhead (a devoted fan of the band) who was living at Yeshiva University in Los Angeles.

It was a little skeleton with a *yarmulka* and a *tallis* sitting on a *menorah*, lighting the *menorah*. And it said, "Happy Chanukah, come to *Chabad* for *Shabbat*" [laughs].

So that was the beginning of starting to package my outreach to attract the thousands of Jewish kids who are seeking spirituality through music. I felt that through doing outreach at the Dead concerts and making T-shirts and hats called [laughs] "Grateful Yid" hats, with the dancing rabbi coming out of the grave dancing with a tambourine, [laughs] . . . it was a message of the times. This started about six or seven years ago.

What kind of reaction did you get hanging out at these concerts?

A phenomenal reaction. It puts a smile on their face and it's associated with something they identify with. And it gives it a Jewish focal point. The shirts and the hats have spread all over the world.

A Deadhead biker who had dinner at Langer's Shabbos *table even converted a meter maid's motorcycle for his use.*

It says "*Chabad Mitzva*bike of San Francisco" and "We Want *Moshiach* Now." It's the only one of its kind in the world. A photo of me on the bike with the Bill Graham Chanukah *menorah* in the background is on my business card, which also says "take it to the streets." [The *menorah*, reportedly the first public *menorah* erected outside of Israel, was commissioned and built in the mid-1970s by the late music promoter Bill Graham].

I feel that that's where Judaism is today—the idea being that it [the motorcycle] puts me in touch with the people and breaks down stereotypes and puts a smile on people's faces. They take a second look rather than crossing me off as just another black-hat ultra-Orthodox fanatic. The majority of Jews today are not in *shul*.

I feel very comfortable and have realized a lot of success in approaching my work with this style. It's enabled me to give back to my people and to serve my Creator and to have a good time while I'm doing it.

As an Orthodox Jew, you are a member of a denomination that is inherently conservative in its worldview. Yet you live and work in a very liberal domain where all sorts of "alternative lifestyles" are tolerated. How do you reconcile this? Is there a tension?

Naturally you feel some tension. But because I grew up here, and because the community is used to bizarre behavior [laughs], you never know where it's gonna strike you; and every other block is . . . I think the last quote is there are 200,000 to 300,000 gays in San Francisco.

Clearly, Orthodoxy does not endorse homosexuality. The Torah calls it an abomination. Does this ever become an issue when you interact with gay Jews?

The way I understand that is, you don't with any person, Jew or Gentile, throw the baby down the drain with the bathwater. It [homosexuality] is an abomination according to the Torah, yet these are human beings, and in particular Jews that are in touch with us. We're always interacting with gays and they come to the *Chabad* House for Friday night services and dinner and different programs we have. And we try to warm their souls like everyone else's.

I look at them as having a Jewish soul, not as being gay. Gay is just one action of a being; it's a prohibitive *mitzvah*. And you just have to be honest and supportive and have *ahavas Yisroel*. If they say they can't stop what they're doing, I say at least take on a *mitzvah* you feel good about—the same approach Chabad has with any other Jew who has a problem with *Shabbos* or has a problem with this *mitzvah* or that *mitzvah*.

There's a chasidic saying that a little light pushes away a lot of darkness, and one step at a time. That's the approach the *Rebbe* taught us. I think instead of sizing up and blasting a person because of one *mitzvah* they aren't ready yet to deal with, you have to give them something they can hold onto.

Rabbi Yosef Langer, 49, is executive director of Chabad of San Francisco. He and his wife live in San Francisco and have five children.

22
The Art of Being in the Right Place

I think there was something independent that was blasting out. The satisfaction that I had been deriving up until then from my work in the theater . . . was beginning to . . . feel more empty.

Judaism does not believe in dumb luck. That means that being in the right place at the right time, as Allan Leicht was, is more than chance. Obviously, God is a factor. He creates circumstances that influence the outcome of situations. But to benefit fully, man must be prepared. Leicht discovered this when his Yiddishkeit came bubbling to the surface after having lain dormant for nearly two decades. Unlike many Jews, however, he was able to recognize it for what it was, and he knew what to do with it. "It's not lightning that strikes you really," Leicht explained, "it's the ability to catch lightning." He'd been trained for that eventuality 40 years ago, although he wasn't thrilled about it at the time. Back then, he would much rather have been at the ballpark.

I was born in 1942, which now makes me 53 years old, and for most of those years I felt extremely Jewish, but not terribly well-connected to Jewish life. I think I am part of a generation that was leading a double life, one as an American and two as a Jew. Somewhere along the line, oh, 14 or 15 years ago, I decided that I should reinvestigate that relationship.

I began in public school. We were living in the Bronx and I went to the public school around the corner through the end of the second grade.

My grandfather, that is my mother's father, felt it was important that I have some kind of Jewish education, and so I was moved at the beginning of the third grade from public school to *Yeshiva Rabbi Israel Salanter*, a very European, at least it seemed to me, a very European school.

And there was quite a wrench, as I recall it, in my lifestyle at the time and it was not a positive experience. I felt very much out of phase with everything around me. I thought everybody was so much more religious around me and I now discover that everybody else thought the same thing. So we were kind of leading all of us double lives, although I didn't know it at the time.

The fact is, that as it turned out, we all agree we got an enormously valuable, long-lasting connection to *Yiddishkeit* through the sometimes primitive and yet always extremely devoted attention of the teachers and *rabbeyim* in that school. Now, it was not state-of-the-art education. The school was struggling through the same thing we were all struggling through in the '40s and early '50s, and that is, Jewish education through the first half of this century, I would think, was really struggling to find its way in America, struggling with a new kind of experience.

Looking back, exactly what kind of impact did this experience have on you?

I think that a soul needs to be exercised the way any part of a human being needs to be exercised, and when it is left undeveloped, it simply lies dormant. I don't think that the individual soul can be touched by *Hakadosh Boruch Hu* without some preparation. I think it was Pasteur who said, "Chance favors the prepared mind." It's not lightning that strikes you really, it's the ability to catch lightning. I think that those six years at *yeshiva*, those six years of real intense Jewish education, as variable as it was, made it possible for me to find myself in God's path later on in life when God needed to find me and I needed to find Him.

Sometimes I watch people when we go to Israel at the *Kotel*, young Jews and older Jews, and they expect to have this transforming experience simply by walking up to the wall. And they very often leave disappointed because they have not had the transforming experience. Most people do more preparation before they see a movie than they do before they go to a synagogue.

You see this now in retrospect regarding your yeshiva *education. But what was it like at the time?*

At the time it was hell [laughs]. It was terrible. Mainly because what I really wanted to do was go to the ball game. It's not so much that I was prohibited either by my parents or by anyone else from going to a ball game on *Shabbos* or playing ball on *Shabbos*, but I didn't want to be seen at the ballpark or going in and out of the ballpark.

I didn't know what to do with my head in the street or on the bus, whether to put a baseball hat on—we never wore *keepot* on the street, you know, in those days—and it took a tremendous amount of overcoming every inhibition in my life to put one on and walk down the street in it.

I couldn't wait to get out of *yeshiva*. Once we did, I graduated from eighth grade in 1955 and we then, as a family, moved from the Bronx to the suburbs and in the suburbs I was finally free. I was in a "regular" high school [in Long Beach, Long Island] with "regular" kids. I would suppose that 95 percent of us were Jewish but I would also suppose that 95 percent of us were not religious. And my parents then shifted from an Orthodox synagogue in the Bronx and became members of a Conservative synagogue where everyone feels very comfortable being Jewish and not having to make any commitments whatsoever to *mitzvos* or *Shabbos* or *kashrus* or anything.

My *bar mitzvah* was typical of those days. I would say it was the punctuation mark, as it is today for many kids, the culmination, the "Aha, now I've done it, now I am a Jew and I can forget about it."

Leicht went to Adelphi University on Long Island on an acting scholarship that ultimately lead to a successful career in show business. Meanwhile, he was unable to maintain even the pretense of observance.

I think my parents were beginning to get worried because most of us at the time were interdating. This is now the early '60s, and it would have been just as likely for me to marry a non-Jewish girl as a Jewish girl if my parents had not been very clearly opposed to such a thing. That was just before the intermarriage rate began to soar.

Leicht graduated from the Yale School of Drama and then got a job directing for a theater in Buffalo, New York. In the meantime, he married an actress whose professional name is Renee Lippin. She had a minimally observant Jewish background.

Whereas my parents were both European and raised in Orthodox homes, her parents were American and not raised in Orthodox homes, with no tradition at all. They were aware that they had holidays, but they were not really aware of how to celebrate them.

There was tension between me and Renee in those years, but those tensions usually surfaced only at Passover time as to whose house we should go to and during Rosh Hashanah time whose house we should go to and how we should split our time between the two families. I was feeling uncomfortable with hers and she with mine at those moments. That tension was in a way a kind of model for the tension that would evolve later on.

Now, trying to find a moment at which a *ba'al teshuvah* becomes a *ba'al teshuvah* is almost impossible. I don't think there is a moment; I think it's gradual. But certainly my reliance on *Hakadosh Boruch Hu* became stronger and stronger after we left Buffalo and moved back to New York in 1968.

We were living the artistic life, and we didn't have children until we were about 12 years married. So I would like to say that the defining moment was having children, and perhaps to some degree it was. But I think I had been prepared for it. I don't think that the *Yiddishkeit* had ever been completely evaporated, and always remained bubbling under the surface somewhere.

And so when we did have a little baby girl and seeing the miracle of a new life being born, there was obviously a great emotional as well as religious change that occurred. This was 1979 when Rebecca was born. We were living in Brooklyn at this point.

So I think that was defining, but I don't think that it was the real reason for becoming a *BT*. The real reason for becoming a *ba'al teshuvah* was because I really needed God, and I wanted to have a closer connection to the real Jewish world.

I think there was something independent that was blasting out. The satisfaction that I had been deriving up until then from my work in the theater—I was working both as a director and a writer—was beginning to, particularly in success, feel more empty.

During the 1970s, Leicht was writing for TV, movies, and the theater, and had won an Emmy. He was also a stage manager on Broadway and directed off-Broadway.

Each one of those successes had become less satisfying. I just wasn't finding in the artistic expression the kind of high that I thought I was going to find. And I think to some extent, to a large extent, that was a contributing factor. And I think that having a child put all that into perspective . . . and what life was all about.

The Leichts bought a menorah *and lit it. It was their first home-oriented Jewish activity.*

It was wonderful. Seeing the Chanukah light reflected in this little baby's eyes made all the difference. So that was a first small step toward *Yiddishkeit* at home. Not long after that, about a year after that, we had a little boy, and that was Zaki. The approach of his *bris* was possibly the most powerful religious anticipation that I have ever had, because it became for me a major, major emotional event. Here was something that had to be decided on and examined. A Chanukah light is a Chanukah light; it goes out. A *bris* doesn't go out.

I mean, that was the bolt of lightning. But again, I had been very well placed for that bolt of lightning, [laughs] standing exactly where it was supposed to hit. It was inevitable from that moment on.

What was going on in your head at the time?

I was never one to take ritual lightly, because even before I was an Orthodox Jew, I was an Orthodox person. That is, coming out of the theater where ritual and ceremony are very much a part of the experience, my relationship to this was not casual. I felt that it was a very, if not religious, certainly a very dramatic statement.

Here you are, you're going to do something transfiguring to a totally helpless infant, and for what reason? And there is no real intellectual way around that. There is no logical or reasonable explanation for a circumcision. There's nothing to it except religion. I began thinking about that quite a bit. And I remember that my anxieties about it were very deep, and because of those anxieties I really had to come to grips with it. Is it something I don't believe in or is it something I do believe in?

A lot of people say "Oh, this is a hygienic, medical thing we're doing." And you know very well it isn't and you're just telling yourself a story in order to get through the moment and not have to deal with the *mitzvah*.

But I did deal with the *mitzvah*. And the reason I was dealing with the *mitzvah* is because I had had the education to deal with it, because I had been prepared for it. Coming up to that moment, to that parentally defining moment in one's life with no preparation, makes it easy to have it done in a hospital or to walk through it mechanically. I couldn't do that.

Shortly after that, the family moved to the West Side of Manhattan and Leicht went synagogue-hunting.

I had no idea that I wanted to be an Orthodox Jew. All I knew is that I had a bank and I had an accountant and I ought to have a rabbi.

He found one in Shlomo Riskin of the nearby Lincoln Square Synagogue, which had been at the forefront of the movement to help Jews return to traditional Judaism.

I think that made all the difference in terms of the path I went on in reconnecting with God and reconnecting with *Yiddishkeit*. I think that Riskin was instrumental in that and I think that the one or two other *rabbeyim* who were at Lincoln Square at the time were instrumental, mainly because they were of a generation I didn't even know existed. I didn't know rabbis like that existed.

What did Riskin and these other rabbis do differently?

Well, they announced page numbers. I had never seen anybody like Riskin before, screaming and yelling at us to keep *mitzvos*, and to use our doubt to renew our faith. It was an enormously eclectic *shul*. It was so dynamic in its variety. It was a place where everyone could feel welcome and understood.

Riskin . . . because of his background was able to relate to people like me in a way that so many rabbis are not able to do. And he recommended that I go to the beginner's service . . . which was being conducted by [Rabbi] Ephraim Buchwald. At first I was a little insulted because I didn't think of myself as a beginner because I'd had this *yeshiva* education. But for nearly two years, I went every *Shabbos* to the beginner's service [and it was] one of the most exciting and transforming experiences I've ever had.

How so?

Not only because of Rabbi Buchwald—who I think is a tremendously talented teacher and someone who has found a role in Jewish life, the kind no one else has found in America—but also because of the freewheeling environment of people being able to bring their emotional Jewish baggage into a room on a regular basis and ask the questions and vent the fears and the anxieties that so many American Jews have. It was a group encounter, the kind most people can't possibly appreciate without having experienced it on a regular basis.

And what did you carry away from this?

A deepening awareness of God, a deepening awareness of Jewish history, a deepening awareness of Jewish commitment, a deepening awareness of a Jew's role in his society and the relationship of a Jew to his family and a Jew to his wife and children.

Which brings me to the essential conflict that Renee and I had to face at this moment, because she was far less convinced of all of this than I was. And it was very, very difficult. I think that without Rabbi Riskin and without Rabbi Buchwald and without that community, this marriage wouldn't have lasted.

That West Side community, the friends that we had, one couple in particular, Hilly and Felise Gross, were instrumental in preserving, at the same time, my commitment to *Yiddishkeit* and my commitment to my marriage and my family. I think it would have flown apart without that.

I think the most important thing was that the rabbis were on her side, not on mine. Time and time again I was called into either Rabbi Riskin's office or Rabbi Herschel Cohen's office and told to leave her alone and not to force her because it was not going to end happily if I did.

How long did it take before you and your wife were on the same page in terms of Yiddishkeit?

We still aren't. It's about as difficult an issue as one could possibly have. You have to have a very special kind of spouse in order to be able to deal with the conflicts.

The conflict remains and Renee has become more and more involved in Jewish life, more on a social level than a religious level because, again, her background is not such that she can participate so well on a religious level. She lights candles every *Shabbos*, the house is kosher, we keep *Shabbos* and the kids are in *yeshiva*. And of course as the kids grew older, the more they see that [although] mommy and daddy don't see eye to eye on all of these issues, but they're making it work.

Has your worklife changed?

Yes. I've lost work because of it. But the main problem I have with my work is not so much the *shomer Shabbos* situation, because as a writer and producer I can pretty much set my own schedule.

The problem is nowadays with content. There are certain things I just can't do. Now, I try to work within the limitation both of what I think is *tzniusdic*—to use my daughter's phrase—but it's not always easy. And I think the way our entertainment business and the . . . moral values of our society, the direction in which they're going, they're going further and further away from what I think I can be doing.

Have you ever been able to consciously and overtly bring Torah values to any productions?

Consciously? It's very hard. It can be done, but it's not recommended.

An example: A character in one of Leicht's TV shows, an observant woman, was shown dating a man who was wearing a keepah.

And the network went crazy. They really wondered why he was wearing that. And we said she wouldn't be going out with a guy who wasn't wearing a *yarmulka*. "Well why?" You don't have to explain a turban or a policeman's hat. Why should you have to explain that? It's very tough. The Jews in the media are very self-conscious.

And so I try to be as low-key about it as possible. And the other Orthodox Jews in the business I know, try to be as low-key about it as possible and to be as much one of the guys as they possibly can be without betraying their own beliefs, which is very difficult. And it's not just Judaism. I think the media in general is very inhospitable to religion.

Do you wear a keepah *to work?*

No. Certainly not into the network, no. I wear a *keepah* almost all the time, but I don't wear a *keepah* to meetings. I find it's a tremendous inhibition at work. I think it makes people very uncomfortable.

What has been the overall impact of Yiddishkeit *on your life?*

I think it has allayed almost all the fears I ordinarily would have had—fear of failure, fear of loss, whether it's physical loss or ill health or loss of loved ones. My whole family was tested very severely a couple of years ago when my sister and her husband died in a fire. . . . It was very tough and continues to be. They left two children behind. This was something that was devastating, but I certainly think my parents and I derived a tremendous amount of strength from *Yiddishkeit.*

My parents, by the way, because I have become more and more *frum* over the years, so have they. And I think I am very proud of the fact that when an individual in a family becomes *frum* . . . when they know there's a religious guy out there somewhere, everybody benefits. They become more aware. Just because you can't call Uncle Allan on *Shabbos* means you know it's *Shabbos.* Just because Uncle Allan and his family can't go to [just] any restaurants, you know what *kashrus* is, you know that something like *kashrus* exists.

I think the impact in terms of raising children in this society is irreplaceable. I don't know how other people get through this with kids. I don't know how Americans are dealing with this. I think we're on a short route to disaster. I don't know how parents are dealing with it in the secular world. It's a minefield, especially if you have young children and teenagers nowadays.

I don't know whether my children are going to wind up *frum* or not, but they're certainly going to have a set of values, there's no question about that.

Have you experienced any youthful rebellion yet?

Yeah, sure. But I would rather be fighting over the length of the sleeves than over whether or not you're gonna come home tonight. My daughter and I are fighting over the length of her dresses and the length of her sleeves. We're not fighting over the things a lot of other parents are fighting over. Kids are sleeping in the backs of trucks at 16 years old.

Allan Leicht, 53, is a writer and producer whose primary medium is television. His credits include the television show Kate and Allie *and the television series* The Thorns. *He is married to the actress Renee Lippin. They live in Los Angeles and have three children, Rebecca, Zaki, and Raffi.*

23
Collared at the Wall

We couldn't figure out why they wanted us, because there was no possible way that either of us was going to become religious.

In 1973, Seth Mandell was planning to learn bartending so he'd be able to support himself while visiting a buddy in New Orleans. But a TV news report caught his attention: Kibbutz *volunteers were needed in Israel to replace soldiers who were fighting in the Yom Kippur War. "I thought that not only could I go to someplace warm, which was one of my major motivations, but I could see this foreign country, too," he said. He put in his time at a few secular* kibbutzim, *became disenchanted with Israeli society, and prepared to leave the country for the Peace Corps. He had his plane tickets. But before he left, he couldn't resist taunting a rabbi who'd tried and failed repeatedly to collar him and introduce him to* Yiddishkeit. *Mandell should have known better.*

I think that I had a pretty diluted and Americanized view of what it meant to be Jewish. In my house [in Eastern Connecticut] everyone was equal, whether you were black, white, Jew, Muslim; all people were created equal. This was the major theme taught by my parents.

As a result, there was nothing particularly special about being Jewish, other than the fact that you had different holidays. All my friends growing up were not Jewish. In fact, I never went out with a Jewish woman during high school or college, that I can recall. In fact, I didn't go out with a Jewish woman when I went to Israel. When I was on a *kibbutz* I went out with non-Jewish women.

So there I was in Israel, reading a lot. *Jews, God and History* by Max Dimont was very, very important to me. Suddenly, in my mind, Jews went from this passive middle class people to this group that came in from Egypt, from the desert, into Israel and cleaned house. Here was a vision of Jewish masculinity which I had never experienced before. I think that was very important.

I would say that my Jewish identity is tied up in this masculine thing. I remember writing to a non-Jewish friend of mine later . . . and saying, "If I'm going to be a man, I'm going to be a Jewish man." And I had to find out what that means, what the Jewish part of that is.

However, Mandell wanted no part of religious observance.

I remember that there were schools in Jerusalem at the time and guys would come up to you at the Western Wall and they'd say to you, "Would you like to come to a *Shabbat* meal? Would you like to come to a class?" And I would say, "No, get away."

Two guys who had been on the *kibbutz* before me came back and we were playing Frisbee and they took off their shirts and they were wearing *tzitzis*. I thought this was the most disgusting thing I had ever seen. I could understand somebody going and studying—I could understand this in a philosophical kind of rational way—but why anyone would want to put on those fringes was totally beyond any kind of understanding I had. I was almost physically repulsed by it.

A year and a half later, [after hitchhiking through Europe and then working in America] I went back to Israel after having had this charge of Jewish identity and a charge of masculinity; I felt very different about myself and loved being there. But I didn't know what I loved about it— being on the *kibbutz* or being in Israel, because I spent all my time in Israel on a *kibbutz*.

What I decided after having lived in Israeli society was that it must have been *kibbutz* that I liked, because Israeli society, as I saw it, was as materialistic and had the same values as American society, except the Israelis weren't able to get all the material goods they wanted because of the economic conditions in their country. So I said to myself, if I'm going to be in a materialistic society, I might as well live in America.

Before I had returned to Israel, I had applied to the Peace Corps, and later was accepted to go Senegal. They were going to teach me French. I was going to be there two years.

Mandell and a friend, a Greek Jew, drove to Jerusalem to say good-bye to the Western Wall.

From Jerusalem we were going to Nueba, which is a nude beach, now part of Egypt, south of Elat. And then we were driving directly from Nueba to the airport, where I was going to get on an airplane and go to America and then go into the Peace Corps. That was the plan.

After visiting the wall, Mandell and his friend couldn't find their car. Their frantic search for it took them to a nearby parking lot.

And there, leaning against a car with his jacket slung over his shoulder is a guy named [Rabbi] Meir Schuster. Meir Schuster is the guy who began bringing people from the Western Wall to the different *yeshivot* in Jerusalem. Now, Meir Schuster I had met about five times over the past few years, and each time he had said, "Would you like to come to a class on Judaism? Would you like to come to a *Shabbat* meal?" or something like that, and I'd always said no, quite abruptly.

So this time for some reason, and I have no idea why I said this, I walked by this guy and I said to him, "Hey, you can't get me anymore." And he said, "What are you talking about? Who are you? What do you mean?" And I said, "You've been trying to get me for two years now, ever since 1973, and I want you to know I'm leaving now, I'm not coming back and you can't get me anymore." So he said, "Well, uh, would you like to meet a rabbi?" [laughs]. And I said, "Well, who is he? And how old is he?" And he said, "He's about 50." And I said, "No, I don't want to meet him." I wasn't interested in meeting anybody that old.

He said, "Okay, but how can you not be open to your religion?" And I said to myself, "That's a very good question." Here I was, trying to be open to experience. I was open to people, I was open to new knowledge; how could I not be open to my religion? It was a very good question.

So I looked at my friend and I said, "Let's get out of here." And he said, "No I want to see this guy." And I, because I was supposed to be open, said okay.

So he brought us to a *yeshiva* called *Aish Hatorah* and he sat us down in the dining hall and there was this kid and he was basically nice to us and he gave us some food. But this kid was really weird [laughs]. This was my first introduction to *ba'alei teshuvah*. He was the first *ba'al teshuvah* I'd ever met in my life, and my friend and I looked at each other, like, this is the kind of people they have here?

Schuster helped Mandell and his friend find their car, and then shepherded them to the home of Rabbi B.

It turns out, he [Rabbi B.] is probably one of the top five experts in Hebrew Bible in the world. He sits us down at this big table, with books

all around, these big Jewish tomes that at the time were totally meaningless to me. And he says, "Tell me what brought you to Israel." And
we told him the story of what happened to us on Yom Kippur.

*Mandell and his friend had gotten stoned, so that killed any possibil-
ity of a fast. Instead, they drove around in search of a bite to eat, which
they eventually found at a small cafe in Gaza. Theirs was the only car
on the road.*

So we told this rabbi this story. And he got angrier than any other
human being I've ever seen before in my life. He grabbed onto the table
and started to shake. His eyes went up into his head and he started to
quiver and shake and his face got red and he said, "Boys, it's not your
fault." What he was upset about was the fact that we were in Israel for
some sense of Jewish identity and all we could do to make Yom Kippur
special was drive to Gaza because that was what nobody else was doing.
He was just furious at the society, that the *kibbutz* society didn't afford
us something to do to make it more meaningful to us.

By the way, when he said, "It's not your fault," my response was to
say to myself, of course it's not my fault. It's either my father's fault or
my grandfather's fault, but it is certainly not my fault that I was not
observing Yom Kippur, because I never got anything that was worth
observing.

So we stayed overnight at this *yeshiva*. The next morning we get up
and eat breakfast and we decide that since they were so nice to us—they
gave us a place to stay and they gave us breakfast and we had dinner
last night—we would go to a class.

So we go to the class. The rabbi walks in, and he's dressed in a three-
piece suit with dark glasses on with a snap-brim hat. I say to myself, "I
don't trust this guy." He was dressed like all the businessmen I'd rejected. . . . he represented to me the establishment.

He begins talking about the relationship between the oral law and the
written law and Plato and Aristotle. I was very, very impressed with his
intellect. I had never thought about Jewish law in terms of poetry, and I
was just very impressed by the whole thing.

The rabbi [Nota Schiller] then brings us down to talk and he invites
us to stay for a week. And I said, "Rabbi I think you're doing a wonderful thing here. I think it's very important for these young men to get
Jewish knowledge. I enjoyed your class, I think it's great, I'm totally in
support of what you're doing. But I have one problem." And I pulled

out my ticket and I looked at it and said, "This is my ticket home and it's due in a week. I'm going to Nueba, going to the airport and then I'm going to the Peace Corps."

Rabbi Schiller offered him free room and board for three months, Jewish philosophy classes from nine to one and the rest of the afternoon off—as well as a free plane ticket home. Mandell and his friend went to the beach and thought about the offer.

We couldn't figure out why they wanted us, because there was no possible way either of us was going to become religious. That's what we thought—they could tell us whatever they wanted, but we were going in a totally different direction.

So we thought that the only reason they were doing this and being so nice to us was because they thought we would study for a while and go back to America, and in my friend's case to Greece, and then we would make a lot of money, and then they would come and hit us up for a fundraiser. We couldn't imagine any other reason they would possibly be so interested because we were so far out of their realm.

But I'd always wanted to live in Jerusalem and I thought that studying Jewish philosophy for a few hours each day would be interesting. And I had this space of time I had given myself to explore the world, so to speak. I decided the only reason that I wouldn't do this is because I was afraid I'd wind up like them, with a black hat and a black coat.

I thought if they can take my brain in a short period of time and brainwash it so I'd change and totally become somebody else, then my brain's not worth anything anyway. So I really thought if they can get me in three months and turn me into that type of person, who I thought myself to be totally unlike, fine, then let them do that. But I'm not going to let fear of becoming something else stop me from exploring something and having this sort of experience, which I thought would be very interesting.

After three or four days of soul-searching—among other activities— Mandell decided to take Schiller up on his offer and enrolled in the Ohr Somayach Yeshiva *in Jerusalem.*

They were very happy to see me and they threw their arms around me and they kissed me . . . and they gave me a place to stay and I started to study and I stayed for a little over three months. At the end of that time, by the way, I became very close to this Rabbi Schiller, the original guy I didn't trust.

I took my philosophy and I really argued with everybody I talked with who believed in the traditional way. I had a great time. It was the most intellectually stimulating time of my life, both studying the texts, as we did, and having arguments and discussions; people were extremely open.

What was your philosophy at the time?

My position was there is no God and only that which we see in front of us is real. And as long as I didn't hurt anybody, I could essentially do whatever I wanted with no obligation to anybody.

A photograph from this period says it all. It shows 13 young men gathered outside the yeshiva. *The second one from the left—the one with the modified Afro—is wearing blue jeans, sneakers, a hooded sweatshirt, and an expression that exudes skepticism and insouciance. It's Mandell.*

When I left I went around telling everybody, "Thank you very much, I now understand that you guys are not crazy." The second thing I understood was that now I believed there was a 50–50 chance there was a God. It went from zero to 50–50 in three months, not bad. And I told them I wasn't going to marry someone who wasn't Jewish. As a result of this experience I thought that there was enough value in the Jewish culture, the religion itself, to want to pass that on.

Mandell returned to America and pondered whether to go into the Peace Corps and gain a superficial knowledge of a new culture or immerse himself more deeply in his own. He decided to return to Ohr Somayach.

It was clear to me the study of Torah and Talmud in and of itself, whether or not there was a God, was an enriching, learning, growth process. It was also clear to me that you could go as deep into Torah as you wanted to and never find the end. That's one of the things that attracted me to it; in all the other endeavors I had ever taken part in, I had always gotten bored. And I had never been bored for a minute in Jerusalem studying.

The other thing I had was a very strong need to justify everything that I did religiously. I never did anything without first having a rationale for myself. So therefore if someone said to me, "Why do you put on *tefillin?*" I had a rationale that makes sense on a very pragmatic level.

And what is that?

There's a number of them. One of the first times I put *tefillin* on by myself, I realized that my grandfather had put on *tefillin* too. So the putting on of *tefillin* is an immediate connection to three generations of Mandells. And from my grandfather back, Mandells had been putting on *tefillin* for at least 2,000 years.

[But] in order to have a valid [religious] system you need to have in it something you don't understand. Some things you've got to do out of faith as part of the system. If everything is rational, then why have God at all?

So 80 percent of this system spoke to me. I liked the idea of the family. I liked the idea of a blending of the spiritual and the physical. The only problem was I didn't believe in God. I didn't have that 20 percent, and the whole system fell apart if you didn't have that.

After having discussed this at length with Rabbi Schiller, I finally said to him, "Rabbi, you're telling me to make believe there's a God?" And he said, yeah. I left the room very troubled. But after thinking about it at length, I said to myself, the system fits together so perfectly except for the God idea that it's worth experimenting with the concept of a true God for a month to see what happens. That's the deal I made with myself. I began looking at the world as if there was a God. And as a result of that, I began to see spiritual occurrences all over the place. I saw things I would have called coincidence as the hand of God.

How has becoming observant changed your life?

I will say that . . . probably 80 percent of what I now do is connected to something having to do with Torah or Judaism. From getting up in the morning and *davening* to spending as much spare time as possible learning to having *Shabbat* to what I eat. Everything is impacted by the fact that I'm now a religious Jew.

My aspirations for my children are totally different; I want my kids to go to *yeshiva*. I spend $10,000 a year to send them to [Jewish] day school. Believe me, I could use that 10,000 for other things, like to buy new cars and to eat better. So, virtually every aspect of my life is geared toward some aspect of Torah, with the possible exception of a couple of football games on Sunday afternoon or racketball.

Is it difficult to reconcile the modern world with the world of a Torah-true Jew?

Not really, because . . . I had been the type of person in the beginning who was never really very fond of America. I didn't admire the value system of America, the materialism, the kind of issues people thought were important, the work ethic.

When I came back from Jerusalem after the first three months there, I looked around at all of my friends and they were working 40 hours a week so they could party on the weekends. I looked at my friends from Jerusalem and they were living every moment as if it was a gift from God because they were able to study. They were able to connect to God at every moment.

My friends who didn't have that were just trying to get through the eight hours of the workday in order to relax. I knew that wasn't what I wanted to do. I knew what I didn't want to do was what my friends in America were doing. It was a very stark contrast.

What I'm saying is that, living a Torah-true life, the outside world is irrelevant to me. My karma in this lifetime is to deal with Jewish issues. I'm very concerned about the state of the Jewish community in this country and about the issue of assimilation. That's what I do. I work to try to serve as some kind of brake against assimilation.

Do you ever have crises of faith?

I periodically have self-inflicted crises of confidence, crises of faith. I like that. I always want to be reexamining my faith. I always want to be examining whether I am doing what is best for me and best for my family, and I would even say, the best for *Klal Yisroel*, to show you how deep that Jewish peoplehood thing has gone into me. That's a deep, abiding value as far as I'm concerned, right up there with family and home and stuff like that.

Some people, I think, feel the need to be religious. They feel that without this structure, without this meaning in their lives, they would be kind of lost and forlorn. I never felt that. I felt I had a very nice life beforehand. I'm not troubled by those kind of things. If I were to decide that this was no longer true for me, and if the system wasn't working, I think I would still be able to take it off like a coat and walk away and do something else. But it's working.

Meaning what?

Meaning it adds a tremendous amount to my life, to my satisfaction, intellectually and spiritually. It means that when I open a *sefer*, open a [holy] book, it continues to be satisfying. I still get more satisfaction out of opening up a *sefer* and learning than I do virtually any other intellectual activity.

Why is that?

It's more meaningful. I feel like I'm growing. I feel it's directly related to my life no matter how far out a particular issue is. I feel it's directly related to who I am and what I'm doing; it's another piece of Jewish knowledge. I can use it also. The more I learn, the more I find I can use it both in my everyday life and in my work life.

Seth Mandell, 44, now a rabbi, is director of the Hillel program at the University of Maryland. He and his wife have four children and live in Silver Spring, Maryland.

24
Making It in
the *Midbar*

Maybe after a few years of being out in the *midbar* . . . and being starved,
like in sheer exile, maybe that changed the way I viewed Judaism.

*Midbar is a Hebrew word meaning "desert" or "wilderness." In the
religious sense, it refers to a place situated well off Judaism's beaten
path—a place, say, like Utah. That's where Jamie Mausberg and his
family settled several years ago, coming from a traditional Jewish community just outside Toronto. Why? Accomplished skiers all, they were
searching for better slopes. They found that. Jamie found something else
there, too. But first he had a severe cardiac episode that landed him in
the hospital.*

It kind of occurred to me that day . . . something came back to me
that I'd read when I was younger. I believe it's Rambam who says, "Rush
to do a *mitzvah* today because you might not be around tomorrow to
perform one."

The idea that you're here today and gone tomorrow kinda sunk in,
and I thought that I better pursue all the dreams that I'd had as a child.
So going back to my childhood, my friends in Toronto, we used to sit
there and fantasize that when we were older we'd be a bunch of rabbis
living next door to each other with 10 or 15 kids each [laughs] and living according to the law. So I just started to think about that and think
about my Judaism and where I wanted to be and what type of family I
wanted to raise.

So I started studying at age 21. It came slow at first. I was piecing together what I wanted for a future and I think at the time *Schindler's List* came out and I started getting ideas in my head . . . [like] what's the difference between what Hitler did to the Jews and what modern secular Jews in America are doing to themselves? It's gonna result in destruction either way.

In one scenario you have somebody pointing a gun to your head and in the other you have a government that preaches freedom and liberal ideas, but the results are the same—you have Jews intermarrying at an enormous rate in America and . . . the results are going to be the same. If you don't keep up with your Judaism and learn about your heritage than you're not going to pass anything on to your children and they're not going to know what it means to be Jewish.

So at that time I decided that I wanted to go to Israel and spend some time on a *kibbutz*. So I went over there and spent some time on a secular *kibbutz*. And over the course of six months, it occurred to me that Israel without Judaism, without its religion, is basically identical to any other state on the planet.

So right before I came home, something, and I can't tell you what, urged me, something deep down, told me to go to Jerusalem and spend some time in the Heritage House there in the Old City. Heritage House is a youth hostel and they have enough room there for about 30 boys and they take you off to different courses and take you to different *yeshivas* that are doing *mekarev* work.

It wasn't really doing enough for me, although it was a fascinating two weeks that I spent there. And then one day I was down by the *Kotel* in Jerusalem, and a man approached me with a black hat and a full beard and the whole works with an Australian accent. And he ended up being the Lubavitch *sheliach* in Jerusalem, and he took me into his house for *Shabbos*. His name is Shloime Gestetner, and like most Lubavitch *sheliachs*, he's a God-fearing Jew who keeps his home open and his heart open to any Jew who needs help in getting back on the path.

So I spent a week there and ended up studying some Torah with him and some *Tanya* and learned some mystical concepts of Judaism. I was feeling stronger and stronger about it, but still obviously living a very unobservant lifestyle. I was just kind of feeling it out and trying to decide where I'd want to go with my Judaism.

I came back to [Salt Lake City] Utah, and that same year, which was 1993, a Lubavitch *Sheliach* just happened to move out to Utah for the first time. Until he came, the only community that existed here was a mixture of Reform and Conservative Judaism. So this was the first time there was a traditional rabbi around in town with sufficient knowledge to teach me what I felt was true Judaism.

That was two years ago, and I've spent the time since learning with the *sheliach*, and learning more and more and I've enjoyed it so much that I think this fall I'm going to head off to *yeshiva* in the Old City in Jerusalem.

Could you describe your upbringing in terms of Yiddishkeit?

I couldn't fit it into a label. We were a traditional Jewish Canadian family that was almost 100 percent nonobservant, but that was brought up to believe that you had the law and man had free choice to live and abide by the law as dictated by the Torah, or not to. But that law was indestructible. It wasn't until I moved to Utah at the age of 17 that I actually learned firsthand what Reform and Conservative Judaism was all about.

Only in the last 200 years, since Reform Judaism developed in Germany and flourished in America, has Judaism gotten to the point where the majority of the Jews living in the world today don't recognize the law as the sole legitimate expression of Jewish values. And I believe that's a pure deception.

Imagine taking the American Constitution and you pull out the 5th Amendment and you're gonna call it the American Constitution. Well, everybody would laugh at you; that's absurd. Well that's basically what Reform Judaism has done, blatantly. And Conservative Judaism has done the same thing but not to that extent. . . . They aren't as far down on the slippery slope so to speak.

Speaking of slopes; you moved to Utah for the skiing?

We started competing in skiing as young children and we got to compete at the international level for the Canadian Junior National ski team and compete in Europe and . . . ended up skiing about 250 days a year by the time I was 15. We always had a fantasy of living out West in the big mountains.

Maybe the move to Utah was an important turning point for me. Once I came out here, I didn't have the security of a Jewish community, even if it wasn't observant. And we came out to Utah and things seemed to be so strange and different out here. We'd go to *shul* and there'd be a choir that sounded like a church and they'd be playing an organ on *Shabbos* and the high holidays. And maybe after a few years of being out in the *midbar*, the desert, and being starved, like in sheer exile, maybe that changed the way I viewed Judaism.

I think there were a few small groups of Jews who grew up locally and they would hang out together, but they never did anything Jewish. It wasn't like they tried to hide it. They were so far assimilated. They knew they were Jewish, but it was like a black guy's a black guy and he doesn't necessarily have a religion that coincides with the color of his skin. He can be Protestant or Jewish or whatever.

These guys out here, they were Jewish by birth, big deal. It's Saturday, let's go to the ballgame, let's meet at a Hillel for a pizza party and let's eat pepperoni and cheese pizza and shrimp and drink beers and go out and find some nice women to date, whether they're Jewish or not. It's just never an issue.

Describe what it feels like to be an observant Jew living in Salt Lake City, Utah.

The food part isn't so bad—we fly it in from Los Angeles—but right now it's extremely frustrating. There's no social group out here of young Jews that are even interested in traditional Judaism. Everybody who's *frum* hangs out at *Chabad*. There's one *frum* family in town and there's the Lubavitch rabbi and his family and there's a couple others.

A family of converts built the first *mikvah* in town about four years ago—the first *mikvah*, period, and there have been Jews here for 80, 90 years. Besides that, there's really nothing. Maybe a dozen families claim they keep kosher. There's one kid in town, he's 17 and he's a Russian exchange student who's going to the university here, and he's the only other *frum* Jew in town my age.

You learn to live with it. It's funny; I guess maybe it makes you stronger in your Judaism. There's been a lot of religious kids, whether they're *Chabadniks* or modern Orthodox Jews from the Upper West Side in New York who come up here to go skiing, and we all taught skiing at the resorts. And you run into these people and somehow they're just all blown away by the fact that there's a *frum* kid living out here in the middle of the *midbar* and somehow getting on with life in a decent way. Some of them actually said [laughs] that I had inspired them somehow to go home and live a more observant Torah lifestyle.

What do you do on Shabbos?

I spend every *Shabbos* at the Lubavitcher rabbi's house. We sleep at their house; they have three lovely children.

Do you now wear a keepah in public?

Yeah, I go to work with a *keepah* on, which is kind of funny, because at work is a mixture of Mormons—and they love Jews so there's no problems with them—but there's some rednecks. So you get some flak from the rednecks here and there, but there's no real discrimination.

Do you plan to stay in Salt Lake City?

For now, at this stage of my life, I want to try living in a Jewish community. So I could see myself living in a big city back east or right now I'm gonna try living in Israel and studying in *yeshiva* and we'll see how that goes.

What has been the net impact of frumkeit *on your life?*

There's good and there's bad. There's an inner struggle constantly against your desires and the things that used to make you happy, whether it's going out and skiing every day . . . or spending the morning and putting on *tefillin* and going to the *minyan*. It can be extremely frustrating trying to incorporate Torah views into my makeup, when I've been constructed from a secular society ever since birth. So at times it can be very frustrating. But on the whole, I think it's brought tremendous joy into my life and I see that increasing as I move toward making a family.

Joy in your life? Explain.

It's hard to explain. A lot of times I think people in their daily existence are always looking into the future—what am I going to be doing then? This month I got plans to go on a vacation and that's going to be great . . . and never living for the now. And now that I've learned to appreciate *Shabbos* I can work hard all week and look forward to *Shabbos*. And Friday night'll come along and there's no other place in the world that I'd rather be than sitting in a *frum* home making *Kiddush* over a cup of wine, enjoying a good meal and heading off to *shul* the next day and *davening* and just forgetting about every other care or worry or problem in the world. When the holidays come around it's the same type of feeling.

Boruch Hashem that there's *Chabad* out in the world and *sheliachs* going around and living in cities like this. Because if it wasn't for them, I'd just be history. I'd be miserable. I don't know what I'd be doing.

A VISIT TO CROWN HEIGHTS

In the summer of 1993, Jamie Mausberg was about to begin a Torah study program in the Catskills. He had arranged to spend a couple days prior to the start of the program with a rabbi in the Crown Heights section of Brooklyn, headquarters of the Lubavitch chasidim. He remembers catching a train from Long Island and then boarding the Brooklyn-bound subway.

I get up out of the subway, not familiar with Brooklyn at all, and nobody is on the street, a couple blacks, no Jews anywhere. I figured, what the heck; I'm in the middle of an Orthodox community, where are these guys?

Within about two seconds, this chasidic rabbi that I didn't know comes running out of this tall building, which I recognized from pictures as 770 [Eastern Parkway], the Lubavitch *shul*, and he comes running out and he grabs my arm and he starts yanking me. You gotta understand, I'm from the West and people are laid back. You go back East and everybody's pushy, shovy, rush, rush, rush, and the Orthodox guys [laughs] are sometimes the worst.

So this guy is pulling and pulling and he didn't even tell me who he is or what he's doing. So I'm, like, wait a minute what's going on here? So he said, "Rabbi Zippel, the *sheliach* from Salt Lake City sent me outside to grab you. We just finished *davening mincha*, the *Rebbe's* coming out." So he pulled me inside 770 and the place was packed with three or four thousand people packed in like sardines. I'd never seen anything like it.

And all these guys, like they were expecting me, were pushing and shoving me up to the front, literally, they're slamming me through there. I lost my bag with all of my clothing. Somebody grabbed my suitcase, who knows where it went.

So they shoved me up front, and I'm like two rows back from this balcony and I recognize the *sheliach* from Salt Lake City, and he said, "Oh thank God you're here. It's so good to see you. I didn't know if you'd make it." And he had told everybody in the place he was expecting me.

Literally, 20 seconds later, the curtain starts moving from up on the balcony and the *Rebbe* comes out, and the Lubavitchers start a frantic *"yechi adonenu morenu v'rabenu melech ha mosiach l'ohlum vaed,"* their tune that they sing ["he should live long, our master, our teacher, our rabbi, king, the savior forever"].

[Sings the tune]. And they go on forever . . . "ay-yi-yi-yi-yi." . . . When I was younger I used to go to a lot of rock concerts, like The Grateful

Dead, and I thought I'd seen it all. I was standing there and I was thinking, this is Judaism? This is like idolatry. It looks worse than the Rolling Stones, where women are throwing themselves at Mick Jagger, and these guys *shokeling* and banging their heads; I'd never seen anything like it. And then I look up on the balcony and there's this 92-year-old man sitting in a wheelchair. He can't open his mouth, he can barely move his arms.

And he's glancing around at the room and nodding. The poor man was very sick. And these people are going nuts, and I'm thinking, what is going on here? This is absurd. These people are brainwashed.

And then he glances around the room and all of a sudden he fixes his gaze on me. Something inside me wouldn't let me look back at him. I don't know if there was a fear, so I looked away. And I don't know how long it was—10 seconds, 2 seconds, 20 seconds—I had this urge to look back to the *Rebbe* on the balcony. And I had heard tons of stories about him already; at this point I was already familiar with all these supposed miracles or his powers or whatever. I look back up to the balcony and he's still looking at me.

Only this time I couldn't look away. My gaze was fixed on him, and it wasn't like he was looking at me like normal people look at each other. It was like he was looking right through me, right into my essence. And that totally blew me away, because before that moment I was such a skeptic, standing there, and thinking that this is a ridiculous scene. And this guy looks at me and I was in a mood where I was fighting it. And without even being able to fight it, in a millionth of a second, this guy's looking at me and he's blowing me away and looking right into me.

And it was almost like he was saying, not, "Jamie Mausberg I've been sitting here waiting for you for 50 years. But, Asher Zelig, like *nu*, where have you been? I've been standing here waiting . . . and finally you're here, I've been waiting all this time."

So I sat there just totally blown away. And a minute later he waved his hand and they took him out of there, and I was just blown, whacked away for the rest of the week, along with the rest of Crown Heights. That one kinda blew me away and I still remember it.

Jamie Mausberg at 25 was an environmental engineer with a consulting firm in Salt Lake City, Utah, before going to Israel to study. He is single.

25
Seder Story

One of the things that began to strike me with increasing force is the idea that there would be no Jewish survival without this stuff, without some kind of traditional Jewish religiosity.

Michael Medved attributes his growth as a Jew largely to his parents' courage and integrity. His development, however, was slow and circuitous and sometimes painful. If there was a single turning point, it came during a potentially ugly family confrontation one Pesach. As Medved likes to say, had the episode been made into a movie—a medium with which he is intimately familiar—it might have been called Guess Who's Coming to *Seder*?

The story starts with my parents who were passionately, profoundly committed as Jews and were themselves both products of Orthodox homes. And until we moved to California when I was six—we moved from Philadelphia—my mom kept kosher, and in fact kept kosher for the first year in San Diego. And then due to tremendous difficulty in getting kosher meat in San Diego, we stopped that. San Diego was not exactly a thriving center of Torah life and learning [in the 1950s]. There were only 3,000 Jews in a city at that time of a half a million.

We were members of a Conservative synagogue in San Diego, where I was *bar mitzvah*. We weren't regular *shul*-goers but we went more often than three times a year. We always used to go for Succot; we always used to go for the first day of Pesach and for other peoples' *bar mitzvahs*. My mom was always absolutely remarkable for Passover. We would have *seders* with between 50 and 100 people, always. The biggest thing when we were growing up was the *seder*.

Even though we weren't Sabbath observers as one would normally define it, [my mother] did light candles every night when we were growing up. We frequently had *Shabbat* meals, but when things started going with more difficulty with my parents' marriage that sort of fell away. [They eventually were divorced.]

Probably the main reason I'm Jewishly involved today is that my parents were. I think the differences in the style and the substance of my involvement and my parents involvement are significant, but they're not cosmically gigantic. They are more differences of shading and intensity.

Were you self-conscious growing up as a Jew in a heavily Gentile environment?

I was self-conscious, but I was kind of proud of it. I thought it was neat. Another area of gratitude I have toward my parents is that I was raised with the sense that it's great to be a nonconformist. And in San Diego in the 1950s, being Jewish was certainly an area of nonconformity.

The summer before Medved's junior year in high school, the family moved to Los Angeles. Suddenly Medved was surrounded by Jews, but almost all of them were thoroughly assimilated. Ironically, the newcomers were "instantly the most ethnically and religiously Jewish people around," said Medved. He landed his first girlfriend, who was Jewish, but it went badly.

After that, everyone I had any kind of significant interest in was not Jewish. And my parents were annoyed at this, particularly my mom. Her line was basically, well . . . you're a kid and it's okay, but when it comes time to marry somebody don't even think about getting seriously involved with an S-word.

By the time he was at Yale, his interest in observant Judaism had waned.

It was just not important to me. [But] it was important to me to be Jewish. Again, as it happened, at Yale virtually all of my friends were Jewish. And some of them had wonderful Jewish backgrounds, you know, knew about the religion in ways that I didn't.

So in a sense, yeah, I was far away, but in another sense Yale was like a Jewish education. Also, I had this stupid thing about expressing my Jewish identity through reading Jewish novelists; like I've always had this tremendous interest in Saul Bellow, Philip Roth, Bernard Malamud, Bruce Jay Friedman. They were my *rebbes* in a sense of what it meant to be Jewish. That's a pathetic situation, but that's the way I viewed them at the time.

In 1968 I developed another girlfriend and she was Irish on one side and WASP on the other. And this became very serious.

I remember her mother was this very sweet Boston lady and she said, "Well, you know so many of my friends have daughters who have married Jewish guys and they make wonderful husbands because they never get drunk and they never beat their wives" [laughs]. She actually said something very much like that almost in those words.

So my parents had heard lots about her . . . and I was not yet 21, and you know you're a bit of an idiot at that time in your life. And I felt the perfect time to introduce her to my parents would be Passover. Remember, the big affirmation of Jewishness in my family was Pesach, so we had this thing—"Guess who's coming to *seder*?"

I assumed that my parents, being good liberals—being these enlightened people both with graduate degrees—I knew that they weren't going to like this idea of me being serious about Fran [a pseudonym], but I did not assume that they would freak out. But in fact they did. It was this consummate nightmare.

As soon as we arrived, my mom took me tearfully aside and said, "Well, if you get married to this woman and you have grandchildren, we'll never want to see the grandchildren, we'll never want to have anything to do with them." And I sort of expected my mom to be more emotional, but my dad I remember took me for a drive and laid down the law and said the same thing, he wouldn't come to any wedding.

This was the kind of thing very few Jewish parents have the emotional resources to do, and I know now that one of the reasons they did it is that I'm the oldest of four boys and they felt that if they sort of rolled over and played dead for the oldest getting intermarried, it sort of erases the sanction.

We stayed for the first *seder*, but that was such an uncomfortable situation that we flew back to New Haven, and all the way back, she [said she] felt she had been treated miserably and she actually hadn't. I mean under the circumstances, it was just that, my parents had made it very clear that she was not being welcomed into the family. And of course she was very conscious of the fact that this was very different than the response of her parents, who had been very welcoming.

And in a sense, there was this awful thing where emotionally I was supposed to be chosing between loyalty to my parents and my attraction or my loyalty or my interest in this young woman. It really wasn't much of a contest, which is why I suspect that when we got back to New Haven, I kept insisting to her that I thought that my parents, in their tribalism and their intolerance, were not representing the true ideals of Judaism.

So partially in an attempt to prove that to my parents and to her, I started reading a few books about Judaism, for the first time as an adult really. And that really was the beginning for me. In the midst of this process, when I was still talking to my parents and arguing with them and going back and forth, Fran sort of belatedly agreed to go with me to talk to the Hillel rabbi [Richard Israel, a Reform rabbi] at Yale about the possibility of conversion.

During the meeting with the rabbi, Fran admitted that the only reason she would convert is that it would pacify Medved's parents and enable them to get married.

He said, "Well, in that case I really can't help you." Which I think was hugely to his credit. And she again felt very badly, although I think she sort of respected his stand. He was saying it's a fraud if it's just for this purpose. That interchange and that display of integrity on the part of Rabbi Israel probably made a significant difference in my life. Before long, I broke up with this young lady, which was the right thing to do anyway.

In retrospect, his parents' position no longer seemed unreasonable.

I always say I became more religious largely because of my parents' courage. I ended up taking it much better because they were obviously right about this young lady and they were clearly right about the importance of Jewish commitment. What happened is, I came out of this whole experience feeling emphatically that it was very, very important for me to be Jewish, that I obviously had to marry someone who was Jewish. I just started experimenting with different elements of Jewish life.

He left law school after his second year to live in the San Francisco area and work on a novel. There, he got involved with group called the Radical Jewish Union.

[It was] a lot of students and others who came together in a sort of left-wing, free-floating, artsy-craftsy, hippie-dippy manner, but it was very nice. The first *Shabbos* meals that I ever had were there. Also more substantively, the Hillel rabbi at the time [at Berkeley] was an Orthodox guy, and I remember the first time I ever had *havdalah* was at his house. And this was really my first contact with any sort of organized Jewish life. Through the RJU I got invited to a *bar mitzvah* at Beth Israel, which is an Orthodox synagogue. And that was very nice and very impressive and I remember for the first time feeling funny when I drove away. I figured why am I driving?

And so it sort of progressed from there. And I'd say in general what happened over a period of several years wasn't learning; I wish it had been. It was really sort of trial and error and finding sort of all the aspects of Jewish observance that I employed in my life [that] ended up enriching my life and improving things.

Why did doing this stuff make sense to you?

It didn't particularly. It wasn't a question of it making sense to me. It was attractive. What was attractive about it was a feeling of community, a feeling of camraderie. Remember, one thing I knew for sure about my Jewish identity was that I cared very much about Jewish survival and I think one of the things that began to strike me with increasing force is the idea that there would be no Jewish survival without this stuff, without some kind of traditional Jewish religiosity.

It was really the only way to reach people, to preserve anything. Because, you know, activities in support of the State of Israel were fine and good and important, but ultimately this was going to do it. And in a sense, my initial experiments with *kashrus* and lighting *Shabbos* candles and putting on *tefillin* and not driving on *Shabbos* were not affirmations of belief in God or the Torah, but were affirmations of my belief of the importance of Jewish identity. There was a feeling that this was a way I could do something.

And it was only gradually when all of this stuff started to make sense and became second nature that it occurred to me that maybe this particular system of self-help had not been composed by some brilliant psychologist several thousand years ago, but may in fact have had divine origins. Because even things that seemed silly ended up being fine.

What has been the net impact of Yiddishkeit *on your life?*

It has helped enormously in terms of my family life. It's helped to make me a much better husband and a much better father. I think that most people today flounder in family life because they don't know what the rules are, they don't know what they're supposed to do, especially with the feminist revolution and revolutions in different mores. I think that just having that road map of what a good family and a happy family should look like has been enormously helpful.

I married the best person in the whole world, and am blessed with this remarkable family. I don't think any of that could have been achieved in the same way without involvement in *Yiddishkeit*, because our family life really centers around *Shabbat*. The children's education is Jewish Orthodox education—we're involved. I think that in my work, I've enjoyed my role as a controversial guy. My most recent book created a great deal of controversy and a lot of national attention, and I think the whole basis for that really was my own religious commitment. [The book: *Hollywood Versus America*].

I've become fairly famous or notorious, depending on who you believe, for being the sort of American film critic who continually berates the industry for the moral and substantive messages it's sending. I think that people get burned out on Hollywood and get very damaged by their involvement with the entertainment industry, and I think that I'm not. I wouldn't be so arrogant as to say that I've been totally undamaged, but I think that our basis in the Torah has minimized the kind of damage that otherwise might have been there.

THE MOVEMENT REEXAMINED

Michael Medved may be a ba'al teshuvah, *but he is no poster boy for the* BT *movement—not any more. Although he has been well-served by* Yiddishkeit, *he is sharply critical of what he sees as a growing trend toward extremism, intolerance, and divisiveness in Orthodox Judaism, even among newcomers.*

The hardest thing for me has been disappointment in the *ba'al teshuvah* movement generally. Because at one point in my life . . . I really did believe 10 years ago and more that the so-called *ba'al teshuvah* movement, the return of Jewish baby boomers to some form of Orthodoxy, was going to completely alter the nature of American Judaism and create a much more viable, dynamic American Jewish community.

I think that we were wrong. I don't think that's happening. And there are many reasons for it, but part of it is sort of a . . . level of unpleasantness . . . that I think is indeed present in much of the so-called *ba'al teshuvah* world.

Medved said he is troubled by those Jews who "have an appalling lack of ahavas Yisroel; *they trash everybody who's not [like] them."*

We have run into in our own communal life here some really unpleasant examples of genuinely warped personalities. The question one has

to ask about people like this, who come with all the black-hat credentials in the world, is would they have been equally unpleasant if they
had stayed secular? And the answer I come up with in at least some of
the cases is no, they probably would have been better off. The lack of
derech eretz, the lack of *kibud av'v'ame*, the lack of *hakaras hatov*, is
just appalling.

That's my crisis of faith, not whether *Hakadosh Boruch Hu* exists and
cares about us. I think he does and I think he does. It's a question of, have
we really gotten it right when our *yeshivas* at times are turning out people
who are . . . emotional cripples and frankly horrible human beings.

Aren't these anomalies?

I think there are too many examples of this for them to be anomalies.

*Medved said his own community has experienced divisiveness and
intolerance masquerading as Yiddishkeit. "It has been really extraordinarily unpleasant; I mean a complete nightmare," he said.*

Most of the Orthodox *rabbeyim* who come through here are really
terrific guys, lovely fine people who are trying with all their heart. But
there is a tendency . . . to elevate *frumkeit*, black-hattedness, *yeshivish-
ness*, above simple dignity, *derech eretz*.

The way that *my rabbeyim* taught me when I was early to this process was that there should be a certain elegance, dignity, consideration
to Torah; that the *payros* of all this, the fruit of the learning and the
mitzvos, was indeed living a life that was beautiful and elevated. My wife
actually says it very well, that this meant a great deal to her. She'd always enjoyed her life, but it was just a question of going from black and
white to Technicolor.

But to me it's like fingernails on broken glass when people who had
an excellent secular education repudiate it and say, "Oh, I learned nothing, and now at *Ohr Somayach* or *Aish Hatorah*, now I'm really learning." Again, one can say that what you learned at those *yeshivas* was
wonderful and great and enriches your life, but it should be to add on to
what you had rather than erasing the person you were. We're in *gulus*,
and we live at a lot of levels with a lot of layers, and I don't think the
sort of simplicity that people tend to yearn for is possible or really honest.

One of the things that I hate, that drives me crazy, is when my nonreligious Jewish friends say, "Oh boy you have it so easy, I wish I had
your faith. It's hard for me, not going to *shul* on Yom Kippur [laughs],
but you have it so easy because you know, you're this religious fanatic,"
which of course in the eyes of most of my non-religious friends I am.

Which is again one of the great ironies in my life, that I'm viewed by some self-righteous *ba'alei teshuvah* in the community as some kind of monstrous *apikoros*, and of course in the eyes of the world in general, I'm a religious nut. Part of the evidence of being a religious nut is that I may be one of the only people who's turned down the *Tonight Show*, actually twice, because it conflicted with *yontif* or *Shabbos*.

Michael Medved, 47, is a film critic and author. He and his wife live in Southern California and have three children.

26
Spiritual Healing

I said, "What is this?" He said, "This is *Yiddishkeit*." I said, "I never heard this in my whole life." He said, "That's the shame of it."

During the 1960s and 1970s, Phillip Namanworth dabbled in everything from Taoism to Buddhism to Christianity. "I tried them all out," he said, but none provided long-lasting spiritual sustenance. So in 1985 when his buddy Kenny invited him along to Brooklyn to see a "rabbi guy," he figured why not? Besides, he had some emotional loose ends to take care of dating back to his childhood in the Bronx. His Jewish education had been so ineffectual that his religious life was left stunted and unsettled. "I thought maybe some spiritual scarring had happened as well," he said. "I thought there was something to correct about that period in my life."

So, I'm 40 and I said at least I'd like to go hear somebody or something so I could make a decision as an adult. I had no intention of doing anything. In all fairness to myself as an adult I had to give myself a shot. And as I hear from my teachers so often, it probably would have been my last shot. If I would have gone and it turned me off, that would have been it for me.

The "rabbi guy" he went to see was Rabbi Simon Jacobson of Crown Heights, a Lubavitch *educator.*

There was a guy with a short-sleeve shirt and a beard and a *yarmulka* and there was food on the table and people around the table, normal-looking like me, maybe some artists and men and women, and he was very congenial. And he started talking, and as he was talking, I was

197

amazed. I'll never forget it. It blew my mind so much that I felt like the top of my head was going to fly off.

I said, "What is this?" He said, "This is *Yiddishkeit*." I said, "I never heard this in my whole life." He said, "That's the shame of it." Here was my own tradition, and the ideas I was hearing were mind-blowing. I had no idea that there was anything in my tradition like that. So needless to say, I decided to come back.

Namanworth bought a chumash *and started studying with a friend at Rabbi Jacobson's suggestion. Others soon joined them.*

We'd argue about this stuff for days. I found *Pirkei Avos* and that blew my mind. And then I felt like I had to *do* something, so one of the first things I did, I decided not to work on *Shabbos*. I wasn't really "in," but there was a certain intellectual integrity that I felt. I felt . . . if I'm gonna connect and there's a God, I gotta do something.

In September 1986, Namanworth had a heart attack at the age of 41. (His father had died of a heart attack at the age of 43.) His daughter was born a couple months later. After he recovered, he resumed his trips to Crown Heights to see Rabbi Jacobson.

We used to take a car service out at 8:30 p.m. on Thursday and stay until two or three in the morning. And I tell you now, I don't remember what he said. It was so wild, it used to go down my back; it was the deepest stuff. And you'd understand [only] some of it, but it didn't matter because you'd get it. There was a part of us getting it that was not the rational part. And I have the same testimony from many of us.

He invited me over for Purim and there was just a great crowd of people who went there. We just tried to stop being animals in our lives. You know, in the music business I'd been around drugs and everything else all those years.

So with all these experiences, I started getting more and more, I guess, religious. And there were a lot of tensions at home because of it over the years. When my wife married me 1981 I was a different guy; I was studying Hinduism and reading about my guru and meditating at a little altar I had set up in my house. And all of a sudden she came home one day, five years later, and I won't go to the movies on Friday night anymore. And I won't eat off the plates. So it's been a real adjustment for her, and she's been a real saint.

Were you following a personality—Rabbi Jacobson—or were you following Judaism?

No, no, no. I knew this was Judaism. What I followed around was the Torah. Simon always made it very clear that it was the Torah. He was open, he could go on the roller coaster with you; he could talk about things. If you were a musician, he didn't say, "Well, tomorrow you gotta wear *payess* and have a black coat and stuff" [laughs].

He'd say, "Do what you're gonna do, give it a shot." He always said the same thing: "I'm here to disseminate knowledge. You do with it what you want. But don't be ignorant." Most of us were ignorant. The more we learned the more we wanted to do, so you'd learn and you'd try. After my heart attack, Kenny brought me *tefillin*. I never had *tefillin* in my whole life. I don't know if I'd ever even seen a pair. Can you imagine? And I started putting them on, and I don't think I've missed a day.

He [Jacobson] always said, "Move on your path and do what you can do and respect every person." Someone [once] asked the [Lubavitch] *Rebbe*, "Who are you?" And he said, "I'm a simple Jew." And now I appreciate it. After all these years I'm trying to struggle to become a simple Jew.

Did you find it difficult to begin performing mitzvahs?

I did it the best I could. You start with one thing. You don't have to jump in all the way. If you're learning as you go and the learning is talking to you—a part of you that's real, that's relevant to you and means something—you can see that the effects are real and you keep going. Many people want to stick to where they are; they don't want to move. That's fine, but it's not for me. In *Yiddishkeit*, nobody's ever standing still except when you're *davening* [the] *Amidah*.

A lot of people want the short hit. They want instant gratification, but Judaism says that's not going to last you. It says if you want to have a *nehr tamid*, the candle burning every day, you've got to do the hard work to integrate what you've learned.

You can see a lot of people who are very good, beautiful people and they're the soul. But they don't have the *mitzvos*, which is the body. Judaism teaches you need both, they're both vehicles. I wanted to become a full person. When something touches you so much and you don't move on it, you're hurting your soul.

How do you know this isn't another "ism" you're dabbling in?

I sometimes used to think my wife thought, he'll stop this now and he'll go on to something else. And I didn't realize until many years later that some of my friends thought the same thing.

How do you know they're not right?

When I said I'm gonna do this, I'd already been in the communes, I'd already meditated with the swamis, I'd already done all the stuff. You know, this is harder than the rest of them. I remember when I was doing yoga, I'd get these short hits and it wouldn't last. And I noticed right from the go with *Yiddishkeit* that I'd get a hit, but I had to work on it. It was very intellectual. Here's something real in my life. I'm not saying I have it, but it's a kind of maturity.

Has it been career-limiting?

Maybe the concept of career is a total distortion today and it needs some limiting. For me, if a job is on Saturday, it's not my job, so how can I say it's my career? I'm a Jew. On Rosh Hashanah God says how much money you're gonna have. I can't raise that by working on *Shabbos*.

Listen, I have what I'm gonna have, and more and more I want to do Jewish things in a Jewish way because I see it adds life to the whole world. But I'm very involved. I write scores for TV, I write for *Nickelodeon*, I write for *Sesame Street*. I get calls to do all kinds of jobs. I don't turn them down, I just tell people, "Here are my hours."

On the career thing—you talk about the jobs you don't get. What about the jobs you do get? That's a more important question. You have to remember that every place you're sent, God's sending you for a reason. Keep your eyes and ears open; see if maybe there's someone you can invite for a *Shabbos* or say a kind word to or do a person a favor.

My mission is maybe to talk to a fellow Jew in a way that they could understand and say, "You know what, there's something here that I like," and to prepare myself to have those conversations and to learn what I can and to raise my daughter a certain way. The other stuff is not my job.

What's the situation with your daughter in terms of Yiddishkeit?

She's in public school, but we're exploring Jewish schools. She's going to a Hebrew camp for the first time, and we have sort of a mixed situation. She comes to *shul*. She's moving and she's got a good soul and I teach her *medrash* and she's learning Hebrew and she sees that I try not to be a hypocrite in anything I do. She's not going to see me eating lobster and putting on *tefillin*.

Do you ever have crises of confidence? How do you handle doubt?

No, I don't have those doubts. The kinds of doubts I have, for me, feel much worse. I feel like some days, no matter what I've learned, I don't know a thing. That I'm so far from God that I can't stand it. That I'll never really know anything when I see all my deficiencies.

Does the twentieth century rationalist in you ever rebel at what you're now doing?

No. Because I've been through so much stuff that I know that rationalism is a small box. . . . Judaism teaches that intellect and faith go hand in hand. They're not opposing factors like in common society.

So use your head for everything. And when your head can't go anymore, don't stop there, which is what the rationalists do. But take a leap of faith and do something. Why? Because then you'll have an experience you can't explain. You'll know that you don't know; which, as Simon explains, doesn't mean I don't know anything. It means that you know in a way beyond knowing.

The mind's not the end of it all. There are more places, and I've experienced some of them. Listen, I was saved from heart attacks; I have so many miracles in my life. [Namanworth had heart bypass surgery in 1988 and another heart attack in 1991. At the time of this interview, he was recovering from hernia surgery].

Didn't miracles happen in your previous life?

I don't know. I didn't think of them in the same way. They could have. I think every day's a miracle.

Do you ever find that Judaism becomes rote?

You always have to watch out for that. You *daven* and you don't remember you did. *Davening* is very hard. *Davening* you have to study about, you have to learn what the sages say about prayer and understand prayer on a certain level. Prayer is so deep. It touches a part of us that connects to a part that's not rational, that's very, very deep. The sages of blessed memory set up these words which are pathways for us; they're not just words. Sometimes I read in the Hebrew and then I stop and look at the English, and depending what's going on with me, I might just start crying through my prayer. Other times I've *davened* and I don't even know I did it.

That's what I meant [about] the difference between Judaism and . . . you know, if you're a yogi, or whatever, I found if I'd meditate for a half hour, it didn't matter. Here, you gotta try to get in touch. Judaism is about being a normal person in the world so that you don't have any asceticism, you don't retreat. Judaism has a balance.

How does it feel to be an observant Jew?

It's a struggle. Life is not that easy. The Torah is not a dream book. The Torah shows you how tough life is. But it says, look, if you follow what I give you here, it'll be meaningful and rich for you. It doesn't mean it's not going to ever be sad or anything. I feel like my life is full of meaning.

I don't know what musical jobs I'll have tomorrow. What I'd like to do with some other Jews is get the voice of Jews who are struggling in the real world out on the stage or theater in song. I'd like to find some way to get that voice out there, of people who are not hating their Judaism, as so much Jewish theater turns out to be, or reminiscing about Yiddish, which much of it turns out to be. But [about] someone who's struggling in the world to be a good person with who he is.

Phillip Namanworth, 51, is a songwriter, musical arranger, producer, and performer. He has written for stage, screen, and television. He and his wife live in Manhattan and they have one child.

27
Bottoming Out

It was intimidating, but there was no question in my mind that this was part of me. This was part of something I had a very real claim of ownership to.

For years, Yaakov Ort was, as he puts it, an "utterly selfish hedonist" as well as a nonparticipating Jew. But his interest in Judaism was piqued after his first child was born in 1982. He figured he owed the boy a credible explanation for why the Jews had survived as a civilization; Ort didn't have a clue. "I mean, they didn't have great music, they didn't have great food, they didn't have great dancing," he said. Library books on Judaica didn't help. But a minister-turned-journalist did. He nudged Ort in a new direction where he eventually learned that there was more to Judaism than he'd ever imagined. He also learned about himself in the process.

In retrospect, the first crucial experience that I had vis-à-vis getting involved in Judaism happened, oddly enough, when I was traveling in Europe as a college student. I think it was 1968 or '69.

I found myself in Switzerland, and I was in a small village outside Geneva, which was halfway up one of the Alps. I was sitting outside and it was an absolutely exquisite morning. The sky was perfectly blue and the air was very, very clean. It was extraordinarily beautiful.

And I remember sitting there and it just occurred to me, as I guess sort of a revelation, but it just absolutely penetrated me that there had to be a God—that everything that I was seeing, the blueness of the sky and the beauty of the trees and just the gloriousness of the day . . . it struck me as being absolutely impossible that all of that could have been a random accident.

Why did all this all suddenly click?

I honestly don't know. I know it was a spontaneous experience. So in fact, the truth of that concept followed me through the next 20 years. That experience stuck in the back of my mind and would always be a source of comfort for me at times of any kind of exceptional personal stress or crisis.

The fact that, yes, there was a God and that, yes, everything was created, meant for me that everything had a purpose—even though I didn't pursue what the purpose necessarily was or what this God or creator had in mind for me or anyone else. It was just a comforting experience, which didn't really bloom or blossom until much later. At that point I must have been about 19, and I didn't begin to explore *Yiddishkeit* until I was 34.

I was brought up in a Conservative–Orthodox home in the Sheepshead Bay section of Brooklyn and went to public schools. From the age of 7 until 12, I had two kinds of lessons every day after school. I had *bar mitzvah* lessons or Hebrew lessons and clarinet lessons. And they were both aimed toward exactly the same day, the day of my *bar mitzvah*.

That morning I got up in *shul* and I read my *haftorah* and I *davened musaf* from the *amud* and I did it very well, and then that afternoon, all the books got closed and I really didn't ever expect them to be opened up again. I didn't follow up with any kind of Jewish affiliation or learning after the day of my *bar mitzvah*.

And the same thing was true of the clarinet. That was aimed for that night at the [*bar mitzvah*] party. And I played, and I played very well, and the clarinet went back in the case, and that was gonna be it for that as well.

But I always felt very comfortable with the fact that I was Jewish and very proud of the fact that I was Jewish. I knew we had good traditions. But it could have been intellectual laziness or maybe just adolescence, [but] I never really had any motivation to explore it at all.

I was always much too interested in other things. I was interested in girls. I was interested in going out with my friends, and once I got to college, in secular studies. The whole Jewish business was really something that didn't have any attraction for me at all.

At the same time that I didn't feel any religious yearnings, I certainly, like many members of my generation, felt spiritual yearnings. And those

It wasn't for another two months that I was actually emotionally capable of going to the lot where my car had been towed to actually see it. The car had flipped over five or six times and was completely crushed. All the windows were blown out, and it happened during the winter, [so] everything was totally soaked. It had snowed in the car and everything was totally wrecked. And I saw the *siddur* on the dashboard. And I took it out and it was in absolutely perfect condition.

It was impossible. Both the accident and the fact that I survived it— and the *siddur* being in perfect intact condition whereas everything else in the car was totally soaked and totally ruined—that was a signal from above for me to move in a certain direction. It was a sort of bottoming out, but not yet.

By the following summer, Ort had significantly increased his involvement with the Crown Heights community. He even started growing a beard.

Then in July I said, "Ach, I've had it [laughs]. Look, I'm divorced, I'm free, this is nice and this is interesting, but I just have to have a good time."

He decided to have it at the Concord Hotel in the Catskills. He spent three weeks there.

It must have cost me five or six thousand dollars. I had a really nice room all to myself and played tennis and went by the pool and played every night, shaved, of course, got a haircut, bought a new wardrobe.

That was really my bottom. Because after that, I said, "All right, this is totally meaningless." I mean, it didn't feel bad, it wasn't like a bad bottom, it wasn't like I'd sunk to the pits. It was more profound. It was like, there is nothing there for you. The other thing is for you. If I'm going to find any kind of happiness and inner peace and contentment and substance, it's not going to come from a life where I'm successful at work and then go out and have a successful social life—go out with nice people and eat at nice restaurants—and go home and go to sleep and do the whole thing the next day.

It never occurred to me that it would be possible to combine the two. I just knew I couldn't. I don't know why. It was either one or the other.

Ort decided to go through with his divorce and sell the house.

The normal course for me would have been to buy a studio or one-bedroom co-op apartment in Manhattan and go back to being single. But that really didn't appeal to me at all. So I decided, having been so fascinated by this chasidic community that I was getting to know, I realized that the only way I would really be able to experience what they were experiencing was to live with them.

And so I decided to join them as kind of a cultural anthropologist, who, as the only way he can really understand the natives, puts on the grass skirt and the hoop through his nose and bangs on the drum along with everybody. So I had that detachment in my own mind, and said, "Okay, I'm going to start growing a beard and wearing a *yarmulka* and I'm gonna wear my *tzitzis* and I'm gonna move in there and see what it's like, see if it really is for me."

So the few months prior to that—I moved in in September of that year—during the summer, I stopped shaving and started wearing a *yarmulka* every place except at work. I had this very interesting experience every day. I would kind of duck behind pillars in the Times Square [subway] station and see if anybody was looking and kind of swipe the thing off my head and put it in my pocket and go on to work.

So I moved in among the natives. I started taking classes at the local *yeshiva*, Hadar Ha Torah, there at night and I was working during the day. [I was] living this sort of chasidic existence kind of in the evening and trying to *daven* in the morning and then going off to work and taking the *yarmulka* [laughs] off my head and just feeling very bizarre about the whole situation. [By this time, he was a copy editor on the national news desk at the *Times*].

One Sunday I just decided that I would leave the *yarmulka* on my head [at work]. I figured, it's a Sunday, nobody's gonna be there and it'll all be very subtle; some people might notice, but maybe other people won't notice.

No matter how bad my expectations were, it couldn't have been worse. I think there was some kind of earthquake somewhere that Sunday [laughs] and the place was jampacked. It was, like, walking through the newsroom, everybody, and it was not my imagination . . . people would stop typing and look at me, and these were people who had known me for 15 years.

The reality is, if I had walked in that Sunday, instead of wearing a *yarmulka* . . . if I had just marched in with my hair peroxided blond and wearing a black leather miniskirt and fishnet stockings and high heels, I'm not kidding, people would have looked at me and they would have said, "Oh, there goes Ort, what's he into now?" And that would have been that and they would have gone back to their work or something.

But—and I'm very sincere about this—the fact that they saw me wearing a *yarmulka* said something much deeper and was much more unsettling to people than any other physical [item] I could have been wearing at that point.

Generally, what has been the reaction from colleagues, especially Jews?

The reaction is . . . it's a real problem for Jewish people who have non-Jewish spouses. Only because they tend to believe that I utterly reject their lives, which of course I don't. Somebody will inevitably say, "You know, my wife's not Jewish." And I say, "Well, *you* are. And God loves your wife, too. We all have different standards and it's certainly not for me to judge or tell you what to do or anything like that."

By the same token, you wouldn't attend one of their weddings, would you?

Absolutely not. [The situation has not arisen]. If somebody's Jewish and they tell me their girlfriend's not Jewish, I just respond—it's a practiced thing that I learned from other people—I respond with just no response. But in a work environment it's very tricky. You don't want to alienate people and you have to work with them. The best you can do is be an example to other people.

I've never gotten any scoffing. For the most part they are bright enough, well read enough to know what I am involved in is nothing shallow. And they understand that if there were to be a disagreement, it would be an extensive debate and I'm sure they're convinced I would have many points to make.

By the mid-1980s, Ort was at a crossroads as he considered remarriage.

That was when you really had to make the decision. Here I was, I'd been living in Crown Heights for about eight or nine months and I had to decide whether to get married to someone religious or not. If I'm not really sure about what I'm doing and if I'm not willing to have made a lifelong commitment, do I really want to drag another person into this? And drag children into this?

So I had to really sit down and ask myself, is this what you want for the rest of your life? Are you really committed? Yes, you'll have doubts. Yes, you'll have questions. Yes, you'll have desires. But are you really willing to make a commitment that this is the choice that you're gonna continue to make for the rest of your life no matter what? And I said yes. When I was able to say yes to myself, I went to friends and said I'm interested. [He was remarried about eight years ago to *ba'alat teshuvah*].

Do you ever have crisis of faith? How do you handle doubt?

You recognize that they're normal, that they're true opportunities for growth, that you don't leave them unresolved. You try to find the answers to whatever questions you have and you ask other people for advice and help and sometimes you just live with it. Ultimately *Hashem* gives us free will, and what that means is that he's gonna give us doubt, he's gonna give us questions. You're gonna wonder. But to me, it's really a matter of just plugging ahead and continuing to chose a certain path.

What are the downsides to becoming frum*?*

I can't eat lobster [laughs]. All of the downsides have to do with— and I'm not just saying this because this is what they teach you in *ba'al teshuvah* school—but seriously, all of the downsides have to do with our *yetzer hara* and have to do with the fact that, oh, I'm going out to San Francisco and this is on business, and oh I can't wait to get there, they have the greatest restaurants. . . . And I look at them; why are you telling me this? You know I can't eat in them.

I can't party, even if I wanted to. I'm limited in exercising my *yetzer hara* in different ways. But I know what it is; I know that that's where it's coming from. And I also know that you can't have it both ways. When you're leading a *frum* life there's an inner glow and an inner smile and you can't mess with that. You start letting other things in, if you allow yourself to stop growing and stop learning in Torah, then that inner glow and inner smile goes away.

To answer a question that you raised earlier, did you eventually determine that God does in fact really care whether you eat a cheeseburger? If so, why?

Yes, God does care; because God cares about me. God made the world in such a way that eating a cheeseburger is simply not spiritually good for me, not good for my soul. Why that is or how that works, is beyond me. But I accept as a matter of faith that He's looking out for me and He's warning me that this is one of these things, Yaakov, you could never figure out for yourself, you could never conclude that mixing milk and meat is injurious to your ability to experience spirituality. I say, "thanks a lot, I'll take your advice."

Overall, what has been the impact of frumkeit *on your life?*

It's given me the ability to do good. And it's given me a channel to do good. It shows me how I can help other people, how I can and should most constructively deal with my fellows and it also gives me the feeling of doing what God wants. So I feel that I have a pretty powerful force on my side, which is nice. And I feel that my behavior is something which would meet the approval of even the most demanding God [laughs]. And that produces a very good feeling in me. I can wake up in the morning and look at myself in the mirror and know that yesterday I did okay. And in the years before I was religious, many if not most days, I couldn't do that.

Yaakov Ort, 44, is special sections manager at the New York Times. *He and his wife live in Monsey, New York. They have five children.*

28
An Ode to
Grandma Batya

Judaism is the passion of my life. Judaism is my intellectual passion, it's
my emotional passion. . . . I'm not Shlomo Riskin who is a rabbi, a *rebbe*,
as a profession apart from me. My self-definition is that I teach Judaism.
That's what I'm about. That's the most essential part of my being.

*Rabbi Shlomo Riskin has been a pioneer in the Jewish outreach move-
ment, which got a jump-start in the early 1970s at his then-fledgling
Lincoln Square Synagogue in New York. Over the past couple decades,
Lincoln Square has served as one of the premier venues in America for
the recruitment of Jews to Orthodoxy.*

*Riskin's affinity for the not-yet-religious may be traceable to his own
background. He was raised in a nonobservant home in Brooklyn. His
father, the son of an ardent Communist, had never had a* bar mitzvah.
Riskin, then known as Steven, found Yiddishkeit *with the help of his
maternal grandmother, Batya, who had come to America in 1922 from
a shtetl in Poland and never learned to speak a proper sentence of English. But she was fluent when it came to her faith. God was a close friend.
As Riskin later wrote, she saw her young grandson as her family's last
hope to continue a tradition that seemed to be on the verge of extinction.*

My grandmother was a very remarkable woman. She had seven children and none of them were religious. I think that was part and parcel of
Europe, of the condition of Europeans who came to America. I think
she probably felt deep down that Judaism couldn't survive the Atlantic

Ocean. At that time, Saturday was a workday, and if you didn't work on Saturday, you couldn't make a living, etc., etc. There was a strong drive for acculturation.

My grandmother and my grandfather were extremely religious. She was extremely devout, prayed three times a day, knew Talmud.

We lived in Bedford-Stuyvesant, and the area had deteriorated tremendously in terms of its having been an upwardly mobile Jewish neighborhood. It turned into a poverty-ridden and drug-infested black area, and the [Jewish] day school that was there was much better than the public school. I was five when I went into the day school. I was the only one [grandchild] who went to *yeshiva*.

And my grandmother saw this as a golden opportunity. We were poor; that's why we couldn't move from the neighborhood. My grandmother, [who] also lived in the neighborhood, said she would supply us with meat so the house would remain kosher.

What was your homelife like?

My parents were not observant. My father was not *bar mitzvaed* even; he couldn't read Hebrew. His father was a very avid Communist, so my father never really got a religious background at all. Of course, in honor of my [maternal] grandmother, on Rosh Hashanah and Yom Kippur, the whole family went to *shul*. That was it. As far as other things were concerned, there was no real religious commitment in any way.

Riskin's first exposure to at-home Judaism came through Grandma Batya. He began spending more time with her when her husband became seriously ill and was confined to a convalescent home.

My home was two blocks away from my grandmother, so you see, Friday evening I began eating with my grandmother—from the age of eight on—and that became every Friday evening and every *yontif* evening. My grandmother moved when I was 12 years old to Bensonhurst, so I would spend many, many *Shabbatot* with her.

What was the impact of this on your development? What was it like?

Number one, the beauty of *Shabbos*, the whole idea of there being a special day. We used to study *parshat hashavua* together every Friday night and we even began to study *Gemara* together on Friday night. And it was really the beauty of *Shabbos*. I remember as a young child, I used to say that when I go to my grandmother's house I can actually touch *Shabbos*.

And that's really how I felt. It was very real. I was entranced to watch her with *hadlakat hanayrote*. I once even thought of writing a book about my grandmother called *God Was My Psychiatrist*. She would mention every child, every in-law, every grandchild, every great-grandchild, and you know, thank God for their successes than pray for what was needed. She would pour out her heart to God. God was a very beloved friend to her. And I watched this and I saw her deep religiosity and I saw *Shabbat* and *yom tov* and the life cycle.

What about all this appealed to you?

I think it was *Shabbat*; I think it was the *zemirot*, the notion of singing songs; it was the *chumash* learning. It was the specialness I felt in comparison to my own home, a certain intellectualism. There was a certain drama of the cycle of the year. There was a certain depth and warmth that was lacking in a secular environment.

There was also a very profound humanism, and that also made a very strong impression on me as I was developing intellectually.

To illustrate his grandmother's universalist ethics, Riskin tells the story of his then 82–year-old grandmother going door-to-door for a month to find suitable lodgings for her Gentile boarder who would be forced to relocate when she moved to a new neighborhood.

I was also close with my paternal grandfather who was also a very deeply principled person, but in a totally different direction, but with a . . . focus on universalism and humanism. I saw from my grandmother that this was part and parcel of Judaism, as well. And part and parcel of religious Judaism too, so that was very important to me.

I would add another vignette that I'll never forget. I used to go to the Turkish bath regularly with my father and my grandfather. It was 1954 and I was 14 years old, and we used to have these big debates, and he [his grandfather, the Communist] was anti-Israel even at that time and pro-Russia.

And then it came out about the "Doctors' Plot" [a Stalinist anti-Semitic conspiracy in Russia] and he was very shook up. And he began reminiscing about *Shabbat* in Brisk—he came from Brisk—in his parents' home. And it sounded like *Shabbat* at my grandmother's home. And he turned to me and said, "It could very well be that I gave up too much for a wrong ideal." I remember the words to this day. So obviously it had a very strong impact and it was a confirmation of what I had been thinking all along.

Was it a fairly smooth transition for you in terms of religious advancement, or was there backsliding? It must have been difficult for a child.

I'll tell you one incident that stands out. I was not very athletic, but somehow I got along pretty well with even the wilder black kids in the neighborhood. A group of guys came and wanted me to go skating on *Shabbos* morning. I must have been eight or nine years old, and I was very complimented that they wanted me to go skating with them. And I went and I finished skating.

And I guess I was aware of the fact that it was wrong somewhere along the line, but you know . . . I lived in many worlds and right and wrong was a difficult. . . . Anyway, we finished skating when I would usually come home from *shul*. I went to one *shul* and my grandmother went to another *shul*, and I used to try to meet her to wish her good *Shabbos*.

So it was just about the time I would have ordinarily come home from *shul*, and the skates were still flung over my shoulder, and I ran up to my grandmother, she was coming home from *shul*, to wish her good *Shabbos*, and she looked at me . . . no reproach. She didn't say anything negative, but I could see in her eyes very real disappointment.

And at that moment, I saw two things—I would never *mechallel Shabbos* again because I don't want her to ever look at me like that with those eyes of disappointment. And I also thought since then I never want God to look at me like that. I've never been afraid of divine punishment. But I have always been and always am afraid that when I stand before the *keesay hacavode*, that God will be disappointed.

Did your embrace of Yiddishkeit *cause any conflict with your parents?*

There was surprisingly little conflict. Look, you have to realize that I was very intellectual. My parents recognized the fact that I was a very good student and I felt not only their love all the time and their support, but I really felt their respect. And fundamentally they allowed me to make my own decisions.

However, his decisions were often sharply divergent from those his parents made. One Shabbos *afternoon, for example, his mother was smoking a cigarette—a clear* halachic *violation—when one of Riskin's friends came to call for him. His friend, Saul Berman, was the son of a local rabbi and later became a rabbi himself. Riskin's mother answered the door with the cigarette in her hand.*

My mother never got ruffled. She didn't believe in religion. She was very secure in her nonbelief and she was very anxious to acculturate into American society. She knew it was a rabbi's son and she was embarrassed. It was the first and the last time really that I ever saw her embarrassed. And she put the cigarette in back of her. Saul Berman understood.

My mother looked at me and she said, "You know, I think God made a mistake putting you and me together." And I said, "I don't think so. First of all, because God doesn't make mistakes, and second of all, because he's teaching me to love people who aren't observant Jews." I think it's been important for me because I've always loved people who were not observant Jews as well.

Riskin went on to BTA, Yeshiva University High School of Brooklyn. During his senior year, he experienced a crisis of faith. He began to have his doubts about Orthodoxy. As a result, he shifted gears and decided to attend Columbia University and the Jewish Theological Seminary, a Conservative institution.

I had certain theological questions—the divine authorship of the Bible, the role of history in Jewish law and sociology in Jewish law and psychology in Jewish law and the ability of Judaism to speak to the 21st century.

Questions you felt weren't being answered in the milieu you were in?

That's right, questions that weren't even taken seriously. It seemed to me that at the seminary they were taken much more seriously.

I met with the [JTS] admissions team and they asked me questions and I answered the questions and they asked me if I had any questions for them. And I said, "Yes I do. As an Orthodox Jew, I know that if I have a *shailah*, I open up the *Shulchan Aruch*. As a Conservative Jew, what do I open up?"

One of the interviewers told him that "it's not as simple as the Shulchan Aruch." *A Conservative Jew, he was told, would find his answer in "the wholeness of the Jewish tradition," which included an impressive array of sources, from the* chumash *to the Mishnah to latter-day commentators.*

And I must say I liked that answer. Intellectually I found it very, very satisfying. It was interesting enough to me, and they seemed to have responded extremely favorably to me. I had more or less thought in my mind this is where I'm gonna go.

And they really wanted me to come and they offered me a very nice scholarship and they said they would like to assign one of their best rabbinical students to be like a big brother.

His "big brother" would show him the ropes and learn with him until he graduated high school and also once he entered the seminary. When

*the "big brother" came down and introduced himself, Riskin noticed
something unusual about him.*

He wasn't wearing a *keepah*. And that bothered me a little bit, but I
thought to myself, listen, you know Judaism doesn't stand on the *keepah*.

Anyway, the interview ended and people were very warm. And he
[the big brother] walked me out. And he stopped by a water fountain to
take a drink of water—obviously without a *keepah* and without a *bracha*.
And I said to myself, you can't talk about the fullness of the Jewish tradition on the one hand and drink water without a *bracha*. And I knew
that I could never go to the seminary.

*Meanwhile, Riskin was offered a full scholarship to Harvard, and his
parents were thrilled.*

They felt that I would be the lawyer that would bring the family out
of Bedford-Stuyvesant. And I wanted to go to YU [Yeshiva University].
And I'm sure it was a bitter pill for my parents to swallow, but I must
say they accepted it.

Why was it important for you to go to YU?

I was going to go to Harvard really, and then I spent *Shavuout* at YU.
And I was learning [Torah] all night, and I loved to learn. And [during]
birchat kohanim the next morning, I made a *neder* that I would go to
YU. And I knew I had to make it as a *neder* because there would be a
great deal of pressure, even internal pressure, to go to Harvard.

What was it about the Shavuout *experience that made you decide at
that point that you must go to YU?*

It was a sense of the eternity of Judaism. I had the sense, and I still
have that sense [during] *birchat kohanim*, that there are thousands of
years that have gone through to me, a chain that has been unbroken since
Aaron. And that that chain of Jewish being is more important to me than
any other of the links of my life.

When I was in college [at YU] there were two people who were very
strong influences on me. Professor Louis Feldman, who is a classics
scholar, and he was my professor initially for Latin because I still wanted
to be a lawyer. I had memorized all of Clarence Darrow's speeches.

And then in my sophomore year I had Rabbi [Joseph B.] Soloveitchik,
and the profundity of Rabbi Soloveitchik . . . I read all of [his] writings
obviously. And in terms of the theological and intellectual questions I
had, within Rabbi Soloveitchik's writings and teachings, if I didn't find
answers to all the questions—and I didn't find answers to all the questions—I certainly found a legitimacy to the asking of the questions.

Not only the legitimacy, but the necessity of asking the proper questions. Because only the right questions would produce the necessary tensions from whence creativity could emerge, halachic and theological creativity. In Rav Soloveitchik's writings and teachings I certainly saw the ability to accept the secular world fearlessly and the teachings of science and philosophy and every branch of intellectual endeavor, together with Judaism being the ultimate axiological system [value system] by which we live.

In 1960, Grandma Batya died at the age of 90. Around this time, Riskin went to Israel for the first time, graduated from YU, dropped his plans to be a lawyer, and decided he wanted to be a rabbi.

I wanted to be a *rebbe* and I wanted to go into Jewish scholarship—I think [for] the same reasons that made me decide against Harvard. I think I realized that the links to the Jewish tradition were the strongest links in my life. I felt that was what my life should be dedicated to.

And the truth was that Judaism then became a passion, Jewish learning then became a passion. Added to that was my success in outreach, although I didn't think yet of being a pulpit rabbi. When I was in Israel, I led a group of mostly nonreligious collegiates and high school students and I saw that I could have an influence on them. And afterwards, that summer I got very much involved in the seminars of YU, [outreach programs] that would go out to communities all over the country. And then, going into the rabbinate and teaching Torah became something that was very logical.

Judaism is the passion of my life. Judaism is my intellectual passion, it's my emotional passion, it's what . . . I'm not Shlomo Riskin who is a rabbi, a *rebbe*, as a profession apart from me. My self-definition is that I teach Judaism. That's what I'm about. That's the most essential part of my being.

Rabbi Shlomo Riskin, 55, is chief rabbi of the city of Efrat in Israel and is dean of the Ohr Torah Institutions of Israel. He and his wife live in Efrat and have four children.

29
A Rational Choice

And so I said, now wait a minute. Am I just gonna follow this group like a lemming . . . or am I gonna do my own thinking and have my own values?

Being a physicist, Tuvia Rome is also a rationalist. But things aren't quite as clear-cut to him as they once were. Or perhaps his view is clearer now than ever before, and he's simply using a different lens. Whatever. The fact is, Rome once felt that his five senses could tell him everything he needed to know about anything. It was a neat and tidy view of the world. And it was woefully inadequate, as Rome would soon discover. What was missing from the equation was the suprarational, such as the hand of God. He first got an inkling of that 36 years ago on his 21st birthday. His father was in the hospital for tests at the time.

I got out of class at 12 o'clock and had a feeling or a premonition or a sense that maybe I should not do what I was planning on doing, namely going downtown and shopping, but I should go and visit my father.

And I examined it, and said is there any rational reason for this? Is there any basis for this? And I concluded that there was no basis, it was not rational, and therefore I went ahead with my plan and went downtown and went shopping. When I got home at four o'clock, my uncle was standing on the porch and he said, "You better get down to the hospital real fast." My father was in the midst of an operation, from which he did not pull out.

Had I listened to that hunch or premonition, I may have had one last opportunity to see him alive. So that, I guess, caused me to think that maybe there is more to it than just pure rationality and that some of these hunches or feelings should be heeded or respected.

I was raised in a very Jewish, very traditional, nonobservant, very Zionist home in Vancouver, British Columbia. We went to *shul* on Rosh Hashanah and Yom Kippur and sometimes for a holiday or on a Saturday when someone had a *simcha.*

My maternal grandfather kept *Shabbos*, but since he didn't play baseball the rest of the week, like I did, I saw no real distinction between his Saturday and the rest of his week. Someone that I saw as being nonactive the rest of the week; so what if he kept *Shabbos*?

When my father died, the question arose of whether I should say *Kaddish* or not. Going to *shul* with all these *boruch atahs*, when you're not so sure there's an *atah* out there, didn't make a lot of sense.

So then I made what I essentially call a psychologically defensive decision. Instead of trying to figure out the right thing, I tried to figure out the wrong thing. And I essentially calculated the following: If I go to *shul* and say *Kaddish* and all this kind of stuff and it turns out to be a mistake, what's the consequences? I wasted some time, big deal. It wouldn't be the first or last time.

On the other hand, if I didn't do it, and subsequently it turns out to be a mistake, it's something you can't undo; it could be psychologically messy. So to protect myself against the dangers of making a bad decision that would have psychological ramifications, other than just wasting time, I decided to go to *shul* regularly and say *Kaddish*.

But at the same time, not being confident there's an *atah* around, it didn't make sense to *daven*. So when they *davened*, I *davened* a little bit, but basically what I did is I bought myself a Hertz *chumash* and a Hertz *siddur* [Rabbi Hertz being the editor of both works] and while they were *davening*, I read. And when it came time for *Kaddish*, I said *Kaddish*. But unbeknownst to me, that gave me a pretty good education in Judaism. So I sat and learned and got a pretty decent education.

At this time, I viewed the Gemara as being an obscure, irrelevant, nitpicking kind of useless "medieval" document. I had no respect for it and no desire to learn about it. But between *mincha* and *maariv* the rabbi would learn from the Gemara. And I would say to myself, hey, that's insightful. Hey, that's clever; hey, that shows knowledge of human nature. So gradually my stereotype, my view of the Gemara changed. The negative obscurantist image faded and I became more respectful of it.

These were all part of my re-education and breaking down of stereotypes. It was all happening without my thinking about it, without my having any intention, without re-evaluating. It was just the flow of life.

A pivotal moment in his religious development came while he was a graduate student at Syracuse University.

I was 23 and I went into New York City for my second visit with a group of friends. We were all young graduate students and reasonably arrogant. We thought we were the elite. I stayed with a cousin of my best friend from Vancouver who was studying at the Jewish Theological Seminary, Jimmy Diamond, and he's probably had more influence on me per unit time than any other person. I've only met him three times in my life.

So I spent Friday night with him, and that's the first time I saw people my age keeping *Shabbat*. And right at the beginning of the meal, Jimmy takes his wife's hand and he recites a poem to her ["Aishes Chayil"]. And of course, here I was into poetry, and I had just come in for [a] poetry [reading], and this was very impressive. This was something I didn't know about, that this is part of the *Shabbos* ritual. I was very impressed with him. And we had great discussions, and it was very nice.

I thought that there was a peacefulness, there was a beauty, there was grace, there was intellectual content. We talked about religion and science all night; it was substantial. There were perspectives that I didn't know about.

During the same trip, Rome and his buddies went to a poetry reading at a fancy Madison Avenue art gallery, where they were treated to an afternoon of pretentious drivel.

But I couldn't help noticing how respectful everyone was, not only my friends. Later, the woman who ran the gallery told us about the various exhibits on the various walls. Regarding a watercolor exhibit, she said, "You might not fully understand it, but don't walk away from it too quickly; look at it, get into it, try to appreciate what the artist is saying, and then you will really appreciate the genius of the artist, who is only eight years old." So I burst out laughing, what a put-on. But nobody else laughed.

And my friends sort of looked embarrassed, you know, they brought this boor down from Syracuse. So I left there thinking, wait a minute. We—graduate students, the intellectual elite, the cultural elite—were very respectful to this garbagey poet and really bought this business about the profundity of a watercolor splashing by an eight-year-old kid. Now these same people have disdain for what Jim [Diamond] and [his wife]

Judy do. They would say what Jim and Judy were doing is obsolete, medieval, superstitious.

And so I said, now wait a minute, am I just gonna follow this group like a lemming or whatever or am I gonna do my own thinking and have my own values? Maybe I didn't buy what Jim and Judy were doing, but I recognized that there was meaning there, there's content, there's sub-stance—you don't have to agree with it—but you can still recognize something there and be at least as respectful to that as [to] a garbagey poet and some eight-year-old splashing watercolor.

And at that time I guess I really started more seriously doing my own thinking and my own evaluations. And in a short period of time I had quite a large number of experiences. One actually moved me to tears. We had a Hillel program at Syracuse, and only three or four people showed up. The speaker just opened up a card table, sat down, opened up a *Tanach* and started reading from Isaiah. Now this was written 2,000 years ago, but it was an accurate description of Jewish history. It blew my mind. What this guy [Isaiah] was saying long before was calling it just as it happened. And I was actually moved to tears. So, over a period of time I had a whole series of experiences.

What did they have in common?

They raised questions: What does it mean? What's the significance? Does it have relevance to me? Should I think more along these lines? I was, I guess, in the data-gathering stage. And then I spent a *Shabbat* with a cousin of mine by marriage who I was meeting for the first time. He and I had a long discussion about science and religion. Actually it all started when I started talking about "those fanatics," *chasidim*.

And he said, "Well, let's define our terms." And we got into a long discussion on science and religion. He, however, knew both. He was a graduate of a *yeshiva*; he was very learned and he also knew mathemat-ics, statistics, and science. It was the first time I ever lost an argument about science and religion.

What position had you taken in the argument?

That science was right and religion was wrong. So here was the first time I had lost, and I recognized that it was related to the content and it wasn't just related to the argumentation style. And I remember sitting with him and I was thinking, it's really interesting, it's really strange how all these things just sort of happened. And then he said the thing that was the turning point. He says, "Well, you've been shown. And you're in a very flexible position now. You're a new person in town now in Syracuse; people don't really know you, unlike back in Vancouver where people knew you and had expectations. You've been shown. For whatever reason, you've been shown. And it's up to you. You can accept it or you can reject it. But I warn you . . . you probably won't get a second chance. Either you act on it now or you don't."

And immediately what flashed into my mind were words I hadn't read for years; they went all the way back to the early years of high school. In *Julius Caesar* by Shakespeare: "There's a tide in the affairs of men which taken at the crest leads on to fortune," and paraphrasing, if you miss it you're washed out with the tide.

So his comment and that quotation flashed together in my mind. For some reason the focus of the whole discussion was about *Shabbat*. So after I left his place, I also remembered back when I was reading the Hertz *siddur*. What stuck in my mind was a comment there by an anti-Semitic Protestant theologian in Germany around 1881 who had made the observation that, talking about the Jews and the Sabbath, anyone who has not experienced the Sabbath cannot know what it's like. And I bought that, just like you cannot know what skiing is like without experiencing it.

So somehow or other I had to make a decision about *Shabbat*—keep it or don't keep it. I agreed with [the anti-Semite]. I didn't know what *Shabbos* was like because I'd never kept it. So the only intelligent thing to do is to run an experiment, and keep *Shabbat* long enough to make an intelligent decision to determine if I want to or don't want to keep it.

So I started keeping *Shabbos*. Actually, I sort of kept it in a half-assed manner. But while I was doing it, I spent some time reading to find out what *Shabbat* was about. I got the flavor of it. Nevertheless, after a while, I decided that's enough, I'm gonna drop the experiment. I think I understand it well enough. I was gonna stop keeping *Shabbat*.

It wasn't all that fulfilling. Of course, I was doing it all by myself. I was doing it totally without any support system. All my friends were either non-Jewish or nonobservant. And after a while, you know, it's interesting but not for me.

Just at this time, a guy gives me a book, called *The Sabbath* by Dayan Grunfeld. I guess it was the right book at the right time. And it really described keeping *Shabbos* properly. And I said, well, before dropping it I'm gonna keep it properly. And I got to like it. And it became very meaningful. So I decided to keep *Shabbat*. And that started the thing going.

At this point, Rome was keeping kosher at home, but not outside. He would have Friday night dinner at a "Jewish-style" but nonkosher restaurant.

About a year later, I was driving home and I decided to stop at this restaurant and have a couple of franks for dinner. And I remember saying to myself, well, I have kosher franks at home. But these are grilled and mine are boiled. Grilled is much better. So I sat in the car and argued with myself. Finally I decided I'm going into the restaurant to have the grilled franks. But the argument took so long that the restaurant was closed. That's when I stopped eating nonkosher. I figured just like with [the premonition concerning] my father; one thing I learned from that is when you sort of get a signal, don't ignore it.

My becoming observant was concurrent with two other major things in my intellectual life. One was getting to understand physics as opposed to just doing physics. As an undergrad, basically you learn how to do it and in grad school you learn to understand it, understand its power and its limitations and its characteristics. That was very important in reconciling the religious view, a Jewish view, with science.

Secondly, I started off in grad school in theoretical physics and eventually got my Ph.D. in experimental physics. So it was a move from the purely thought to the doing. And I correlate that with my move from being thoughtful about Judaism to doing, namely, *mitzvos*. And I would say that they went pretty parallel, the movement from primarily thought to combining thought and action.

So now do you have any problem reconciling science with Torah?

No, absolutely not. In fact, in many ways you could say lots of times when you learn something in science, you can say, "Oh, so that's how God arranges to do it."

What has been the net impact of observant Judaism on your life?

I feel much more comfortable in the universe. I understand it better and more, although still imperfectly, both the physical and the nonphysical, both the Jewish world and the world of history. It's like you have choice. You can understand it a bit more or a bit less. And I find that by being observant, first of all, [it] makes you participatory. And there's tremendous meaning associated with the various actions.

What about the ones that some regard as nitpicky? Do they all have meaning to you?

The difference in engineering and science and computers between something that works and something that doesn't work is the nitpicking in the details. If something is roughly okay, it doesn't work. If you put all the parts of a car together and the carburetor isn't tuned just right, it isn't gonna run. A computer system that's 99.99 percent okay, is a hunk of junk. If one talks about the Talmud being nitpicky, that nitpicky is minor nitpicky compared to the General Theory of Relativity.

The characteristic of a system that works is attention to detail—whether it's in the physical world, the engineering world or the scientific world. Especially in the computer world, it has to be 100 percent. And therefore I find that the focus on details in observant Judaism is, one, less than in computers and, two, necessary for it to work.

Tuvia Rome, 57, is a "refugee from physics who is working in computers." He lives in Manhattan and is single.

30
The Best-Laid Plans

We didn't go as far as to say *Hashem* was actually guiding us, but there was something there.

After Hy Rubenstein graduated from college, he heard about a great deal on a trip to Israel. The package—geared to Jews like Hy who had little religious background—was underwritten by a philanthropist, so it was dirt cheap. Participants only had to put in half a day at a yeshiva, and they'd have the rest of the day to themselves. Tours were included. "I needed a break," said Rubenstein, who envisioned a restful vacation rather than a religious experience. He figured he could kick back, sleep through the learning sessions and then play tourist till he dropped. Once he was there, however, things didn't go exactly according to plan.

The first decision I made [in Israel] is that this is the land of my history, my heritage, so I decided I was gonna wear a *yarmulka* all the time in *Eretz Yisroel*. Of course it was a very small, knit *keepah*. You put the baseball cap on top of it and nobody notices.

So I go there and the group is all from Brooklyn [Rubenstein's hometown] and Queens, all with little or no background, and we were going because we thought it would be a great trip. Nobody except my best friend was even interested in anything at this point.

So what happens in the *yeshiva*, you get up in the morning and they would *daven*, and that meant I had more time to sleep. Then we'd eat breakfast and then go to classes. The *rosh yeshiva* had a masters in philosophy, so we were always awake for his classes; they were very interesting. Everything else . . . it would have been real nice if we were interested, but we weren't. We just didn't care.

The first couple of weeks all the trips were planned by the *yeshiva*. I visited the graves of people, I had no idea who they were—all the *tzaddikim*, and they didn't have any background to give us, so okay, another grave, another rabbi, very good.

But somethng was seeping into us—in spite of all this, I might say. We started asking each other questions, like why are they doing this to us? Why are they showing us all these graves? Who goes on a grave thing? We started laughing among ourselves, not asking the *rabbeyim* or anything. There must be some reason. Then we kind of went to him— the guy who got stuck with us to take us on the trip—as a group, and asked him, "Why are you doing this to us?" And he said, "You have to feel *Yiddishkeit* to get it."

I saw the Rambam's grave and I didn't know who the Rambam was at the time, so I couldn't be impressed by his gravesite. But we were seeing how other people visiting the graves were impressed. And it kinda took on something. If they're interested, maybe we should be interested.

Rubenstein said he and members of his group became far more interested while they were camping out in S'fat, one of Israel's most mystical cities. There, they met another group of students who were undergoing a similar change.

We all realized there was some kind of feeling we were all feeling. Nobody understood it; we couldn't really put our fingers on it. But it just felt different to be there. Since there was another group talking to us, we figured, well, it's not just us.

We went to this cemetery in S'fat and saw another bunch of *tzaddikim*, and there was a *mikvah* in the mountain there. So this guy took us to the *mikvah*, [and] he said, "Ya gotta go [into] the *mikvah*." We didn't want to start getting all our clothes off and jumping into a very cold pool in the side of a mountain. And one of the guys who was with us said, "Why should I do this?" And the leader went into his standard shpiel on why we should be doing all these things, but it still didn't make any sense to us.

The mikvah was situated in a cave which had a large steel door at its entrance. The door was open when the student spoke up.

And he [the student] started walking toward the door and he says, "I feel I should go in but I don't know why. Why don't you just give me a sign whether I should go in." And as he says that, the door closes. And we figured, alright, coincidence, big deal, who cares. So he turns around and says, "All right, I'll go in." And he takes one step back toward the back [toward the pool] and the door swings open again. And we kind of look out to see if there's any kind of wind or anything, and there's no wind. Absolute calm, nobody's out there. So we all took off our clothes [laughs] and jumped in the *mikvah*, still not sure why we're doing this.

Later that day, the group witnessed another episode at the cave where the ancient heroine Chanah *and her martyred sons are said to be buried. Candles flickered in the absolute calm.*

We backed out very reverently from the cave. And we just started realizing, all these silly little things that were happening . . . we didn't become *frum* immediately, but it was adding to the feeling that there's something special about this place. We didn't go as far as to say *Hashem* was actually guiding us, but something was there.

You were in Israel for six weeks. By the time you left, how had you changed? What did you take from that trip?

Not much. I got off of the plane and my family meets me in the airport, and I'm still wearing the *keepah* because I felt I should. My sister comes up to me and hands me a McDonald's hamburger, and said, "I heard you missed hamburgers." I ate it, but it felt a little funny.

Was it a cheeseburger?

Of course. I loved cheeseburgers. The next day, I take off the *keepah*, of course, and adopt my normal routine. I start law school in the fall, I'm back to normal, except I do realize there's a culture shock.

Meanwhile, the friend who told him about the trip to Israel was becoming more observant.

He was slowly making changes in his life and I was going along for the ride when I was with him because he was my best friend. But nothing major with me. What I did do is every night, I would think through all the things that happened during the day, and remembering things that seemed to have some kind of outside [spiritual] influence in *Eretz Yisroel*, I tried to identify things throughout my day that may have had an outside influence—[such as] this happened and it shouldn't have happened that way, I got a higher grade than I maybe deserved here. And I kind of went over my day with that in mind before I went to sleep. And I started to notice that there were things that seemed to have [an outside influence].

Rubenstein mentioned an incident in which he escaped injury after running full-speed into a concrete pillar during a pick-up football game.

And I thought, maybe I'm being saved for something else. I don't know what. Those are the types of things I was thinking about. It could be absolutely nothing or there could be something here.

But I was missing the feeling—which now I can call a spiritual feeling, but was then just a feeling—of connection when we were in Israel. So I started to put on *tefillin*. I did put on *tefillin* the last week I was in Israel because I felt I had to do something. So I went to my friend and said, "I'll get up early, will you help me?" I didn't *daven* because I didn't know what to say, but I put on *tefillin*. When I came home I said, "Lemme do that again," because I felt good when I did that.

I felt when I was in *Eretz Yisroel* I had a historical connection with all the Jewish people who came before me in *Eretz Yisroel*. And I'm saying I feel it, but how do I connect into that. I couldn't *daven*, because I didn't know the prayers; my Hebrew was very rusty. I was trying to do something to get closer to this feeling I was having.

It was similar to, if you go into a garden and you smell the flowers and it smells so good and you kind of get closer to the flower to smell it better. I was getting the feeling and now I was saying, what do I have to do to get closer to this feeling? Because this feeling is really great.

So I start putting on *tefillin*—and then taking off *tefillin* and taking off my *keepah* and going to law school. Three months later or so, my father had a mild stroke and went into the hospital for bypass.

While he was in for bypass, I'm starting to pray for him while I have my *tefillin* on. And I start to take off my *keepah*, as I did every weekday, and I said, you know, why am I doing this? Why am I taking it off? Is it gonna kill me to keep it on? So I kept it on.

You gotta realize that I'm now halfway through the freshman year of law school. So all of a sudden I walk into class with a *keepah*, and everyone's saying what's going on here? It was very embarrassing. First I would jokingly say, "Midterms are coming up, and I need all the help I can get." And when that didn't satisfy people, I said, "Look, my father just went to the hospital, he's having bypass surgery, anything I can do would help." And that they accepted—neither one of which was the real reason. I had been putting on *tefillin* for about three months now and then taking off my *keepah*, and I said that's not consistent, I want to be consistent.

Another friend, who also was becoming more observant, invited Rubenstein to shul after noticing he was wearing a yarmulka in public.

It hadn't even occurred to me that there was another step. I figured, you put the *keepah* on and you're finished. He [the friend] never ridiculed me or asked why. He just picked me up for *shul* on Friday afternoon and we went and I had no idea what I was doing.

It was a Young Israel [Orthodox synagogue], and I was very comfortable. A lot of *ba'alei teshuvah* were there. They all understood immediately without asking me any kind of embarrassing questions. They said, "Let me show you where to go. Let me show you how to do it," and they said, "Here's the prayers, read this and this." And over the years, they brought me along very nicely and easily.

My belief in God was coming from the daily review of what was going on in my life, and saying, I see the hand of God in things, little things. And maybe at that time I was seeing things that didn't exist. If I was walking down the street and somebody was saying the wrong thing about people and they tripped over a rock, I'd say, "God just pushed you a little bit to not say those things."

And I started to believe it, like, why not? Why couldn't this be? Every single day I would go over the things that happened good, the things that happened bad and see that there was a global entity above that seemed to be guiding things. I could say it's happening to me here in Brooklyn, too. I could look back at things that had happened previously and say, yeah, that fits into the mold also. No, I didn't see *Eliyahu Hanavi* come down and tell me what to do. It was just kind of a slow thing, and that's where my belief came from.

Now the question was: How do I plug into this Jewish religion and why is the Jewish religion the correct religion? Thank God there was nothing else at the time. I guess if the Moonies had come by at that moment, I would have been ripe [for] picking.

My friend who took me to *shul* led me in a specific direction. And every time I would learn a *halachah* or a custom or something, or start delving into the history of Judaism, I would play it against what I was looking for. I'd say, "Is this what I'm looking for? Is this showing me that there really is a God that has a daily influence on what we're doing?" And of course I found that the answers were always fine, they were always correct.

At the same time, I went to lectures geared toward *ba'alei teshuvah* in Brooklyn. I was still skeptical; I didn't jump in with both feet. I went step by step and I was saying, well, what about other religions? And people were always willing to talk about other religions and show where other religions did fall short in various ways.

Unfortunately, I didn't have a rabbi. I didn't go to a rabbi and say teach me. And I didn't have a *yeshiva* I could just jump to. So I was still kind of doing it on my own, going very slowly and probably making dozens of mistakes. I was also still living at home with my parents—I was still in law school—which kind of maybe slowed down my return.

During law school he decided to marry a woman whose religious background was similar to his.

And I said, it's all or nothing at all—kosher home, *Shabbos, mikvah,* everything. And she agrees and we go to the rabbi and he gives us everything we need to get going and we do it. We get married between my second and third year of law school, and that's when we start making the break. Now we're going to be absolutely positively *frum.* Of course it didn't work.

I was wearing a *keepah* now all the time, walking into *trayf* restaurants. So I wore a cowboy hat so that no one would see that I was wearing a *keepah.* Even though we had made the commitment, when we found things that were going against the commitment, we'd say, alright, just this once or just this twice. So we were taking steps backwards all the time—not liking it, but doing it.

We did have conflicts with the family, because now we didn't want to eat at their house, or only eat certain things on paper or plastic. Both her parents and mine. So we're having a lot of problems with that, both trying to explain to them our level and trying ourselves to keep the level, because we knew we cheated now and then. But we both felt it was important to keep *kashrus.* It made us feel good to keep kosher and keep *Shabbos* and to start to keep the *mitzvos.*

They got married in June 1979. The next year, Rubenstein graduated from law school and entered the military. He was assigned to a base in Arizona; the family moved there in April 1981.

There was another family in the military that we became very close with, completely *frum.* They were able to bring us along and say, "You know you can do this. You can be in this army town and still hold onto certain levels." Our levels just kept going up and up and up.

Every time our parents came to see us, our level was higher and that would cause fights. [Our] parents [were] telling us we were being ridiculous about the restrictions we put on ourselves, *Shabbos* and things like that. We started to have kids—every year—and after the second one they said that's enough. And after the third one they said that's enough and after the fourth, I think my mother-in-law wanted to kill me.

Even our friends . . . the non-Jewish ones said whatever you wanna do, that's fine. The Jewish ones would see us get more serious and therefore the gap between us got bigger, between our level of observance and theirs, and they were more threatened by it. We always seemed to have more problems with the Jews than with the non-Jews.

Arizona is not known as a bastion of frumkeit. *Didn't you feel isolated?*

We did. Sometimes we'd look around and say, it would be so much easier if we weren't *frum*, especially in this environment. Who would know? Yet there was always something tugging on us and pulling on us, saying don't do that. We didn't always have the feeling I had in *Eretz Yisroel*. And sometimes we had no reason to keep going other than we knew intellectually at that point that it was right, and that may have helped us through the emotional part.

How did you know it was right intellectually?

By then we had done enough reading and there were enough things in English that we were able to read that we felt very comfortable with Judaism being the right religion. And not only that, but both of us realized that, at least for us, once you made the decision that there is a God— that he did create the Torah and he did create the world and the Torah tells you how to live your role, and that this was handed down for thousands and thousands of years—it felt hypocritical to us to say we're Jews and we're not gonna follow all the rules and regulations. It never occurred to us to be halfway.

The Rubensteins would sometimes spend Shabbos *or* yom tovim *in Tucson, which had a tiny observant community and a rabbi "who was able to* mekarev *anything," said Rubenstein.*

He was a very dynamic person. He showed us the love of God; he showed us how you could love the religion. We had been doing it, we had been feeling things, but we really had not connected these things. He was able to take your intellectual side and your emotional side and show you how they connected with the total love of *mitzvos*. From that point forward, we just shot up.

Are you ever troubled by doubt? How do you deal with it?

Sometimes I'm reading through a Gemara, and I'm saying, "Wait a second, why am I doing this? You know, I'm just reading words and it's not meaning anything to me." And it is hard. I'll try to go hear a lecture or an influential speaker or try to see a *rav*, and say, "Could we just talk for a little bit?"

When we were in Israel seeing the graves, [and] I was seeing what other people were experiencing, I was living vicariously through their experience—seeing there must be a lot of importance with this grave because they're really getting a lot out of seeing it. So I try to do the same thing [now]. I try to find people who still have the fire really burning in them and try to catch a little of that flame.

My 12-year-old daughter Shoshana did on *Shabbos* tell me that she hates being a Jew, which goes back to your question of how we deal with doubt. She was saying there are lots of Jews who just act horribly, *frum* Jews, and she doesn't like being associated with these people.

I tried to say if women acted horribly does that mean you wouldn't want to be a woman anymore? [I was] trying to say you can't not be a woman; you also can't not be Jewish. But she's having some doubts now, as to where God is. And I tried to have a conversation with her, saying you've got to feel God by yourself; I can't force God on you. And only if you look and try to see where He is in your life will you be able to accept the fact that He is in your life. I don't know how I'm gonna jump-start her, although she hasn't taken any actions in line with her fears or doubts.

Are there any downsides to becoming frum*?*

I can't send my children to their relatives for a couple weeks in the summer, because nobody else is *frum*. Nobody else is kosher. Some of my relatives have gone out of their way [to accommodate us] whenever we come to visit, but it's still not a *Shabbos* environment. Others haven't done anything to accommodate us. It's a struggle.

Overall, what has been the impact of Yiddishkeit *on your life?*

My daughter [Shoshana] asked me a question: What does this all mean? Don't we all just live and die and who cares? And I always felt that the answer was no, but I couldn't prove it. Now with becoming *frum*, I feel this is right. Even if there isn't, *chas v'shalom*, a God and Judaism doesn't really mean anything, it's still the proper way to live. *Derech eretz* is still the proper way to act toward people, etc., etc. It also makes sense out of life, that you're doing it for a purpose. Even if your purpose only is to help everybody you can on this world while you live, and when you die you become dust. That's a good enough purpose for me to live and get up every day.

But you can still be a good person and never crack a chumash*. Why do you need all this religious stuff to be a decent person?*

Because that's my tie-in with the 3,000 years of the Jewish religion. That's my tie-in to people greater and much more brilliant than I am, who wrote these words or worked with these words. That is what ties in the fact that people have lived and died [for this over thousands] of years, that they are passing on to me their thoughts, their feelings, their workings.

Hy (Chaim) Rubenstein, 39, is an attorney. He and his wife live in Baltimore, Maryland, and they have seven children.

31
Going Home

I think faith is a commodity. I had thought prior to that that faith was a crutch.

It has become an archetypal ba'al teshuvah *story: A wayward Jew's search for spirituality leads to an ashram, a house of Eastern religious meditation. In reality, though, it's no refuge; just another spiritual dead end. The tale is no cliché to Esther Rochel Russell because she lived it. Ironically, her search had taken her to Israel before she arrived in India, where she became seriously ill after spending a few weeks seeking truth and tranquillity in an ashram. A pivotal point came while she was lying flat on her back in an Indian hospital. She remembers a doctor with a turban asking her where she'd come from. She told him Jerusalem. He smiled knowingly, as if he'd heard that sort of story before. He told her she wasn't about to find the truth in India. He told her to go home. And she eventually did.*

Very often I find myself amazed that I'm religious—that I'm a religious Jew, of all things. I was thinking, like, how I ever could have found myself in this position [laughs] with my hair covered, with a child—not that that's so unusual—but a child and more children hopefully on the way?

And I was thinking back to how this originated. I think it all comes from a feeling, since I was very young, that I really wanted to make a difference in the world, and feeling there was something bigger than me. I think this was just an organic feeling.

I grew up in the suburbs in Los Angeles, the Valley, which was lox-and-bagels Judaism. I was brought up with a very Reform doctrine, not really knowing anything about Torah. I didn't even known that there were five books in the Torah. I didn't even know who Moses was really or what he did, and I actually had a confirmation at a Reform synagogue and I really knew absolutely nothing. I knew that there was a Holocaust. That was basically the focus of my education.

Did you have a bas mitzvah?

No. That wasn't something that was important or was stressed in my synagogue. I did have, though, religious relatives on my father's side that must have had some kind of influence. I'm sure that, as I'm thinking about it now that I'm religious, that there must have been some very holy souls that were *davening* for me to come back to this. Because I really think that that's been a part of how it all happened; it seems to be an otherworldly kind of choice in some ways.

I had this innate yearning to make a difference or be someone or do something important. I still have that, but it's sort of found its home in a religious life. Which is sort of a surprise to me because all through high school and in college, I was very active in politics and worked in Washington, DC, for all these public interest groups and saving the whales, Greenpeace and impeaching Reagan. I was always sort of into leftist ideologies.

And I found that to be a fruitless endeavor after realizing that politics is so limited in terms of the impact and change one can make. It just somehow felt that this wasn't really what I was supposed to be doing to help make a difference. I felt like it was too distant, too removed from my life.

I studied psychology. My bachelor's is in psychology. And I thought maybe that psychology would be sort of the source of where I could find my ultimate questions answered about the meaning of life and what we're doing here. And I would be able to find purpose and meaning, things I'd always been questioning and searching for.

I always felt myself to be different than anybody else. When I was growing up, my friends were always saying stop analyzing so much, you think too much, here, take another beer, another joint, forget all of that nonsense.

Russell's search for truth led her to the performing arts, which she began to pursue as a career after college.

I was working in Hollywood on television shows, some real stupid television shows. I was an assistant producer and I did some writing and I did this for a few years, and I was also acting in theater.

I was making a lot of money. I remember sitting at my desk [at an ad agency] and having these incredible anxiety attacks, and I would think, what am I doing? This is so against my inner principles. It was . . . it just felt so wrong.

So I actually joined a program called *Sh'root La'am*, don't ask me why, which is sort of a Peace Corps rendition in Israel, where you help impoverished and underdeveloped communities. I did this and I worked with the Ethiopian community, which was wonderful.

Why did you pick Israel of all places?

I was thinking of going into the [American] Peace Corps, but it was a two-year program, so I went to Israel. You know, you could say my soul brought me there. I mean if I'm gonna help people, I thought, I might as well help Jewish people. I guess even then I did have a Jewish inkling.

Was it your first time in Israel?

My parents had sent me on a teen tour of Israel when I was younger, about 15. I thought it was a beautiful country and it definitely did have an impact on me. I think it must have had more of an impact on me than I imagined. I remember even then when I was a kid going to the [Western] Wall and crying. It evoked a very strong reaction in me.

So I joined *Sh'root La'am*. And [then] I just sort of wanted to clear my head out and maybe figure out what it was that I wanted to do that was more meaningful. So I met some friends and wanted to go check out India.

I just thought that I hadn't really found the spiritual sustenance that I was hoping to find in Israel at that point. So I said maybe I'll go check out the Far East. I was always interested in Eastern religions and transcendental meditation and so I went there, and I was in an ashram for a few weeks. And I ended up getting very, very sick. I mean I had about a 105 fever, and they were giving me cold showers. I was in really bad shape.

And I remember they had to take me down in one of these stretchers to get to the city. And I went to see this Sikh Indian [doctor] and he said— I remember he had this really very beautiful face and these very big deep hazel eyes—and he said, "Where are you coming from?" I said, "I'm coming from Jerusalem." And he said, "Where are you staying here?" And I told him up in the hills in an ashram. And he said, "You should go home. What are you doing here?" I said, "I dunno, I'm looking for truth." I just remember he smiled and said, "You're not going to find anything here. Go back; you should go home."

I remember going to the airport, and it was in Bombay; it was crowded and it was smelly and I was so thankful that there was this nice Israeli couple that helped me the whole way on the flight. This almost was like divine providence to have these Jews, you know. And at that point, I realized that there is a familial bond here.

She flew back home to Los Angeles to recuperate and then enrolled in the New York University theater graduate school.

I had friends who were going to hear this rabbi speak. He happened to be an Orthodox rabbi. And he was speaking right down the street from my house, and I figured why not? Why not just go hear him speak? It wasn't as though I was looking for anything in Judaism. I was just open and interested in different perspectives and in learning. If it was a guru who was speaking about something interesting I would have gone.

And it was much to my surprise, when I went to hear that rabbi speak . . . *alav hashalom*, this rabbi's name was Yitzchok Kirzner, and was an extraordinary, extraordinary man.

I remember I went in there for the first time and I was in shock because we were learning *Tehillim*, and I was learning about King David and all the struggles he had, and it just amazed me. And I remember coming out and I just started sobbing.

I couldn't believe that this was . . . mine. I'm looking all over and thinking that everything is interesting, but what to me was the most profound and the most interesting—what was mine—was what I had never been taught. I was awestruck.

When I think back on that time, when I was first learning what it is to be a Jew—not how I had grown up—but what it really means to be a Jew, it was so overwhelming and so thrilling and so exciting because we have so much to be proud of.

It took immediately?

I was so hungry to learn more. . . . I went to this rabbi's particular *shiur* consistently, I wouldn't miss it. And I would almost always come out crying. He had a women's *yeshiva* on the Upper West Side of Manhattan, and I went there and I learned with him for a week. [I said] I'm gonna do this; this is the most important thing in my life despite everything else. I just loved it. I lapped it up like a dog. It was such an inspiring, inspiring week for me, although it was a little bit of a turn-off because of the way the people looked and it was a little closed-minded.

How so?

The black clothes and the wigs and the whole ordeal was a little bit much. But I got past that. I mean I've been around weird-looking people, especially in the theater. So I just thought, I'm not gonna let the externals push me away. The essence of what they're saying is ringing true. And it was from there that I just kept learning and learning and learning. And I decided maybe I'll take a little time off school. And from there I went to *yeshiva* in Israel [in 1990].

What did your folks think of this?

[Laughs] They were glad I didn't have the Buddhist shrine in my house anymore.

You had a Buddhist shrine?

Oh, yeah, when I was in Los Angeles I used to have friends over and we'd chant.

She spent a total of six months studying at yeshivot *in Jerusalem and S'fat.*

S'fat is a holy place, and when you walk around there you feel the air is very thick with all the *neshamas* that have been there for hundreds of years. And at night, it's so quiet, and when you walk in the dark down the alleys, you feel that you're gonna turn a corner and bump into the *Ari* any minute. Or you'll hear them learning in one of the little enclaves.

What did you take away from that experience?

I was definitely fully committed to this lifestyle. I really evolved in terms of believing that the Torah was the way the Jews were supposed to live their lives. And also some of the things I didn't completely understand or agree with, *halachahs* for women or *halachahs* in general—which is a struggle because it's hard to lead a religious life—I just sort of took on faith.

I was able to deepen my faith. I think faith is a commodity. I had thought prior to that that faith was a crutch. A lot of secular people think it's a crutch we hold onto because there's nothing else in life, so we sort of developed this thing called religion. We developed this notion called religion in order to hold onto something and create our own meaning in life. And I sort of dropped that whole notion, which was a very big thing, because once you lose it, it changes your whole perspective on living.

It was replaced by what?

Belief. Belief that there is a God, belief that there is a purpose in life, a meaning. It's not that we've created this, as little helpless defenseless creatures, which is what I think secular universities tend to teach; we make man the almighty. There is something here. And the fact that we have a need for it is not a weakness, but it means that there's something there to believe in.

Any other highlights of your spiritual growth?

It was really an accumulation of learning. I think for anybody to become *frum* and to deepen it, it's learning and having the openness and having the teachers who are willing to answer questions. I still ask questions and I still resist things and I still fall back and forth between realities.

But when I get back into learning again, I hook into the Torah as a blueprint for living. And that really came through, through the immersion of myself in the *yeshiva* environment.

Was it a big gap for you between "spiritual Judaism" and "mitzvah Judaism"?

It still is. In fact, I probably struggle with that a lot. It still drives me crazy that I can't eat certain nonkosher foods that I just love. Or certain *halachahs* or *Shabbos malachahs*, you know, all the things you can't do. It's restrictive and it doesn't feel as though I'm elevating anything. But the more I learn, and I mean learn on a spiritual level rather than an intellectual level, by that I mean learning *Chasidus*.

Explain Chasidus.

Chasidus takes *halachah*, *mitzvos* and Torah to a very essential and deep level and it talks about how this world is just an image of a higher spiritual reality. So everything we think, speak or do in this world emanates from a spiritual essence. Supposedly, when we're learning Torah, we're opening up to God's consciousness. So that really is the essence of what *Chasidus* teaches. And it sort of like cuts through all the intellectual [argument], which to me can go 'round and 'round and 'round. Maybe what I just said regarding *Chasidus* sounds a little magical, but it is a mystical element of what Judaism is.

It makes it relevant and elevates it. It's like, ultimately what are we doing in the world? Ultimately, ultimately. What are we here for? To elevate this world to a higher plane, to make the mundane more spiritual, elevate it, everything in our lives—how we think, how we speak, how we dress, how we do business, how we do everything. That's what being a Jew is.

How do you reconcile frumkeit *with feminism?*

I try to look at it from a higher perspective. And I try to think that ultimately if I trust in this Torah, then God probably knows more about what I'm supposed to be doing, what's ultimately good for me, than I know. And it has a lot to do with ego—on a woman's part. And if she really, really believes in Torah, then she'll see that this is good for her. And that's a hard thing for women in our culture to swallow because for the most part the secular culture does denigrate women.

Do you feel that Orthodoxy denigrates women?

Ultimately no. I don't think the real real rabbis do. They put their wives on pedestals. As we get closer to the *Moshiach*, we'll hear more feminine voices in our teachings. At this point, it doesn't bother me.

I understand women who do have [a problem with] it. But again . . . it has a lot to do with ego and them having their internal . . . [sighs] problems. It has a lot to do with not making your own needs more important than what the Torah says is right. It's hard for all of us.

Do you ever have doubts about Yiddishkeit?

I definitely do [laughs]. I think the first sentence I said was, "What the hell am I doing? Am I totally brainwashed and whacked out?" I think that a lot.

Still?

Yeah. I really think that maybe I'm really whacked out, that I've gone bonkers. I grew up for 30 years one way, with one perspective and one framework of education and thinking. And I miss going out and doing wild things with my friends. But then I think again, what am I really missing on an essential level? How do I deal with doubt? I'll have to think about that. I get depressed. I get depressed and I start feeling really alone and like I've just made a big mistake.

How I help myself through that is I look around at the external world and see what is going on out there. And I say, you know what? Even if this is a . . . crock, this is 100 times better than anything else. And it really is. That I never doubt.

What's so funny is that I find myself now as a Torah-observant Jew finding answers to my life in a book that supposedly was given to us 3,000 years ago on a mountain in a revelatory experience—while I still have the struggle within me of being a person who still appreciates the search for the answers.

I still struggle with the fact that, well, here's this Torah that I'm abiding by and living my life by and following its rules, some of them I don't understand because I don't know enough. And I'm just sort of going by faith because it seems to be wiser and bigger than me, hoping that this is the right way to live. It's like something intuitively tells me it is.

How do you know this isn't another ashram experience? How do you know this is real?

That's what my parents ask me. How do I know? Because this is the only thing that has stuck. First of all, I'm not an Eastern person. My soul was born into a body that was American, that was Jewish to Jewish parents. So it seems logical that if I was born a Jew, if God made me a Jew, that I should lead my life as a Jew.

The other thing is that all the other religions and philosophies really negate the physical world, especially the Eastern [ones]. And it seems that, we're spiritual beings in physical bodies in a physical world. And Judaism for the most part, recognizes [this] and emphasizes *mitzvos*, which is doing in the physical world. It's doing physical acts in this world. It's helping others, giving *tzedakah*, putting on *tefillin*, keeping *kashrus*, the way we kill our animals, it's really dealing with the physical. And it just doesn't seem reasonable that we're supposed to be sitting in an ashram on the top of a mountain just getting close to God. It just ultimately didn't seem reasonable.

Esther Rochel Russell (formerly Leslie Barer), 34, is a drama teacher at various yeshivot in Los Angeles. She and her husband, whom she met at a shabbaton in Crown Heights in 1992, live in Los Angeles. They have two children.

32
Art, You Look
Like A Jew

As I look back on it now, I was gasoline and all I needed was a spark. . . .
I was palpably obsessed with my Jewishness. I just didn't know what it
was and I had to get a hold of it.

With a sefer Torah *cradled in his arms, Arthur Sapper turns to face the
packed sanctuary. He is a synagogue regular, a large man in his mid-
40s with a large voice and a self-assured manner. He booms out the*
Sh'ma *in a ringing baritone, as he's done so many times before. In fact,
he looks as if he's been doing it all his life. Far from it. There was a
time too not long ago when Sapper and the Torah were complete strang-
ers. He had drifted so far from Judaism that for nearly two decades he
barely saw the inside of a synagogue.*

I want to tell you about a very formative experience that happened at
work one time.

When I was in my twenties, I had found a job [as a staff attorney] in
a small federal agency. One of the other staff attorneys had grown up in
New York City. He was not a Jew; he was very, very WASPish. His
name was Hastings S. Trigg, III [laughs]. But he was a wonderful guy.
His nickname, and everyone calls him this, is Skip; nobody calls him
Hastings.

Skip was a very intelligent man, very honest, and he grew up in New
York, so he knew about Jews. And he wasn't at all awed by the sight of
the descendants of the ancient Israelites in our hallways.

One time we were shooting the bull in the office and we were talking about . . . what do we all look like, our appearances. One of the guys in the office was Italian, and I suppose he looked Italian. Skip, I suppose, looked like a WASP . . . and so forth. And I said at one point that people sometimes mistake me for Italian.

Skip turned around and said to me in a completely honest, open-faced way, "Art, you look like a Jew." And I remember distinctly that when he said that to me my stomach leaped into my mouth. It was the most threatening thing you could have said to me because I was very conscious of the persecution that Jews had gone through.

And by saying that I looked like a Jew, and now of course I realize I do—I have an eastern European Ashkenazi face, I have a long nose and large ears and long fingers, I've got the long face, I have it all. When he said that, it was as if, to me, he was painting a bull's-eye on the back of my head.

I had inherited the historically Jewish fear of persecution and had never realized until that moment how much it had affected me. But when he said that—and it was a completely honest statement; he didn't mean to offend me or to threaten me—I suppose there was a touch in his mind that I was being dishonest. And if he thought that, he was probably a little bit right.

That episode forced me to deal with who I am. Now there are two ways a person can come to grips with an identity that is not rewarding to them. They can either disavow it, reject it, or they can embrace it and try to find the good parts of it and benefit from that. Well, probably had my daughter not been born and had I remained childless, I probably would have taken the first path. Probably, I say, for statistical reasons, because so many of the kids I had grown up with had taken that path.

But I had become a father, and so it pushed me into the direction of trying to find reward from this identity that I was stuck with, that I wore on my face.

I remember that being Jewish [while growing up in Queens] meant something to my parents. But it only meant something; it did not mean that the house revolved around it. Nevertheless, we were sent to [Conservative] Hebrew school. And while we were in Hebrew school my parents dutifully attended the synagogue because it was required [laughs]. And I remember that [otherwise] my father was really a three-day-a-year man. And everything was quite superficial.

A three-day-a-year man?

Somebody who goes to *shul* on the two days of Rosh Hashanah and on Yom Kippur. The community was assimilating. These were people who had come from the Lower East Side and from some parts of Brooklyn. They or their parents had come from Europe; they knew the economic value of becoming American.

The community was led by a rabbi who was very German, very correct. I remember one time I had picked up the practice . . . of covering my eyes when I said the *Sh'ma*. This was an early indication that I was attracted to this kind of demonstrative religiosity. And I remember that I did it and I looked up at Rabbi Goldman [a pseudonym] and he shook his head in a horrified silent "no" [laughs], as if this were a superstitious habit from Europe that we just didn't do in modern America.

Things were quite superficial; people were Jewish because they felt culturally Jewish. They knew nothing about the religion and cared less. They sent their kids to Hebrew school because of, I suppose, cultural intertia—they wanted their kids to be Jewish, to marry Jewish, but nobody quite realized that what they were doing would turn out to be largely in vain.

I had a rather poor Hebrew school education. I and all my friends deeply resented having to go to a secular school, get tired and then go immediately to a Hebrew school which was alien to us and did not seem to have any connection or support to any other aspect of our lives. It seemed to be destined to end in something called *bar mitzvah*, which we had no clear conception of, except that we had to practice for it and learn something for it . . . and that it meant something to our parents.

Sapper's bar mitzvah *was held in a rented nightclub.*

I remember going to some friends' *bar mitzvahs* at the time and one of them rented out the same nightclub, but *with* the nightclub acts, and it was extraordinarily vulgar as I look back on it now.

At about the age of 11 or 12, I just completely lost interest [in Judaism]. And the reason was, as I look back on it now, what psychologists call cognitive dissonance. That is, you learn one thing and see or practice another. And you have to reconcile the two in your mind, and when you're a child, it's very hard to do. Something has to go. And I was basically a victim of that, so Hebrew school went.

I think, had my parents shown the slightest interest in religious studies, it would have been different, but they didn't. Their Jewish identity was purely cultural.

For a very brief time after I was a *bar mitzvah*, I actually went to Sunday morning services and put on my *tallis* and *tefillin*. But I was completely turned off by it because the men who were there—there were all men there, there were no teenagers—never said a word to me and they treated me, quite understandably, as something of a weirdo. So that died real fast.

And for the next essentially 17 to 19 years, I was out of the synagogue and I had almost no connection to Jewish religious life at all. I was not even a three-day-a-year man. However I had a great, astonishingly strong sense of Jewish identity. I knew I was a Jew, I just didn't know what it meant.

At the State College of New York at Buffalo, Sapper met the woman who would become his wife. Their backgrounds were "astonishingly similar." During law school, they lived in Oxon Hill, Maryland, a place virtually devoid of Jews. Sapper recalls the time he and his wife saw the movie Blazing Saddles *at an Oxon Hill theater. There's a scene in the film in which Mel Brooks, playing an Indian chief, suddenly lapses into Yiddish.*

And of course as far as the audience was concerned he's speaking Apache. But my wife and I knew exactly what he was saying [laughs] and we were roaring, and everybody in the audience thought that we were Apaches. Wrong tribe. I suppose *Blazing Saddles* was my one Jewish experience in Oxon Hill.

In hopes of finding a somewhat more Jewish environment, the Sappers moved to Bethesda, Maryland, which is located in the most heavily Jewish county in the Washington, D.C., area. As it turns out, though, the neighborhood they picked—on the recommendation of their Jewish real estate agent—was atypical. It was so heavily Catholic that it was nicknamed "Vatican Hill."

When our eldest daughter was about two years old, and this was an epiphanous experience, you might say, we sent her to a neighborhood secular nursery school. It was supposed to be secular. It was in a church, but everyone said, "Oh, no, it's secular." Well, their idea of secular was not ours. In the wintertime our daughter came home with a drawing of a pine tree, and in the springtime she came home with a spring basket, not an Easter basket, oh, no. Well, this struck my wife as not right and she was very offended by it. And so the next year we sent her to a Jewish nursery school at, of all places, Beth Shalom in Potomac [Maryland], an Orthodox *shul*.

And then one day in the spring, I came home from work and my daughter and wife were sitting at the table in the kitchen and in front of my daughter, who was three years old, was a little basket, and my wife, said, "Look Artie, Michelle made a *shalach manos* basket."

And of course I quite dutifully faked it. I said, "Oh, it's beautiful" and I fawned all over it. Then I took my wife aside and said, "What's a *shalach manos* basket?" Actually I doubt that I even picked up the words. I just said, "What kind of a basket is that?" And she explained to me that's a basket that you make for Purim. And of course the fact that it was Purim time had not even entered into my consciousness at all. At that time I was about 30 years old.

I resolved . . . that I would never be caught short like that again. I remembered the lessons of cognitive dissonance and I remembered how destructive it was for me and my friends, my classmates whom I'd grown up with in Queens, to see their parents have them taught one thing and themselves do none of it.

And I began to read, and the more I began to learn, the more we began to do. And the more we began to do, the more we learned and so on. There were times when I would come home from the local library and take out stacks of books on Jewish practice.

As I look back on it now, I was gasoline and all I needed was a spark. And I remember for a few years there I was palpably obsessed with my Jewishness. I just didn't know what it was and I had to get a hold of it. It was something that was always eating at me, something that always helped define me. I didn't know what it was, and I had to grab this thing by the tail and wrestle it down and open its jaws and find out what it was.

One day we made a trip to New York City, and we stayed with my wife's mother. And we drove to the Lower East Side of Manhattan and we came back with bags full of stuff. A *tallit gadol* for me. A *challah* cover. A *Kiddush* cup, all these Jewish religious articles. Lots of them. Stuff we never had, never knew how to use.

My mother-in-law, whose Jewish observance in the United States was to light candles Friday night and buy kosher meat—she came from a religious home—she saw my wife taking all this stuff out of the bag and she cried. Tears of joy. She was so moved. And the fact that she was moved by it strengthened us.

Fast-forward a few years. Our [eldest] daughter is now four years old, and goes back to Beth Shalom nursery school and we're starting to learn a little bit more.

Then we had a decision to make, and this was truly a crossroads point in our lives. Should we send her to a Jewish day school or to a public school? My wife and I both knew that if we were going to keep her Jewish, sending her to public school would not permit us to do that because we didn't have the social support system that we had in New York; translation: A Jewish neighborhood. So therefore we decided to send her to kindergarten at the Charles E. Smith Jewish Day School in Rockville.

My second daughter was born in 1982. Her name was Sarah May, now Sarah Malka—notice how it went from Michelle to Sarah; getting a little bit more Jewish. Oh, and of course for our first daughter, we didn't go to synagogue to name her. We just gave her a Hebrew name. For our second daughter, we went to a nearby Conservative synagogue where I clumsily play acted my way through an *aliyah*. And I [laughs] knew so little, I actually offered [the rabbi] a congratulatory cigar, which he very politely declined to accept because it was an object that you couldn't use on the Sabbath and so therefore he could not even handle it.

Because our daughter was in a Jewish day school, we just had to join a *shul*. There I was again afraid of that terrible angel, cognitive dissonance. If you would have asked, am I doing any of this because of religious conviction? I'd have to honestly say I am not. I was desperately trying to maintain cultural Jewishness by using the Jewish religion as a vehicle for perpetuating Jewish culture.

The Sappers shul-shopped and then joined what he calls "a left-wing Conservative" congregation that was a considerable drive from their home.

Within a short period of time we were fairly acclimated, and I had learned so much by their standards that I became known as a *macher*, a really active person in the synagogue, which my wife and I were—but also as something of a knowledgeable person, because remember, I'm still in the obsessive stage here.

I would drive to the [*shul*] library after dinner at my home and just read books. I got to know that library very well. We became very regular *shul* goers. At one time in our lives, *Shabbos* was Friday night. Now, it crept into Saturday. After a while, we stopped our practice of shopping for food on Saturday afternoon. We were probably one of the few Jews in Montgomery County who were keeping *Shabbat* in the Conservative mold in a fairly conscientious way.

During this era, she [their eldest daughter] was still young, between four and eight, and she was infected with our spirit of Jewishness. One day I think I had casually mentioned to her while driving that it might he nice if she were to use her Hebrew name instead of her English name, Michelle, at school and perhaps all the time. Well, lo and behold, she marched into school the next day and announced that she was henceforth going to be known as Masha.

By this time we were very involved in the Conservative movement, but amazed and disconcerted and upset at how people would treat us as being some kind of knowledgeable Jews. And it didn't take my wife and I long to catch on to the shallowness of the Conservative movement— how little you had to know, how little you had to do to be part of it. How it so much lacked any sense of Jewish community. If you had a movement in which cars are permitted to be used on *Shabbat*, people could live anywhere, and there was no religious basis for a community; it was gone. The clergymen were shallow.

The Charles E. Smith Jewish Day School was not affiliated with any religious movement. Nevertheless, its essential ethos was . . . Conservative. My daughter came from a family where we kept *Shabbos* strictly according to Conservative precepts. She was invited out numerous times to birthday parties on Saturday afternoons. She was invited out numerous times to birthday parties in *trayf* restaurants. And who was doing the inviting? Classmates and parents of classmates in the Charles E. Smith Jewish Day School. This was devastating to her. She was disappointed in these people. But more important, it tagged her socially as being on the outs. It made her terribly unhappy. She was ostracized because she was observant.

People used to say [to her], "What are you, Orthodox or something?" She was truly an oddball. She was Conservative, but really religious about it and this was unheard of. If you were Conservative, you were just assumed to be a hypocrite. A teacher at the school later remarked [about this] to me when I talked to her about how unhappy my daughter was in school. She said to me, "Don't you know that the observant or Orthodox children here at school are like *marranos*? They hide their observance. Don't you know that?"

I was stunned. Yes, I had known it. But I would never think it or say it overtly. But to hear a teacher say it . . .

Around 1986 we began to really search for a Jewish community we thought we'd feel comfortable in. We were still very committed to the Conservative movement; we had no intention of becoming Orthodox. Being Orthodox was not quite to our liking. This was a feeling born not out of knowledge, but out of ignorance and rumor.

What was your image of Orthodoxy?

Intolerant, backward, medieval, all the usual stereotypes.

During this period we'd drive to *shul* every Saturday morning. I would not wear my *keepah* in the car at first; I would put it on in the [*shul*] parking lot and then take it off in the parking lot on the way home.

Then there came a point, where I said to myself that if I really believe this Conservative *halachah* about how it's okay to drive to *shul* on *Shabbat*, I guess it's okay to wear my *keepah* in the car on *Shabbat*. And I began to do that but with grave discomfort because I really didn't want anybody to see me wearing a *keepah* while driving the car on *Shabbat* because I thought it would degrade the image of the Jew in the popular mind if somebody were to see a Jew wearing a *yarmulka* driving on Saturday. In other words, translation: I knew in my mind it wasn't the right thing to do. But I wasn't strong enough in Torah yet to take my hands off the steering wheel, so to speak.

Serendipity. There was an amazing coincidence, a touch of luck that touched my wife and me and our eldest daughter in North Bethesda, where we lived, which had the most profound effect on us.

As it turns out, we lived across the street and two houses down from perhaps the only observant Jews in North Bethesda. Their names are Dr. and Mrs. Lewis Lipkin, and they took our eldest daughter, Masha, under their wings and they made her their adopted granddaughter. They treated her with tenderheartedness and kindness and they showed her that observant Jews can have *Shabbat* and be pleasant.

It was an enriching and loving experience for her and for us. Every *Shavuos* we would go across the street with our dairy concoction . . . and we'd have *Shavuos* meals and they'd come to our house on *Succot* and we'd share each other's company and *Shabbos* table on *Shabbat*.

To have lived across the street and two houses down from these people was the most extraordinary stroke of fortune. And of course, they'd been living there for decades and I hardly knew that they existed while we were living in North Bethesda, and they hardly knew that we existed, but somehow or other we just connected. In them I found a kindred intellectual spirit.

At the end of a *sefer* of *chumash*, we say "*chazak, chazak, venithchazek*—be strong, be strong, we shall strengthen each other." This is what was happening with the Lipkins, they were strengthening us and we were strengthening them because they had been all alone in North Bethesda.

There's another formative experience, one which had a lot more influence on me than I tell people. One day while I was still at the Conservative movement stage I saw an announcement in the *Washington Jewish Week* that Rabbi Meir Kahane, *zeycher tzaddik lavracha*, was speaking at the Silver Spring Jewish Center, and I went to see him.

And this experience punctuated the sentence that began with Skip Trigg saying, "Art, you look like a Jew." It provided a period to that sentence. How? I had never seen or heard Rabbi Kahane speak before. I had heard of him; naturally I had heard he was an extremist. And I sat there, pretty close to the front, and had an experience that I'd never had before in my life.

I saw a Jew with confidence pound a lectern and yell and speak forcefully, speak Jewish opinions with a complete lack of self-consciousness, with complete confidence in the rightness of what he was saying, with not a care for whether it happened to coincide with modern American values. Quite the opposite; he overtly disavowed any attempt to adopt or coincide with modern American values.

I had never seen this before. Never. I had never seen a Jew [bangs the table] pound a table in anger and speak an opinion out of deep conviction like that. It was a new experience. In [the] Conservative [movement], people were willing to dialogue, to talk, to discuss, but nobody ever came forward with a heartfelt, Jewishly based opinion.

The ethical discussion in the Conservative movement was that you had to find some premise on which to base an argument that was an American premise, or I should say a Western premise. But Rabbi Kahane, he used Jewish premises, thank you, and he was quite happy with that. It was an astonishing experience for me. I walked out of there having seen a new thing, and I began to read some of what he'd written and began to realize that there are premises out there that I knew nothing about. He, Rabbi Kahane, showed that there was a way to be proud of your Jewishness and not be self-conscious about it.

And so we realized that the Conservative movement had no future. We began to realize slowly, slower than all our other realizations about it, that it had no intellectual base, that it was merely a way of accommodating Jewishness to American culture. It was not based on Torah Jewish values. It was a purely cultural phenomenon.

Sometime, not too long thereafter, say late 1986, we had basically decided to become Orthodox, to move to an Orthodox neighborhood. We told our acquaintances and friends from the Conservative synagogue that we were going to be leaving and this would be the last *Shabbat* we'd be there.

There was a great age cleavage in the reactions to our leaving. The older people said, "Oh good, that's where you belong." They knew we were serious. They knew this was not the place for serious Jews.

But there was also a lot of anti-Orthodox feeling. So for the Sappers—the big *machers*, the big *talmid chachams*, the big committed Jews, the ones who always came to *shul* on *Shabbos*, the regular of regulars—for them to go over to the Orthodox was like going over to the enemy.

Our biggest problem was we didn't think we'd be accepted [in an observant community]. We had heard the horror stories about how people who became Orthodox weren't accepted.

Sapper arranged to spend Shabbos—*while his wife and kids were out of town—with a family in Kemp Mill, the largest Orthodox enclave in the Washington area.*

By that time, I had known enough about *Yiddishkeit*, how to keep *Shabbos*, how to keep kosher, how to *daven*. I knew enough to keep *Shabbos* without making any faux pas. And so I stayed with a family here in Kemp Mill and I had a wonderful time. It was a really eye-opening experience.

I had a wonderful time. But second of all, I saw it through rose-colored glasses. I was seeing Anatevka, because I wanted to see Anatevka. So we made arrangements to spend *Shabbat*, the entire family this time, at another family's house in Kemp Mill. And that was also a very wonderful experience, especially for my wife and my older daughter. And it was at that point we decided we're going to sell our house in Bethesda. We would purchase a house in Kemp Mill. We were going to move to Anatevka and we were going to pull our daughter out of the [Charles E. Smith] Jewish Day School.

In the meantime, Sapper began attending Shabbos *services at a Bethesda-area Sephardic synagogue. Unlike many of the congregants, he and his two young daughters walked to and from the shul, a distance of nearly two miles each way.*

It was the perfect transition *shul*. It was in form Orthodox, but the people there were not personally observant. So no one could look down their nose at me. And in that period we went from being Conservative Jews to being Orthodox Jews. The light switches stayed in their position for 25 hours. Things changed. Not markedly, but things changed. We stopped answering the telephone, for example. I think as I look back now, I was probably surprised at how little things changed, because we were fairly conscientious Conservative Jews. Our *kashrut* was upgraded somewhat.

If you have the belief that the Master of the Universe is commanding you, you're going to do it. And that's why I think that the great cleavage between the observant and the unobservant is not merely in their outward observances but I think it's also in their basic belief that there is first of all a God, and second of all, that his word is in the Torah.

So we sold our house in Bethesda and we moved to Kemp Mill. We were pleased with the community to no end. People were very accepting. We made mistakes and nobody embarrassed us. We put our eldest daughter into the Hebrew Academy [a nearby Orthodox day school].

She was in sixth grade, and she was [eventually] accepted. However, she was bewildered . . . by this change, by this ever-present change; you know children like stability. The one thing that she wasn't getting from her parents was stability because things were ever-changing. We were always adding new observances. And then one day we said we're moving to Kemp Mill and becoming Orthodox. Well, she was pleased, and at the same time apprehensive. But then when she got here, she did not find Anatevka. What she found were children who came from observant homes but had all the cruelties of children.

She did not have an easy time of it. She had not been taught in the Charles E. Smith Jewish Day School that when you *daven Shmonah Esrai*, that you're supposed to put your feet together. She *davened Shmonah Esrai* with her feet apart. You know, this was a faux pas. Of course to children this is just a mark of Jewish inferiority. And her Hebrew was not as good as the others. So she had real problems adjusting.

Our then-five-year-old daughter Sarah had no problems adjusting. She didn't remember driving in the car to [the Conservative synagogue] and I hope she never does. My son was born with the legal name Mordechai Yaakov Sapper. No name change for him; it's not Mordechai Jacob Sapper, no, it's Mordechai *Yaakov*, two *a*'s. And our youngest daughter, she is Chaya Esther and that's her legal name. And so I'm proud to say that our children's legal names are exactly the same as their Hebrew names—a point I now realize to be extremely important.

How has becoming an observant Jew changed your life?

I now know that I'm part of a tradition that stretches back a good 4,000 years. But the burdens of being a Jew are far heavier than I imagined fifteen years ago, and it weighs on me. Primarily, in fact entirely, the burdens of being an observant Jew lie in the realm where the secular world intersects the Jewish one at work.

The original root meaning of the word *kadosh* is separate, unique, special. You attain holiness by being separate, apart, special. When you keep kosher and when you keep *Shabbat*, you cut yourself off from your comrades at work. And if you're in a highly intellectual profession like I am—I'm an attorney in a law firm—unless you have great social skills, it marks you. It cuts you off.

If you wear a *keepah*, that's even worse, so to speak; then you're truly marked off. So it closes certain professional doors. I do not have the social skills to overcome those disadvantages. There are attorneys who are observant who do have them. I don't. So for me it has . . . had great drawbacks.

If I were not observant, I think I'd be earning a lot [laughs] more money today. And I'd have a lot less to spend it on too. Because I wouldn't have to pay for tuition and kosher food, and I'd be able to take vacations. I haven't taken a vacation in four-and-a-half years because I use up all my time on the *yomim tovim*.

Now, the biggest problem being a *ba'al teshuvah*. I had not been raised as an observant Jew, a person who always has his mind on his religious principles. I'd been raised in a secular environment, and I lived in one through my early adulthood. I really did not have an observant Jewish concept in my personal behavior yet. It was a struggle for me not to use certain coarse language. Of course I don't use it anymore, but it was really a struggle.

It was a struggle for me to behave the way a person in awe of God is supposed to behave. And I'm sad to say that I've sometimes failed at that struggle. And that to me is a hole in my heart because my personal behavior is so influenced by my background, my youth, my early adulthood; it's so hard to change that even though I wear the *keepah* and look like a religious man, I sometimes fail to live up to the image that I create. That's extremely wounding to me. And I try, I try every day, but it's a terrible, terrible weight on my mind.

[But] I understand my ancestors now. I understand the Jewish religious tradition. I understand where I come from and where I'm going. I have a window, a tiny window . . . that views a cloud surrounding God. I'd feel quite comfortable now if Skip Trigg said, "You look like a Jew." I'd say, "Yeah, I do." I wouldn't have my heart jump into my stomach. For one thing, I wear my *keepah* at work.

I also now have some confidence that my grandchildren will be Jews. I have some confidence that my great-grandchildren will be Jews. Fifteen years ago, I had no confidence in either. I now know that I will die a Jew and not just an American with bleached-out Jewish ancestry. I now know that I am part of a community, and that's a great comfort.

Arthur Sapper, 45, is an attorney. He and his wife live in Silver Spring, Maryland, and have four children.

33
The Taste of *Shabbos*

And I said, "How long has this been going on without my knowing about it?" And he said, "About 3,300 years."

By the time he was in college, Brian Wolf had a rather distinctive philosophy of life. It had nothing to do with Judaism or any other religion. It was based almost solely on tennis, a sport he played well and lived for. One day a member of a cult approached him on campus and asked him what he thought was the most important thing in life. Wolf didn't have to think. "You've got to get your first serve in," he told him. "If you don't, you get clobbered at the net."

Wolf never lost his love for tennis. But he did learn that there's a lot more to life than a good first serve—and his belief in that "something more" was later severely tested. He discovered this added dimension while he was working for a defense contractor in California. A local rabbi would stop by once a week during lunch hour to discuss Jewish topics with some of the employees. Wolf was one of them.

I didn't have the faintest idea what he was talking about, but I attended pretty regularly. I would parallel my *Yiddishkeit* to a really nice-looking book that your aunt Tillie buys you. You put it up on a bookshelf, it looks so nice up there, but you never touch it or read it.

Part of the reason I went to these sessions is the same reason I ended up going into mathematics, which is I always had a great interest in how the world was put together. How the world was put together means not only the laws of physics that describe the movement and stability of objects but also describes various nonphysical and intellectual types of subjects, including the spiritual. I've always had an interest in how did we get to where we are now?

At one of the lunchtime get-togethers, an entire group of rabbis showed up to answer questions.

There were three rabbis sitting all in a row who had on . . . there were two blue suits and one with a dark grey suit. And then there was this fourth guy who didn't have a suit on. As a matter of fact, when he came into the room, I thought he was one of those engineers who they lock up in one of the vaults and don't let out until the end of the day for those super top-secret projets. He had on paisley suspenders; he had on a white shirt with all kinds of buttons, like "Torah is the real thing" with a sort of Coke symbol. I thought this was the neatest guy I ever saw in my life and I wondered what trip he was on.

It turns out he wasn't one of those super-secret scientists. He was one of the rabbis. And when the question came around to why don't we believe in you-know-who, he fielded that question. It turns out that he had been the liaison for *Chabad* on the UCLA campus for the year to spearhead antimissionary work. So he fielded the question, and he did it in such an interesting and humorous way, I thought this guy's got such a tremendous sense of humor and such a wit that I really wanted to find out more about him.

The instant the session was over, I made a beeline to the door and blocked the exit and said, "You're not getting out 'till I get your name and phone number and I find out what kind of trip you're on." And he reaches into his shirt pocket and pulls out a card. I had never heard of a rabbi with a business card. It said "Rabbi Shlomo Schwartz, director of social activities, *Chabad* UCLA."

Rabbi Schwartz invited Wolf and a friend to Shabbos *dinner at his home. It was their first genuine* Shabbos *meal.*

There are nine children, the rabbi, the *rebbetzin*, maybe 10 or 20 other singles like myself and my friend. The place was buzzing with excitement. People were meeting people and everyone was giving me *shalom alechem* and good *Shabbos*, and I didn't quite know what to make of it.

And whatever it was the *rebbetzin* had been cooking all afternoon, the aroma just filled my nostrils and just whetted my appetite all the more. Ordinarily you find good food at *Shabbos*, but the excitement in the air and the amount of *ahava*, that's love, and interest that you could feel from Rabbi Schwartz and Mrs. Schwartz, probably went into the taste of the food a little bit.

When the meal was done, I remember going up to the rabbi and shaking hands with him. He has an expression and a feeling he gives over to you, his face basically glows. I said to him, "Rabbi, how often do you do this?" And he said, "Every week." And I said, "How long has this been going on without my knowing about it?" And he said, "About 3,300 years [laughs]." I said, "You know what? We're gonna be back next week."

That was where I got started. The experience was anything and everything you could expect it to be. The taste of the chicken from that night still stays in my mouth. And the taste of the friendships and the feelings I had on that particular evening, they linger even longer.

It was a little hard to fall asleep that night. When I got home, I relived and relived the experience and I thought if that's what *Shabbos* is all about, I would like to get some more. I got a deep sense of *Yiddishkeit* [that night]. Part of that is because there was the food, [and] there was the fellowship and the *zemiros*, the singing.

At the same time, Rabbi Schwartz gave *divre Torah*, he talked about Torah, and he talked about some deep intellectual subjects. And he talked about them in a very interesting and palatable way—a sentence or two, a thought I could take home with me and keep and put in my pocket and look at again and think about. So therefore I had not only an emotional experience, but something that I could hang onto intellectually. So I went with my friend every single Friday evening.

Meanwhile, Wolf learned Torah with Rabbi Schwartz, but in limited doses. After two years of that, he wanted more. With the rabbi's help, he enrolled in a yeshiva in Los Angeles where he studied with a tutor.

For me it was very easy to compartmentalize my life. I had my life at work, I had the social component of my life, dating and so forth. I had the athletic aspects of my life and I had my religious aspect or spiritual aspect. And one had nothing to do with the other.

I began learning at the *yeshiva* mostly because I began having intellectual questions. I asked questions every week for two hours straight.

Wolf invited a friend to attend.

Between the two of us, we asked him [the tutor] more questions for two hours straight. And we did this for weeks and weeks and weeks and I learned an awful lot about what I didn't know about Torah.

Along the way [another friend] Jeremy [an assistant athletic director at UCLA] was taking classes very seriously, and he decided what he wanted most out of his life was to sit and learn Torah in *yeshiva*. And when he said to me, "I'm leaving in six months for Israel and I'm gonna sit and learn and become a rabbi," I basically freaked.

I had had friends who had become *frum* to the extent that they kept kosher and kept *Shabbos*. At that point I had begun removing certain things from my diet. I no longer would eat shellfish. I wouldn't eat milk and meat knowingly together. I was making small changes as I went, but still my life was compartmentalized. Still, I was Jewish on Friday night and Saturday and on Sunday for two hours during our learning sessions. The rest of the time I was completely secular.

But when Jeremy decided to learn in *yeshiva* full time and wanted to become a rabbi, in *Eretz Yisroel* in the Old City, it absolutely blew my mind. It's one thing to have external *mitzvos*, and it's another thing entirely to be *frum* on the inside, to have your entire life centered around the Torah and all your decisions are based on how it will affect your spiritual life. That's a different matter altogether.

And when he said: "This is reality to me and the secular world is no longer the reality to me, it's not the focal point, it's not the center, the apex, of a person; the epitome of what a person should be is not rich and famous, but rather he should be spiritually guided," my mind just whirled.

I had met a lot of people and they were all Los Angeleans or at least if they weren't born there they were living there and they still had the Los Angeles lifestyle mentality, even though they were *frum*. Nobody had just given up their entire life and gone to *yeshiva*. So here was a person who was willing to dedicate and center his entire life around Torah. It made a great impact on me.

Meanwhile, Wolf investigated the "Torah codes"—words that are said to be imbedded in the Torah which prove conclusively, according to some, that the Torah is divine.

It was further evidence that the Torah was not just a diary, it was not just a statutory lawbook, or civil law, but rather, there was more to it. But I did not become *frum* because of this. I was stimulated to learn more about it. It's not a proof, it's just evidence.

Shortly after hearing about his friend Jeremy, there was a shakeup in Wolf's company. He got a job back East as a consultant, but his lifestyle remained unchanged.

I was still doing *Shabbos* from Friday night to Saturday night, but then sometimes I would *mechallel Shabbos* then too. I might drive in on Friday night, sleep at my parents', and drive in Saturday morning, try to do it unobtrusively like nobody knew.

So there came a turning point. After doing this for so long, I honest cannot figure out how I was so compartmentalized for so long, because it really rubs against my grain. And I look back now and realize there were many, many times I was a very unhappy person while I was doing these things. Because I think if you're not integrated, I don't think you can be honestly happy. I think the only way you can be happy is when your entire life is an integrated single thrust in one direction. Being pulled in multiple directions with multiple interests often conflicting does nothing but tear a person apart.

So I decided I'm gonna really study seriously and find out what this is all about. And I began learning more and more, and it got to a point . . . that I realized in the spring of 1992 that I had sort of plateaued out.

I was no longer growing . . . and I was unhappy; I felt divided. I thought I could separate them [his two lives] and I finally realized I can't do it any more. To make a long story short, Rabbi T. [a local rabbi he knew] called me up because he must have sensed that something was going on.

He said, "What's it gonna be? What's with your studies? You're not growing; you've petered out, you're not learning anymore. For some reason for the past few months you haven't been taking classes either, have you?"

I said, "How'd you know?" He said, "You're not happy and what's the story?" So I said, "To tell you the truth, rabbi, I'm sick and tired of proofs of God. I know God exists, I know the Torah's true, but what am I gonna do about it? I can't get past the hump. I've only heard lectures and classes and talks and *derashes*. I said it's passive, I'm sitting there like it's a lecture in college. I want to *do*."

I was having a difficult time stepping over the line, [saying] this is who I am, the main focal point of my life is the Torah. That was a very hard step for me to take.

The next *Shabbos* I sort of confronted him, [and] told him I didn't like what had happened. And he and I had another little tête-à-tête and I remember we went off into a room and it was very emotional, I broke down and cried. And I just said, "I can't take it any more." At that point . . . I was interviewing for a contract with the World Bank.

It was a very prestigious contract that would look good on anybody's resume. I was to be in charge of a certain aspect of their computer system and this was a worldwide system. This was the job of jobs, the epitome, the best. This was going to make me. I was going straight upward from here.

After weeks of interviews, Wolf was selected for the job. When it came time to sign the contract, receive his beeper and officially be brought on board, Wolf learned of one more detail. The company wanted him to be available 24 hours a day, seven days a week, "24-by-seven."

[I said], "How about 24-by-six, give or take a couple hours?" He said, "What do you mean?" I said, "I'm just not available from Friday night about two hours before sundown until Saturday about two hours after sundown, given traveling time." I said, "I'll be happy to carry the beeper with me if I ever go on vacation. You can call me on Sunday, but you can't have me between Friday night [and] Saturday night. I said it's my Sabbath. This is me."

You might ask, how [did] I suddenly get the strength to say that? I think part of the reason why *Yiddishkeit* both flourishes in the states through *BT*s, but at the same time is falling flat on its face in terms of those people who are fading away from *Yiddishkeit* . . . you have this great divergence, this great gorge being chiseled out . . . because we're not challenged here very much. Part of the reason I responded the way I did is because he was taking away from me something that was mine and I didn't care about it until he suddenly wanted to take it away from me.

I said, "You go back to your superiors and you tell them, 'We've been interviewing for quite a little while, and Brian Wolf is the best candidate. However he's not available for 24 hours out of the week. Shouldn't we still hire him?' When you get your answer, then you call me back."

And I got up and walked out. And I got back on the subway and . . . I sat and thought about it and I went, oh my goodness what have I done? I just walked away from THE JOB.

Wolf didn't get the job and walked around in a daze for a while after being rejected. He then made the first international phone call of his life. It was to his friend Jeremy in Israel. It was May of 1992.

I said, "I can't handle it any more." I said, "I'll give it two weeks." I said, "Something's going to happen to push me one way or the other. I'm either going to become a *frum* Jew or I'm dropping the whole thing, I'm walking away from Torah, I'm never coming back to it." And he went "Gulp."

About a week-and-a-half later, Rabbi T. called and invited Wolf to a summer camp that specializes in outreach to young Jews who have shown some interest in Yiddishkeit.

They are sent to this place in order to have an opportunity to live the Torah experience. It's like a *yeshiva* lifestyle, except it's a really beautiful setting; sit and learn Torah and there are as many tutors and rabbis as there are students. It took. It took real good, real deeply.

But Wolf knew it was just a start. He needed to learn Torah full-time at a real yeshiva in Israel. He filled out an application and was accepted at a place called Machon Shlomo.

I got home and told my parents . . . and they went ballistic. My mother was crying and she looked over at my father and said, "Where did we go wrong?" I couldn't believe that they were getting so mad. I thought this was the greatest thing, man, why are they getting upset?

Why were they so upset?

My parents are very into personal success and being successful has very little to do with your sense of spirituality; that's not success per se. There's no external evidence to show that you're successful; the best success in Torah is all internal. So they couldn't relate to it.

Wolf then tried to explain his decision to his younger sister.

I said, "One of the reasons I want to go and learn about Torah is I'm a Jew, and I don't even know what that means. I don't know how to be one. I said if God created the world, and if that's true, which it is, what kind of impact does that have? How am I supposed to know what's in the Torah? I don't even have the skills to learn anything on my own. I need to go there to learn. "

I said one last thing, and that is, "We've had a *mesorah*, a tradition, a lineage passed down from Sinai till now." I said, "Our great-grandparents were religious. Somehow or other in the last couple generations we're not. I don't want in another couple generations for somebody to point at the family tree and go 'you see that link right there? That guy dropped the ball.' I'm not going to be the one who dropped the ball."

Did she understand this?

I wouldn't say she understood it or agreed with it, but she was supportive of me.

His other sister vigorously opposed his decision, but they have since reconciled. His grandmother lent her enthusiastic support. She even gave him money to help defray expenses. Wolf spent two years in the yeshiva.

After the second year, they [his parents] began to realize this was not a fling, this was not a phase I was going through. It was something I was serious about, not something I was doing as a hobby. This is an integral part of me. *Shabbos* is not something you do on weekends. This is who you are.

In a nutshell, Torah is the aspect that flavors and enhances and molds and modifies every decision and every selection and every aspect of my life—including not only where do I want to eat, where do I want to live, what type of job I'll take . . . more importantly, how do I deal with raising children, life's problems, and so forth.

It's not too often that we feel we have an impact on the world or some people in the world. When I went to the interview for the job I have now, [he has since changed jobs] I was wearing my *keepah*. So externally I looked like a Jew.

During the interview, the president of the company stressed the importance of an employee in Wolf's position—computer system overseer— being available to serve the company whenever he is needed.

I thought it's déja vu all over again. I said to him, "Let me tell you exactly how it is." I said, "The Torah demands that I be a good employee." I said, "You'll get a good job. But let me tell you what it is— from a couple hours before sundown on Friday to a couple hours after sundown on Saturday, there's no way, no chance, no how that you're gonna have me."

He said, "What about your holidays?" And I said, "I'll take my vacation time and personal holidays and not my sick time." And he says, "You're willing to give up your two weeks a year of vacation time in order to fully observe your holidays?" And I said, "That's right."

And he stopped, looked down at his pad, looked up at me, and said, "I want to tell you something." He said, "There are very few times in America that I bump into someone who has convictions and is willing to stand by them. But anyone who has that kind of conviction, we want him here. I want to make you an offer right here, right now."

Brian Wolf, 37, is a computer consultant for a Baltimore-based company. He is married and lives in Baltimore.

34
A Change of Tune

My soul became inflamed with the fact that, hey, there are actually people that know about this other force and they call this other force that affects our lives God.

By the age of 28, Morrie Yess was a genuine honky-tonk hero. "I had achieved what was my dream when I was 17," he said. "I had wanted to be a functioning, money-earning, successful performer." He was setting attendance records at gigs. He was playing places like Reno and Vegas; people were lining up for his autograph. And the future looked even brighter, which meant that new heights of egocentrism and hedonism would be within his reach. And then one night in Kansas City he came to a realization. He was in the bathtub at the time.

I was looking at my hands, and there were wrinkles and not from the water—actual wrinkles that were not there when I was 18. And it dawned on me that I was getting older. That may sound like a ridiculous statement, but there're different ways people can relate to information like that.

What happened was that I realized my aging on an emotional level. This aging was the first crack in the egocentric eggshell of my mindset. And what I mean by that is that I realized that I was not causing myself to get older; it was happening to me. I was sort of like a passive victim of the process.

And what that did is, that opened up the idea that hey, there is something outside of myself that is affecting me. And then it was only a footstep away from that to realize that that same thing that's affecting me is affecting everything else.

It's making flowers come up and go away and seasons come and go. It was an awareness of a higher power above mankind that affects the reality of human experience, why some people get sick, why some people are healthy, why some people are one year prosperous and the next year against their entire will become poverty stricken, God forbid.

It just became more of the fact that this philosophy of egocentricity—that I am in control—is an absolute and total falsehood which denied the evidence of there being an external force that plays on our lives. It became necessary for me to readdress this external force and, knowing that I'm Jewish, I figured, okay, I'm going to go back to the beginning.

And here I was [laughs], this honky-tonk hero, traveling from place to place, living a very pastoral and hedonistic lifestyle, at the same time becoming a closet biblical student.

I cannot express in strong enough terms, the absence of any God-consciousness in my childhood. I had been raised mostly in Canada, having lived four years in Moncton, New Brunswick, and the next four years in Montreal and then the next nine years in Toronto. I had pretty much of a middle-class Jewish upbringing, where the religious side of our Jewishness was of minor concern in the family and the primary focus in our upbringing was the attainment of career success.

At 17, my father and my mother moved from Toronto to Hollywood [California] for the sake of business opportunities. It was 1962 and I was enrolled in a high school that was in a Jewish neighborhood. Again, there was no religious emphasis. Being in Hollywood, the West Hollywood area, and having a love for music that developed seriously about the same time as I moved to Hollywood, it was a most opportune time to become involved in a musical career for a variety of reasons.

I was infected by two things. I want to use the word infected, implying an illness, and I also want to use the word affected, referring to my personal activities. What was the illness? The illness was, here I was a transplanted Canadian, who is now an American, who happened to be Jewish on a nonconscious level in the sense that I knew nothing about my Jewishness other than the fact that I was Jewish. And here I was in a very competitive society, West Hollywood, where the rule of thumb and the coin of the realm were fame, stardom, and career success.

And this is what people totally dedicated their lives toward. And any means possible to achieve this end was acceptable in the pursuit of this goal. This caused me to come into contact with some pretty flaky people who were both shallow in terms of their inner qualities and at the same time, paradoxically, some of them were incredibly talented.

And I was swept up so to speak in this tornado, or feeding frenzy, of success desperation. And the thing that was most infectious in my life was the unstated yet completely understood philosophy of selfism, meaning that if I succeed, I pat myself on the back, and if I fail, I attribute the failure to myself.

Now in my late twenties, I had achieved a moderate amount of fame in the secular music field. When I say fame, I mean I was working steadily in five-star hotels, being asked repeatedly to return, establishing room records for beverage sales and attendance.

It was a pretty hedonistic lifestyle, my life in those days. There was no lack of either pursuit or availability of pleasures in all realms of existence there. Although it was career-satisfying, when I looked to my left and right, the people who were kind of on the same road of pursuit, there were a lot of bugs in their ointment.

Specifically, a lot of marriages were falling apart, a lot of people's personal lives were nosediving into self-destructive behavior with drug involvement and criminal behavior. A lot of people were emotionally very unfulfilled, spiritually unfulfilled. And I was also looking back on the dynamics of the interpersonal relationships in my family and realizing that this ideal state of a close-knit family was far from being actualized. There were a lot of old buried discords and dislikes, and I just came to this realization that there was something fundamentally wrong here.

And I went out and bought a couple English-translated Bibles and started from the beginning. That was like a private endeavor that I didn't talk about because it was not too cool or too hip.

Yess then bought a Hertz chumash [*so named for its editor, Rabbi Hertz*], *which included commentary.*

It provided a greater degree of depth. I realized, oh my goodness, there's really something heavy here. There's something really profound. And my soul became inflamed with the fact that, hey, there are actually people that know about this other force and they call this other force that effects our lives, God. And I accept their definition until something else can come along to disprove that or this proves itself by experiential evidence.

So I then went back to this Jewish bookstore on Fairfax Avenue [in Los Angeles] and bought more books—now we're talking about the middle of 1978—and across the street there was this little storefront synagogue that was called *Chabad* Lubavitch Mid-city.

And there was a Russian rabbi there and his name was Naphtali Estulin and he came in and he gave me a look, and I was in my hippie uniform in those days—leather cowboy hat and jeans and red pointed cowboy boots and I had no beard—and he gave me one look up and down and his first expression was, [laughs] "Are you Jewish?" [Laughs].

And I told him, "Of course I'm Jewish." And he answered, "Did you put on *tefillin* today?" And I said no, and he dragged me to the back of the *shul* and he wrapped me up in *tefillin*. And then something really profound struck me—that here is a man who is totally dispossesed of any Jewish anxiety. He's walking around in a long black coat with a beard and *tzitzis*, he knew his Judaism, he knew how to run a congregation, he knew how to do Jewish things.

And there was no explanatory dialogue that explained the compromising of the fulfillment of the *mitzvos* that were done in his *shul*, as opposed to the Reform and Conservative synagogues that I had seen, where people are driving to *shul* while the rabbi was either looking the other way or people were emotionally uptight about that.

The next thing that transpired was that this rabbi developed a relationship with me, where it was one *mitzvah* at a time. In a very slow and methodical manner he reaquainted me with the Jewish basics. Most of the Jews of my generation were a missing link in the tradition from our grandfathers, who were observant, to our parents, who became victims of the spiritual Holocaust of North America, which is assimilation.

I had the sense of having been duped, having been tricked, I even want to use a stronger word, defiled . . . in the sense that I had been disconnected from that which was my heritage, which is the Torah. And this resulted in a commitment to reaquaint myself with that which had been denied me. And that manifested itself in going to Israel on a one-way ticket. I really wanted to get to the bottom of this entire issue called God.

Had you essentially stopped your career?

I was working bars and nightclubs and taverns and some honky-tonks and some very nice places and some very sleazy places. And this Rabbi Estulin said to me, wear a *yarmulka*, and a week later he said put on *tzitzis*.

On stage?

Let me explain that. The alleged philosophy [in the industry] was one of liberalness. In other words, if you were gay that was fine. If you were a radical that was fine. Do your own thing was the operative philosophy. When I walked into my social group with a *yarmulka* on my head,

I became a pariah, I became like the outcast. That is not allowed. Our liberalness stops at your *yarmulka*, or our liberalness stops at your *tzitzis*.

I went there [Jerusalem] in 1978, and checked into a *ba'al teshuvah yeshiva* and that's when the transfusion really occurred. It was a blessed environment. There were incredibly good rabbis who were aware of all the different religious streams that flow within Orthodox Judaism.

And I was able to take my American secular upbringing and ask such questions as, "What does the Torah say regarding democracy?" "What does the Torah say regarding the profit motive?" And the entirety of my value system was then reexamined within the context of my Jewish tradition. And that which was valid stayed and that which was fallacious was removed from my inner experience.

And step by step, *mitzvah* by *mitzvah*, year by year, I became more able to become comfortable with my Jewishness. And if you really want to know, the microcosm of my experience at the time was that I was like a bewildered little Jewish *boychik*, like I was six years old, inside the body of a 33-year-old secularized American Jewish adult. What had to happen is that the spiritual cripple that was within me needed spiritual therapy and that came in the form of Torah learning and Torah practice.

What did you do about your career?

Rabbi Estulin said to me at one point that I have to keep *Shabbos*. I told him that if I keep *Shabbos*, I'm going to go bankrupt because clubs hire you for six nights a week and Friday night is the biggest earning night of the week. And if I tell them I can't go they won't hire me, I'm gonna lose my income. So I remember he said to me, "God will take care of you." And sure enough, I started keeping *Shabbos* and sure enough three months later I was in bankruptcy court [laughs].

Did you have family at the time?

No. I had financial difficulty and I may have been very anxious about this, but I did not die. On the contrary, there was a certain sense of liberation from having been enslaved to this idea of no money, you pass away, which was very prevalent in our society. People are more connected to their money than reality, I believe, in many circumstances. God should and does come first in a person's life whether he or she is aware of it.

So I was in *yeshiva* with all these 16 or so years of West Coast song-writing and song-performing experience and it was only natural to take the beauty I was discovering in my Jewish studies and to try and express them in contemporary song.

Yess had not always felt that way.

I had felt very guilty about having used this gift of music for self-serving purposes, having come to realize that it was in fact a gift from God and I had misused it and I felt that my atonement would have been to throw it away. I remember being on a balcony and cutting my fingernails, which were needed for playing, and crying my heart out, saying to God, "I'm sorry, I'm sorry for everything I've done up to this point in time. I just didn't know any better."

And Rav Horowitz [a teacher], said, "No, no, no, no, the real repentence, the real *teshuvah* would now be to take the same gift that you've used for purposes that were not godly and to turn it around and use it for godly purposes."

Yess and another man—who wore a yarmulka *and a long black coat on stage—formed the highly successful Megama Duo, which played Jewish music throughout Israel and internationally. The group toured almost non-stop for more than three years in the late 1970s and early 1980s. In the process, Yess said, he was "transformed from an out-of-work nightclub performer to a very much wanted Jewish act all around the world." When a rabbi said his services were needed outside Israel, the Yess family—they had four children by then—moved back to Toronto and then settled in Montreal.*

And I went from what would be called modern Orthodox observance into an acquaintanship with *Chasidus*, specifically Lubavitch *Chasidus*. [This] has taken me from . . . let me see if I can express the dynamic of this to you. [It's] almost like riding two horses at one time—well, I've got to make a living, I've got to support my family and do the day-to-day stuff, yet I have to keep *Shabbos* and keep kosher and do all these *frum* things. What happened when I got involved with *Chasidus* was that it all came together in a unified understanding. In other words, that mystery that I confronted when I was 28—what is this all about?— became answered when I started studying *Chasidus*.

And not only did it become answered in terms of my own personal relationship with God, but it became answered in terms of the purpose of creation, what the role of the Jew is in creation, the spiritual forces that have brought about the various stages of human history, the significance of the Garden of Eden, the significance of Mt. Sinai and the significance of what we are currently in store for. And I became very much . . . fascinated with the Lubavitch *Rebbe*; who was he? I should not only say who was he, but who is he? I'll explain that in a second.

There have been too many things that have happened along the road that just happened to be, quote unquote, by coincidence—which Judaism denies, by the way—[there] just happens to be a Lubavitcher there pointing the way to my next step. And my connection to the *Rebbe*, especially in the last nine months, has skyrocketed to a unprecedented level in my personal life.

I believe we're in store for some astonishing events on the imminent horizon. I honestly believe that the *Rebbe* is *Moshiach* and I honestly believe I'm going to see the *Rebbe* back at 770 [Lubavitch headquarters] alive. The *Rebbe* is the one who will take us out of this exile and bring us back to Jerusalem.

What negatives have you experienced as you've embraced Yiddishkeit?

Every *mitzvah* is acquired at the expense of a test. For example, one of the things I had to forgo is my love of lobster, which is forbidden.

The word for "holy" in Hebrew is *kodesh*, which means separate. So we are not to imitate the ways of the Gentiles. And the way that one becomes holy is by realizing that life is a test and a struggle between that which is physical and that which is spiritual. And that the job is to take the physical and elevate the sparks of holiness within it for the purpose of returning those sparks of holiness to God. That's the job of the Jew.

Every step of the way was difficult. And because of its difficulty, each Jew is rewarded for the struggle. I had to learn how to *daven*. I had to go into synagogues where I was mocked by people who looked at this hippie in cowboy boots. That hurt.

What has been the net impact of Yiddishkeit *on your life?*

It has meant the difference between living a life under a Gentile agenda as opposed to a sacred agenda, and I mean that with no insult to the Gentiles. We have a special mission, the Jewish people, to be a holy nation, a kingdom of priests. When we live our lives according to a Gentile agenda, we forgo that Torah command. And we suffer spiritually and we end up disconnecting ourselves from God.

You wanna know what the biggest payoff of all of this has been? I've got a 14-year-old boy, *keneina hora*, who can sit in a room with me and open up a Gemara and teach his father. There is no amount of money in the world that would reward me more than that. I know that I got a kid who is oriented to his function, his identity and purpose. Our family, *boruch Hashem*, . . . all I can say is thank God for the *Rebbe* and his emissary, this rabbi in California, who some 16 years ago had the kindness to ask a hippie guitar player if he was Jewish and if he'd put on *tefillin*.

Morris (now Moshe) Yess, 50, produces Jewish educational media products and performs concerts for Jewish communities worldwide. He and his wife live in Montreal and they have six children.

35
Dr. Kahn's Legacy

I had to . . . take myself out of the broad, wide, American mainstream
that I was part of and insert myself into a tiny slice of a people that, to
me, had previously been very small and insignificant. I felt like I was
crawling into a crawlspace.

John Young's story of his return to Yiddishkeit *is also the story of his
struggle with emotional pain so intense that it drove him to psychotherapy. His therapist was Dr. Samuel Kahn, a man of great kindness
and healing powers who was also a committed Jew. In fact, Young determined that the source of Kahn's greatness was the Torah. When Kahn
died, it left a gaping hole in Young's life. Still grieving over his loss, he
resolved to follow Kahn's example and find himself through* Yiddishkeit.
*His journey to reconnect with his roots, however, was more arduous than
most. He hadn't even know those roots existed until he was a teenager.*

I was raised as a Christian and did not know I was Jewish. My father
and mother decided to stay away from their families as I was growing
up. I didn't see them too much and I was told that my father's side was
Russian background and my mother's side was Hungarian background.
And I was also told I was a Protestant.

That all changed when I was 16 years old. I decided to look through
a drawer, and in the drawer I found my grandfather's—my father's
father's—burial certificate. In those days I had enough general education to know what Hebrew letters looked like. He was buried in Beth
David Cemetery on Long Island, a Jewish cemetery. And that was my
first inkling that I had a Jewish background.

When my father came back from work I showed him what I found, and I said, "Why didn't you ever tell me?" And he said, "I didn't think it was important." And subsequent to that I found out that my mother was Jewish, that all four grandparents were halachically Jewish, and going back, there were very few intermarriages in the family—that I was a Jew through and through.

Up until that time, having been raised a Christian, and thinking of myself as Christian, to me the Jewish people were an insignificant minority in the world, certainly in America, something I had no part of and no interest in. Of course now this event posed a challenge. I had to, in my identity, take myself out of the broad, wide, American mainstream that I was part of, and insert myself into a tiny slice of a people that to me had previously been very small and insignificant. I felt like I was crawling into a crawlspace.

I wasn't too happy with the news that I was Jewish because the very fact that I had to discover it seemed to me that there was shame involved with it. It was some kind of dirty little secret that I had come across. I have a sister and a brother, *boruch Hashem*, and we each found out separately that we were Jewish. We did not share this secret. We each had to find out for ourselves, because it seemed to be a dirty little secret.

That was when I was 16. I am now 40 and the rest of my intellectual and emotional life has really been involved with turning course, seeking the truth, pursuing an honest identity, and learning what it's all about to be a Jew. It's been 24 years and I still [have] a long way to go.

My father's parents had an arranged marriage with a *shadchen* and it was a big mistake. Their marriage was a disaster and they stayed together because of my father. My grandmother had just come over from the *shtetl* in Russia and my grandfather had already been over here for a number of years, maybe 15 to 20 years.

My father was scarred by the terrible relationship of his parents. It was the relationship that he was really running from. And he was running from himself, and that led to running from Judaism. He was always on the run, a wandering Jew, wandering from job to job.

My mother had no *Yiddishkeit* in her home. What happened was, she went through what I went through. She was raised as a Christian and then discovered by accident that she was Jewish. To my mother it remained a dirty little secret, because that's what her environment had taught her. Her parents were from Hungary, where anti-Semitism was rampant. She didn't turn around and sort of fight it [her adopted identity] like I did later on. She actually assimilated that attitude, and by accident she married my father.

Young discovered he was Jewish while the family was living in a suburb of Albany, New York.

For a while we had attended [a Unitarian] church regularly. There's an old joke in the Unitarian Church. The joke is that they were "Jewnitarians," because we weren't the only Jews. I think by that time, we had stopped [attending church] and we were just nothing.

At the time I was in shock, that's the only word to describe it. It lasted through [high school] graduation.

Young attended Yale University, where he had no Jewish involvement.

What really started to bear Jewish identity was pain—emotional pain and trouble. Growing up, there was a lot of emptiness in the home, depression, emotional pain.

At Yale, being out of the nest and on my own, it caught up with me. I had no home to hide in. My father's financial problems also caught up with me. When he announced to me that he just didn't have the money to continue to keep me at Yale, I was sort of set adrift. I wasn't studying anyway and I was sort of a wild kid, chasing around. I was a mess, I was very mixed up, and I was not going anywhere.

Young sought help from a great aunt, who introduced him to a 78-year-old man in Westchester County, New York, who had once helped her family.

He actually practiced therapy in a group environment, where the people became friends. He was a very unusual man. He had studied with Freud. He's been dead since 1981 and I still miss him terribly. His name was Dr. Samuel Kahn.

Knowing Dr. Kahn and knowing that he came from an Orthodox background [but was no longer Orthodox], I asked him, "What is the secret of your ability to help people the way you do?" And he whispered it: "The religion." I think it was that remark that made me vow that no matter what Dr. Kahn thought about Orthodoxy, it was the secret of his tremendous skill.

I'd look around at the healthiest Jews I saw and they often had strong Jewish identities even though they weren't Orthodox necessarily. I began to associate that with health and happiness. It became obvious in my own therapy. I think Dr. Kahn did what no other therapist would do. He would home in on my Jewish identity. I don't think today anybody would do that. But he would home in on that and say, "You're Jewish, you're a Jew," in a professional therapeutic setting.

One great cause of the pain I was feeling, the depression I was in, was the fact that I had been denied my Jewish identity and denied all the richness that goes with that.

Dr. Kahn died in December 1981, after Young had been undergoing therapy for about five years.

I continued therapy sporadically after that. A lot of it was to get over my grief over Dr. Kahn's death. My main mission [then] was no longer to understand myself, because I had done that as best I could. But it was more understanding myself through Judaism, through Torah, in a Jewish context.

Young had already established a connection to Judaism through a small congregation Dr. Kahn had founded in Westchester County, New York.

It was Reconstructionist, but in those days Reconstructionism hadn't gone off the deep end—it *had* gone off the deep end in the sense that it's Judaism without the supernatural. It was my connection, it was my *kesher*, because I had no *kesher* before. They were a necessary bridge to get to where I am today and I thank them for that.

When Dr. Kahn died I guess I say my journey began in earnest. I was going to learn more about observance because those were his roots and I wanted to find out the roots of his greatness. This was not a typical therapist, this was a man of *chesed*. I saw the Torah as the roots of his greatness and he saw it that way. I wanted to go to Orthodoxy to get the truth.

I just attended the funeral of a colleague and he left a living will for his children. And he said in the living will that I believe that Judaism is the true religion because it's not only belief, it's action. But really he's talking about Orthodoxy, that's where the action is, the *mitzvot*.

I also had to go back and look at where was the last time I had healthy, well-adjusted people in my previous generations, that I knew of to the best of my ability. And I had to go back to the *shtetl*. Because since the *shtetl*, it was just pain and chaos and adjustment after adjustment, and painful adjustment, and wandering and running and confusion and psychological problems.

Meanwhile, Young got married to a ba'alat teshuvah *and they settled in Forest Hills, New York. The marriage lasted for two years. He has since remarried.*

She [his first wife] introduced me to the Orthodox culture. [The fact that] she was ahead of me was probably a source of tension, because I would never measure up. I was trying, but it was difficult. There's a lot of conflict and tension in becoming a *ba'al teshuvah*, a lot of going up against things you think are crazy. But for some reason you hang in there because there are all sorts of peripheral things that you can't find anywhere else—warmth, community, a certain richness, and a certain connectedness that you don't find in American culture.

Nor had he found it in non-Orthodox Judaism.

The problem with the other denominations [was that] everybody was just doing their own thing. They were going to *shul* expecting to be entertained, wanting to take instead of give, sitting back. Orthodoxy is the only denomination where you go in there and you better give or you're not gonna get anything out of it, and it's called *kavanah*.

This was a major reason I went to Orthodoxy from the other denomination—I wanted to define myself as a Jew in the positive, not the negative. And the only way you could do that was to be Orthodox. You cannot define yourself in the positive as a Jew in the other ways. The only possible way to do that is through Zionism, but that is not going to promote your individual growth.

It [Zionism] will give you a group identity, but it is dry compared to mastering or delving into the layers of the literature of our *rabbonim*, of the *chumash*, of the *midrashim*. That is where you're going to grow, develop and build yourself up and define yourself in the positive. Showing up in your car on *Shabbos*, and keeping up with the Schwartzes isn't going to do it.

[But] there was tremendous friction because it [becoming Orthodox] involved a lot of change of habits, change of thinking, tremendous difficulty. You're constantly feeling you're doing the wrong thing, you're saying the wrong thing, you're thinking the wrong thing, and you feel guilty all the time. And after a while you resent feeling guilty—I don't like this feeling, I'm still a person. All right, so I'm not doing it right. I'm just tired of this, you know? *Kashrus, Shabbos, taharas hamishpachah.*

It's kind of like being in a different culture. It's a huge adjustment. You're always tripping up. You feel like a real gawk, like you're uncoordinated. And it's totally disconcerting. It's a blow to your self-esteem. At the same time you're balancing that with material needs, educational needs, which take a lot of self-esteem, which take a lot of drive.

Between all these normal life goals you have, where you have to scrape and struggle, there was a tremendous catchup job. You learn as much Judaism as you can. And then you realize it's so vast you're never going to catch up. And then you realize how much you missed, as the more you know, you realize you don't know. And then you understand the benefits of a *yeshiva* education you never had. There's always something in the back of my mind that says I'm not measuring up.

Nevertheless, how has the quest for Yiddishkeit *changed your life?*

I'd be as empty as I was without it, and I was very empty. I was depressed. I thought there was meaning to what I was chasing after, which was a big name, a lot of secular education, a Ph.D. I convinced myself there'd be some sort of pot at the end of that rainbow.

It's an irony that in being in a wonderful marriage with my wonderful wife, and our beautiful child and hopefully there will be more, that now there's a richness in my life that's never been there before. But along with that richness comes a responsibility to maintain it, and it takes energy. I marvel at people who have all the kids they have and they still do the *mitzvos*. What I'm saying is that I'm a very flawed Jew. It was many years just getting used to *Shabbos* and *kashrut*. I'm still on this journey. It's been 24 years and it's gonna be for the rest of my life.

How have your relations with your family been affected?

My father passed away, he died at Sloan Kettering in New York. I want very much to define myself in the positive and that includes loving my parents and respecting them, and not living my life in the negative. I asked my father's blessing on his deathbed that I'd like to live an observant life. I didn't know what he was going to say, but thank God he said yes. While my mother certainly didn't choose to take the path I've chosen, she never offered any resistance to my decision to become observant. However, her lack of awareness of Orthodox practice often created uncomfortable situations, and that took about 10 years to resolve in a positive manner.

What about relations with other nonobservant relatives? Have you worked that out?

It took about 10 years to work that out too. In many respects it's brought me closer to them, because, as I said, my father and mother really isolated themselves from their families. So for many years I had nothing to do with these people. On some level, they know I'm going in the direction of Jewish continuity and on some level they're choosing their path, which is consciously or unconsciously not to go on the path of Jewish continuity. They respect me for what I'm doing.

John Young, 40, is an economist with the accounting firm Arthur Andersen & Co. in Washington, DC. He and his wife live in White Oak, Maryland, and they have one child.

Glossary

"Heb." indicates a Hebrew word; "Yid." a Yiddish word; "Aram." an Aramaic word; "Sp." a Spanish word.

Ahavas Yisroel (Heb. "love of Israel") Love for the Jewish people.

Ain kelokaynu (Heb. "there is none like our God") A hymn in praise of God sung on Sabbath and Jewish festivals.

Aishes Chayil (Heb. "a woman of valor") A hymn that Jewish men traditionally sing to their wives on Friday night.

Aish Hatorah (Heb. "fire of the Torah") The name of a *yeshiva* based in Israel.

Aleph bais or **aleph bet** (Heb. "alphabet") The Hebrew alphabet.

Alev hashalom (Heb. "may peace be on him") An expression used when mentioning a deceased person.

Aliyah (Heb. "ascent") Either relocating to Israel or being called to the *bimah* in the synagogue to make a blessing over the Torah.

Amidah (Heb. "stand" or "standing") The 7- or 19-blessing prayer, said while standing, that forms the core of Jewish worship. Also known as the *Shmonah Esrai*.

Amud (Heb. "pillar" or "stand") The lectern in the synagogue before which the prayer leader stands.

Apikoros An apostate Jew.

Ari (Heb. "lion") Isaac Luria (1534–1572), a Kabbalistic scholar who settled in the city of S'fat.

Ashkenazi   (Heb.) A Jew of European ancestry.

Avenu shalom alechem   (Heb. "Our father, peace be on you") A Jewish folk song.

Averah   (Heb. "sin") Sin.

Ba'al teshuvah   (Heb. "master of return" or "one who has returned"; pl., *ba'alei teshuvah*) A Jew from an unobservant or minimally observant background who has embraced traditional Judaism. Abbreviated: *BT*.

Bais midrash   (Heb. "house of study") A study hall, normally in a *yeshiva*.

Bar mitzvah   (Heb. "son of commandment") A Jew who has reached maturity and is therefore responsible for keeping God's commandments. Also, the ceremony celebrating this change in status. The parallel ceremony for girls is known as a *bas mitzvah* or *bat mitzvah*.

Baruch atah Hashem   (Heb. "blessed are you, God") The three words with which Jewish blessings begin.

Bekesha   (Yid.) A long black coat worn by *chasidim* during prayer, religious ceremonies, and other occasions.

Bentsh lulav   (Heb. and Yid. "bless the lulav") A blessing made over the four plant species that Jews "take" on the holiday of Succos.

Bereshis   (Heb. "in the beginning") The first of the five books of the Torah, known in English as "Genesis."

Bimah   A raised platform near the front of a synagogue upon which the Torah is read.

Birchat kohanim   (Heb. "blessing of the priests") A synagogue ritual in which the descendants of the priests provide a conduit for God's blessings.

Boruch Hashem   (Heb. "blessed is God") An expression of thanks.

Boychik   (Yid. "small boy") A term of endearment.

Bracha   (Heb. "blessing;" pl., *brachos, brachas* or *brachot*)

Bris   (Heb. "covenant") Most commonly refers to the circumcision procedure and ceremony which take place on the eighth day after a male child's birth.

Cave of Machpela   The burial cave in Hebron of Adam and Eve, Abraham, Isaac and Jacob and their wives, Sarah, Rebecca and Leah.

Chabad   (Heb. acronym: *chochmah*, wisdom; *binah*, understanding; *da'as*, knowledge) A large, outreach-minded chasidic sect, also known as Lubavitch.

Chabad Chasidus Chasidic philosophy and writings. Also known as *Chassidut*.

Chabad house A community facility operated by the *Chabad* Lubavitch *chasidim*.

Chabadniks Followers of *Chabad* ways and philosophy.

Challah (Heb.) Braided bread eaten on the Sabbath and some holidays.

Chanukah (Heb. "dedication;" also an acronym for "on the 25th day they rested") The Festival of Lights in December which celebrates the rededication of the Temple by the Maccabees after their victory over the Syrian Greeks in the second century B.C.E.

Charedim (Heb. "those who tremble") Ultra-Orthodox Jews.

Chas v'shalom (Yid. "God forbid).

Chasid (Heb. "a pious one"; pl., *chasidim*) Follower of the chasidic movement, which originated among the Jews of Poland in the 18th century.

Chavurah (Heb. "partnership" or fellowship").

Chazon Ish Avraham Yeshayahu Karelitz (1878–1953), a widely recognized *halachist* and commentator.

Chazzan (Heb.) Cantor.

Cheder (Heb., Yid.) The one-room schoolhouse that originated in the European *shtetl*. Also refers to Hebrew school.

Chesed (Heb. "favor" or "kindness").

Chevron (Heb.) Hebron.

Chinuch (Heb. "education") Specifically, Torah-oriented education.

Chofetz Chaim (Rabbi Israel Meir Kagan, 1839–1933) A pious and saintly sage whose commentary on the *Shulchan Aruch Orach Chayim*, known as the *Mishnah Berurah*, is a definitive work in Jewish law.

Cholent (Yid.) A traditional hot Sabbath dish made of beans, meat, potatoes, barley, and other rib-sticking ingredients.

Chometz (Heb. "leaven") Its consumption and possession is prohibited on the spring festival of Passover.

Chumash (Heb.) The five books of Moses.

Chupah The canopy under which Jewish couples are married.

D'var Torah (Heb. "a word of Torah"; pl., *divrei Torah*) A discussion of a Torah-oriented topic.

Davening (Yid.) Praying.

Derash (Heb.) A discussion or investigation of a Torah passage; pl., *derashim*.

Derech eretz (Heb. "the way of the land") Proper behavior, respect.

Eliyahu Hanavi (Heb. "Elijah the Prophet," 9th century B.C.E.) Tradition says he was so holy he went to heaven without dying and will some day herald the arrival of the Messiah.

Emes (Heb. "truth") Truth.

Eretz Yisroel (Heb. "the Land of Israel") The land of Israel.

Esrog (Heb.) A citron. One of the "four species" involved in the celebration of Succos.

Farbrengen (Yid.) A gathering of chasidic Jews, usually to hear an address by their *rebbe*.

FFB (Yid., Eng. "*Frum* from birth.") A Jew who was raised in an observant home and has remained observant. ·

Fleyshik (Yid.) Meat.

Frum (Yid.) Religious, observant, Orthodox.

Frumkeit (Yid.) The practice of traditional Judaism. (Colloquial, *frumness*).

Galillah (Heb.) The rolling up and rebinding of the Torah scroll after it has been read in the synagogue.

Gashmius The physical, as opposed to the spiritual.

Gemara (Aram.) The voluminous explication of the Mishnah that was completed in the 5th century C.E. Together, the two works comprise the Talmud, although Gemara is sometimes used generically to refer to the entire Talmud.

Gilgul neshama (Heb.) A soul that is transferred through reincarnation.

Goy (Heb.) Gentile; pl., *goyim*.

Goyisha (Heb.) Of or like Gentiles.

Gulus (Heb.) The Diaspora.

Hadlakat hanayrote (Heb.) The ceremonial lighting of candles.

Haftorah (Heb.) The prophetic reading that takes place after the reading of the Torah on the Sabbath and on festivals.

Hagbaha (Heb.) The ceremonial elevation and public display of the Torah after it has been read in the synagogue.

Haggadah (Heb. "narration") The body of talmudic literature that is nonhalachic, including legends, aphorisms, and moral illustrations. Also refers to the book in which the Passover story is told. Also, *Aggadah*.

Hakadosh Boruch Hu (Heb. "the holy one, blessed be he") God.

Hakaras hatov (Heb.) Gratitude.

Halachah (Heb. "the way") The body of Jewish law; pl. *halachahs, halachot*.

Hallel (Heb. "praise") A special prayer of thanks consisting of a group of Psalms.

Hamotzee (Heb.) The blessing said over bread.

Hashem (Heb. "the name") One of the names of God.

Haskalah The Jewish "enlightenment" movement which began in mid-18th-century Germany and spread throughout Europe.

Havdalah (Heb. "separation") A ceremony marking the conclusion of the Sabbath.

Hillel (Heb.) A support organization for Jewish college students. Named after the revered sage and martyr who lived in the first century B.C.E. and the first century C.E.

Im yirtzeh Hashem (Heb.) God willing.

Kaddish (Heb.) A prayer said by mourners which praises God and asks for the speedy establishment of His kingdom on earth.

Kasher (Heb.) To ritually purify; refers primarily to utensils and vessels used for the preparation and consumption of food.

Kashrus (Heb.) The system of rules governing what a Jew can and cannot eat. Also, *kashrut*.

Kavanah (Heb. "intent" or "intention") Concentration and genuine emotion during prayer.

Kedusha (Heb. "sanctification") A congregational prayer which is recited responsively during the repetition of the *Shmonah Esrai*. Also refers to holiness in general, such as that found in the Land of Israel.

Keepah (Heb.) A skullcap worn by Jewish males; pl., *keepot*. Also, *yarmulka*.

Keesay hacavode (Heb.) The heavenly throne of honor.

Keneina horah A phrase designed to ward off the evil eye.

Kever Rochel The tomb of the biblical matriarch Rachel.

Kesher (Heb. "connection).

Kibbutz (Heb.) An Israeli collective settlement; pl., *kibbutzim*.

Kibud av'v'ame (Heb.) The biblical commandment to honor one's father and mother.

Kiddush (Heb. "sanctification") The benediction and prayer said over wine to welcome the Sabbath or festivals.

Kiruv (Heb.) Outreach to disaffected Jews.

Kishkes (Yid.) Guts.

Klal Yisroel (Heb.) The larger Jewish community; Jews as a whole.

Klee   (Heb. "instrument," "vessel" or "tool") Instrument, vessel or tool.

Koach   (Heb. "strength") Strength.

Kotel   (Heb.) The Western Wall; the remnant of the wall surrounding the Temple compound in ancient Jerusalem.

L'chaim   (Heb. "to life") Often used as a toast.

Loshen hara   (Heb. "evil tongue") The sin of speaking ill of others.

Lubavitch sheliach   An emissary of the Lubavitch movement, an outreach-minded chasidic branch that takes its name from a town in Russia.

Lubavitcher Rebbe   The leader of the Lubavitch movement, most recently, the late Menachem Mendel Schneerson.

Lubavitchers   Members of the Lubavitch movement.

Lulav   (Heb.) A bundle of three species—palm, myrtle, and willow—which Jews are commanded to "take" on the festival of Succos along with the fourth specie, the *esrog* or *etrog*.

Ma'ariv   (Heb.) Evening prayers.

Macher   (Yid.) An operator. A big shot. Somebody with connections.

Machlokeses   Disagreements among Talmudic sages.

Maftir   One who is called up to read the Haftorah as well as the last few verses of the weekly Torah portion.

Malachah   (Heb.) An activity which is prohibited on the Sabbath.

Mamish   Literally, definitely, really.

Marrano   (Sp. "swine") Jews in 15th century Spain who were forced to adopt Christianity yet secretly remained faithful to Judaism.

Matzoh   (Heb.) Unleavened bread.

Matzoh brei   (Heb., Yid.) Fried *matzoh*.

Mechallel   To desecrate.

Mechitzah   A physical barrier separating men and woman in Orthodox synagogues.

Mekarev   To bring closer to traditional Judaism.

Melava Malka   (Heb. "escorting the queen") A festive ceremony held at the conclusion of the Sabbath.

Menorah   (Heb.) The seven-branched lamp that was found in the Temple in ancient Jerusalem. Today, the eight-branched version, also known as a *Chanukiah*, is kindled as part of the festival of Chanukah.

Meshuggah   (Yid.) Crazy.

Mesiras nefesh   (Heb.) Utter devotion.

Mesorah   (Heb.) Transmission from generation to generation of a tradition or the text of the Torah.

Midbar (Heb.) Desert or wilderness, physical or spiritual.

Middos (Heb.) Character traits.

Midrash (Heb. "investigation") Literature which seeks to explain the biblical text; pl., *midrashim*. Also, *medrash*.

Mikvah (Heb.) A ritual bath.

Milchik (Yid.) Dairy products.

Min hashamayim (Heb.) From heaven.

Mincha (Heb.) Afternoon prayers.

Minyan (Heb.) A prayer quorum; pl., *minyanim*.

Mishnah The teachings of the Oral Torah which were compiled at the beginning of the 3rd century C.E. The explication of the Mishnah is known as the Gemara. Together, they form the Talmud.

Misnagdisha Of or like the *misnagdim*, the 18th-century opponents of *Chasidism*.

Mitzvah (Heb.) Commandment; pl. *mitzvot, mitzvos*.

Moshe Rabbenu (Heb. "Moses our teacher") A reverential appellation for the biblical Moses.

Moshiach (Heb.) The messiah.

Motzei Shabbos (Heb.) The conclusion of the Jewish Sabbath on Saturday night.

Musaf (Heb.) The additional service that commemorates extra Temple sacrifices brought on the Sabbath, festivals and Rosh Chodesh, the beginning of the new Hebrew month.

Neder (Heb.) A vow.

Nehr Tamid (Heb. "continuing light") The continually illuminated lamp which hangs before the holy ark in the synagogue.

Neshama (Heb.) The human soul.

Nu (Yid.) Perhaps the most versatile expression in the Yiddish lexicon. Depending on inflection and context, it can signal a question or convey anything from doubt to recognition to disapproval.

Ohr Somayach (Heb. "light of joy") A *yeshiva* headquartered in Israel.

Parshat hashavuah (Heb.) The weekly Torah portion.

Path of the Just A moral–ethical work written by Moshe Chaim Luzzatto (1707–1747).

Payess (Heb.) Sidelocks.

Pegisha A chasidic gathering.

Pesach (Heb.) The springtime festival which commemorates the Jews' deliverance from Egypt. Also known as Passover.

Pesukim   (Heb.) Sentences or verses.

Pidyon haben   (Heb. "redemption of the firstborn") A ceremony in which the firstborn son is redeemed by payment of the equivalent of five shekels to a descendant of the tribe of Levi.

Pintela Yid   (Yid.) The spark of Jewishness residing within each Jew.

Pirkei Avos   (Heb. "chapters of the fathers") A collection of ethical and moral teachings from the Mishnah. Also known as *Pirkei Avot*.

Purim   (Heb. "lottery") A joyous springtime holiday which commemorates the intervention of Queen Esther, who foiled the plan of the vizier Haman to destroy the Jews of Persia.

Rabbeyim   (Heb.) Rabbis. Also used today, *rabbonim*.

Rambam   (Maimonides, 1135–1204). One of the greatest sages and codifiers in Jewish history, he wrote the *Guide for the Perplexed* and the *Mishneh Torah*, among other esteemed works.

Rashi   (Rabbi Shlomo Yitzchaki, 1040–1105). One of the greatest biblical and Talmudic commentators in Jewish history.

Rav   ("master"). A title for authoritative teachers that originated in 1st century Babylonia. Today, it is often used interchangeably with *rabbi*.

Rebbe   A chasidic leader or a rabbi who functions as a teacher.

Rebbetzin   The wife of a rabbi.

Rosh Hashanah   (Heb. "head of the year") The new year holiday on which the ram's horn, the *shofar*, is blown.

Rosh yeshiva   (Heb.) The leader of a *yeshiva*.

Ruchnius   (Heb.) Spirituality.

Seder   (Heb. "order") The Passover ritual of reading from the *Haggadah*, the account of the Jews' exodus from Egypt, and partaking in the accompanying ceremonial meal.

Sefer   (Heb. "book"). A holy book.

Sefer Torah   A Torah scroll.

Sh'ma   The six-word declaration of faith that forms the cornerstone of Judaism belief. It proclaims the oneness of God and the loyalty of Jews to God.

Shabbaton   (Heb.) A weekend celebration in which Jews of one community visit Jews of another community.

Shabbos   (Heb.) The Sabbath, a day devoted to rest and sanctification of the world; pl., *Shabbatot* or *Shabbosim*.

Shadchen   (Heb.) A matchmaker.

Shailah   (Heb.) A question posed to a *halachic* authority.

Shala Shudis   (Heb.) The third meal of the Sabbath.

Shalach manos   (Heb.) Baskets of candies and other treats that are exchanged during the festival of Purim.

Shalom Alechem   (Heb. "peace unto you") A greeting. Also the pen name of Sholom Rabinowitz (1859–1916), a famous Jewish writer and humorist.

Shalom bayis   (Heb.) Peace in the home.

Shavuout   (Heb. "weeks") The late spring holiday celebrated seven weeks after Passover which commemorates the giving of the Torah at Sinai and the offering of the first fruits. Also, *Shavuous*.

Shidduch   A marital match.

Shiksa   A non-Jewish woman.

Shiur   A class or lecture in which the Torah or a Torah-related topic is discussed.

Shiva   The seven-day mourning period that begins with the burial of the deceased.

Shlomo Carlebach   (Now deceased) A pioneer in the *ba'al teshuvah* movement who began reaching out to assimilated Jews in the 1950s.

Shmini Atzeres   The eighth day of Succos, although it is considered by some a separate festival.

Shmonah Esrai   (Heb.) The 19- or 7-blessing benediction which forms the core of Jewish worship. Also known as the *Amidah*.

Shmooze   (Yid.) To chat.

Shnorrer   (Yid.) A beggar or chronic borrower.

Shokeling   Swaying while praying.

Shomer Shabbos   (Heb. "one who guards the Sabbath") One who strictly obeys the laws governing permissible and impermissible activities on the Sabbath. Also, *shomer Shabbat*.

Shtetl   (Yid.) A small Jewish town or village in Eastern Europe.

Shul   (Yid.) Synagogue.

Shulchan Aruch   (Heb. "prepared table") The authoritative code of Jewish law published in 1555 by Joseph Karo.

Siddur   (Heb.) Prayerbook.

Simcha   (Heb.) A joyous religious celebration.

Simchas Torah   (Heb. "rejoicing of the Torah") The festival falling immediately after Succos which is devoted to celebrating the Torah. It features a series of processions (*hakafot*) during which Jews dance with the Torah.

Soncino Tanach   An edition of the Hebrew Bible published by the Soncino Press.

Succah   (Heb. "booth") The makeshift dwellings Jews "reside" in during the fall festival of Succos, or Succot, which commemorates the period when the Israelites wandered in the wilderness and lived in booths.

Succos   See above.

Tefillin   The network of Scripture-filled leather boxes and leather straps which Jews don when they pray on weekday mornings.

Taharas hamishpachah   (Heb.) Laws which govern family purity by regulating when husbands and wives may have sexual relations.

Tallis   (Heb.) A prayer shawl also known as a *tallit gadol*; pl., *talletim* or *tallesim*.

Talmid chacham   (Heb. "student of a wise one") An individual who is learned in Torah.

Talmud   (Heb.) The voluminous compendium of laws, legends and debates formed by the combination of the Mishnah and the Gemara in the 5th century C.E.

Talmud Torah   (Heb.) After-school Hebrew school.

Tanach   (Heb.) The Hebrew Bible, consisting of the Five Books of Moses, the Prophets, and the Writings.

Tanya   Two famous works bear this name, although in this context, it refers to a philosophic–mystic tome produced in the late 18th century by Rabbi Schneur Zalman of Liadi, originator of *Chabad* Chasidism.

Tehillim   Psalms.

Torah   Specifically, the Five Books of Moses, but generally all the teachings of traditional Judaism.

Trayf   In this context, unkosher meat.

Tzaddik   (Heb.) Righteous one; pl., *tzaddikim*.

Tzedakah   (Heb.) Charity or righteousness.

Tzibbur   (Heb.) A community of Jews or a *minyan*.

Tzitzis   (Heb.) The fringes attached to the four corners of a garment worn by Jewish men which is known as an *arba kanfot* or a *tallit katan*. This sometimes refers to the entire garment.

Tznius   (Heb.) Modesty.

Tzniusdic   (Heb.) Of or relating to modesty.

Vidui   Confession of one's sins.

Yad Vashem   A Holocaust memorial in Israel.

Yarmulka   (Yid.) A skullcap, also known as a *keepah*.

Yehi ratzon   (Heb. "may it be your will") A prayer traditionally said by women on Friday night immediately after lighting the *Shabbos* candles.

Yerushalayim (Heb.) Jerusalem.

Yeshiva A school devoted to intensive Torah learning; pl., *yeshivot*.

Yeshiva bochrim Students at a *yeshiva*.

Yeshua (Heb.) Salvation, help or rescue.

Yeshua Hamoshiach (Heb.) Jesus the Messiah.

Yetzer hara (Heb.) The "evil inclination" which tempts an individual.

Yiddishkeit (Yid.) Traditional Jewish belief, practice and culture.

Yiras Hashem (Heb.) Fear or awe of God.

Yisroel (Heb.) The land of Israel or the Jewish people.

Yom Kippur (Heb.) The Day of Atonement, the holiest and most solemn day in Judaism. It is celebrated in the fall immediately following Rosh Hashanah. Together, the two comprise the "High Holidays" or the "Days of Awe."

Yom tovim (Heb.) A general designation for Jewish holidays and festivals. Also, *yomim tovim* or *yontif* (singular).

Yoshka Jesus.

Z'chus (Heb.) Merit.

Zemiros Traditional Hebrew songs sung at the Sabbath table. Also, *zemirot*.

Zeycher tzaddik lavracha (Heb. "May the memory of the *tzaddik* be for a blessing") A phrase said in honor of a deceased righteous man.

Zionistic Of or relating to Zionism, a political movement that began in the 19th century and called for the restoration of the traditional homeland of the Jewish people. Today, after the establishment of the State of Israel, Zionism refers generally to monetary, political, and cultural support of that state.

References

Becher, Mordechai, and Newman, Moshe. *After the Return.* Jerusalem and New York: Feldheim, 1994.

Birnbaum, Philip. *Encyclopedia of Jewish Concepts.* New York: Hebrew Publishing Company, 1991.

Bridger, David and Wolk, Samuel, eds. *The New Jewish Encyclopedia.* New York: Behrman House, 1976.

Cohen, Arthur A. and Mendes-Flohr, Paul. *Contemporary Jewish Religious Thought.* New York: The Free Press, 1988.

Danzger, M. Herbert. *Returning to Tradition: The Contemporary Revival of Orthodox Judaism.* New Haven and London: Yale University Press, 1989.

Encyclopaedia Judaica. Jerusalem: Keter Publishing House, 1972.

Gribetz, Judah, et al. *The Timetables of Jewish History.* New York: Simon & Schuster, 1993.

Hayim Nahman Bialik and Yehoshua Hana Ravnitzky. *The Book of Legends.* Trans. William G. Braude. New York: Schocken Books, 1992.

Heilman, Samuel. *Defenders of the Faith: Inside Ultra-Orthodox Jewry.* New York: Schocken Books, 1992.

Helmreich, William B. *The World of the Yeshiva.* New York: The Free Press, 1982.

Johnson, Paul. *A History of the Jews.* New York: Harper & Row, 1987.

Kosmin, Barry A. and Lachman, Seymour P. *One Nation Under God.* New York: Harmony Books, 1993.

Kosmin, Barry A., et al. *Highlights of the Council of Jewish Federations 1990 National Jewish Population Survey.* New York: Council of Jewish Federations, May 1991.

Lewittes, Mendell. *Jewish Law, An Introduction.* Northvale, NJ: Jason Aronson, 1994.

Litvin, Baruch, ed. *The Sanctity of the Synagogue.* Mt. Clemens, MI: Baruch and Ida Litvin, 1962.

Reisman, Bernard. "The Leadership Implications of the National Jewish Population Survey." *The Journal of Jewish Communal Service* (Summer 1992): 350–356.

Rosten, Leo. *The Joys of Yiddish.* New York: Pocket Books, 1970.

Samlan, Arnold D. "The Contemporary Jewish Lexicon." *Sh'ma: A Journal of Jewish Responsibility* (April 3, 1992): 87–88.

Schiller, Mordecai, ed. *Jerusalem Echoes.* Jerusalem and New York: Ohr Somayach Institutions, 1978.

Seltzer, Robert M. *Jewish People, Jewish Thought.* New York: Macmillan, 1980.

Singer, David, ed. *American Jewish Year Book 1995.* New York: The American Jewish Committee, 1995.

Steinsaltz, Adin. *Teshuvah: A Guide for the Newly Observant Jew.* New York: The Free Press, 1987.

Touger, Eliyahu. *Maimonides' Mishneh Torah, Hilchot Teshuvah.* Ed. and trans. Rabbi Eliyahu Touger. New York and Jerusalem: Moznaim Publishing Corp., 1990.

Willis, Ellen. "Next Year In Jerusalem." *Rolling Stone* (April 21, 1977): 64–76.

Wright, John W., ed. *The Universal Almanac.* Kansas City and New York: Andrews and McMeel, 1991.

ABOUT THE AUTHOR

Richard H. Greenberg is a freelance writer and editor. His work has appeared a number of publications, including the *Washington Post*, the *Los Angeles Times*, the *Chicago Sun-Times*, the *Chicago Tribune*, the *Miami Herald*, *Columbia Journalism Review* and *Regardie's* magazine. He earned his bachelor of science degree in journalism from Northern Illinois University. Mr. Greenberg lives in Silver Spring, Maryland, with his wife, Kathy, and their two children.